The Portfolio Project

The Portfolio Project

A Study of Assessment, Instruction, and Middle School Reform

Terry Underwood
California State University, Sacramento

National Council of Teachers of English
1111 W. Kenyon Road, Urbana, Illinois 61801-1096

For Joanne and Karen

Staff Editor: Rita D. Disroe
Cover Design and Prepress Services: Precision Graphics
Cover Photographs © Elizabeth Crews

NCTE Stock Number: 36281-3050

Library of Congress Cataloging-in-Publication Data

The portfolio project : a study of assessment, instruction, and middle school reform / Terry Underwood.
 p.   cm.
 Includes bibliographical references (p. 241) and index.
 ISBN 0-8141-3628-1 (paper)
 1. Portfolios in education—California Case studies.
 2. Educational tests and measurements—California Case studies.
 I. Title
 LB1029.P67U53   1999
 371.39—dc21   99-42587
                                                         CIP

It is necessary, then, to be satisfied with swirls, confluxions, and inconstant connections; clouds collecting, clouds dispersing. There is no general story to be told, no synoptic picture to be had. Or if there is, no one, certainly no one wandering into the middle of them like Fabrice at Waterloo, is in a position to construct them, neither at the time nor later. What we can construct, if we keep notes and survive, are hindsight accounts of the connectedness of things that seem to have happened: pieced-together patternings after the fact. To state this mere observation about what actually takes place when someone tries to "make sense" out of something known about from assorted materials while poking about in the accidental dramas of the common world is to bring on a train of worrying questions. What has become of objectivity? What assures us that we have things right? Where has all the science gone? It may just be, however, that all understanding (and indeed, if distributive, bottom-up models of the brain are right, consciousness as such) trails life in just this way. Floundering through mere happenings and then concocting accounts of how they hang together is what knowledge and illusion alike consist in. The accounts are concocted out of available notions, cultural equipment ready to hand. But like any equipment it is brought to the task; value added, not extracted. If objectivity, rightness, and science are to be had it is not by pretending they run free of the exertions which make or unmake them.

Clifford Geertz, *After the Fact* (1995)

Contents

Introduction

Portfolio assessment arrived in the northern California district in which I was teaching during the late 1980s on the crest of a frenzy of reform, a frenzy stirred up by a state department of education bent on changing the thoughtlessness its leaders perceived as being characteristic of public education. Motivated by the reverberations of a spate of published critiques of schooling such as Sizer's *Horace's Compromise* (1984) and Goodlad's *A Place Called School* (1984), California's policymakers and educators had joined hands in an effort to change the way schools forged the minds of the future in their classrooms. Like many others nationwide, my district was valiantly trying, if only semiconsciously, to do what people now call, either scornfully or nostalgically, "whole language." This district wanted to be a part of the tidal wave of child-centered sentiment that was sweeping phonics workbooks, spellers, and grammar lessons from classrooms and leaving behind "good literature" in its wake. We wanted children to care about literacy. The idea then was to give children a "print-rich environment," to invite them to join Frank Smith's "literacy club," to hook adolescents and young adults on literature, to get them excited about the joy and power of books. The movement affirmed the centrality of student engagement, identity, and purpose in classroom literacy practices; it validated the teacher as a professional who possessed expert knowledge and skill; and it paid sustained attention to assessment as a powerful variable in the production and reproduction of classroom cultures.

I can no longer remember who first called "portfolio assessment" an oxymoron, an exemplar of the triumph of syntax over logic as in "mandatory recreational" reading (or simply "recreational reading" for too many students). When I first heard the phrase at an inservice during the late 1980s, I thought that this clever oxymoronic characterization held more than enough truth to explain the nods of approval and knowing smiles among my colleagues in the California Writing Project. *Of course* portfolio assessment was an oxymoron! The portfolios of student writing we had reviewed in Writing Project workshops were provocative, inspiring, interesting; but what little we had seen of portfolios in the name of *assessment* was disturbing. Portfolios were meant to empower, to engage, to emancipate. Assessment was by nature controlling, limiting, and conforming.

So when my district ordered its newly adopted basal reading series for its grade schools in the mid-1980s—a basal series which had been completely revised to reflect someone's version of whole language principles—it should not have been a surprise to find both the absence of phonics workbooks and the presence of a rather schizophrenic portfolio-assessment system. The basal portfolio-assessment system—a huge oxymoron if ever there was one—came in class sets wrapped in clear plastic; that is, the flimsy light-brown assessment pamphlets with tear-out pages came packaged in shrink wrap, with enough materials per teacher to cover a whole classroom of students. The pamphlets contained a set of three reading tests, little more than end-of-story comprehension questions to which students wrote answers three times a year, to be scored by each teacher-of-record and stored in folders to go on to the next grade level at year's end. There were also some multiple-choice "skills" tests, much more easily graded than were the open-ended reading responses. And there were Likert-like scales that asked students to rate their level of enjoyment or interest in the story according to degrees of smile or frown on a circular face. In addition to these periodic comprehension and skills exams, the district had announced a plan to mandate that teachers collect writing samples tied to uniform prompts as a part of each student's portfolio.

But *why*, teachers across the district asked.

Why were all of these *papers* being stuffed in folders and saved? Most of the students couldn't read the "good literature" in the basal anyway—it was much too difficult for most grade levels—so why were teachers being required to give students comprehension tests and then to *save* them? Who was going to look at them, anyway? Since each teacher scored the reading responses alone and nobody knew whether there was any continuity at all across the district, who could even make sense of the scores? Was it simply a way of putting on a show of reform?

And where were these folders supposed to be stored, anyway? What were teachers supposed to do when boxes upon boxes of portfolios piled up in their rooms, in the hallways—even in the library? What were the middle schools to do at the end of the year when their half-dozen or so elementary feeder schools shipped over truckloads of boxes of portfolios that the English teachers could make no sense of and had no use for?

Could the students decorate the covers, at least?

Eventually, of course, this attempt to implement a standardized portfolio-assessment system across a large, diverse, and rapidly growing school district failed. No one could use data generated by the system to

examine district-level or even school-level issues because scoring—
even when it was done—was idiosyncratic and erratic. Almost no one
ever took the system seriously enough to allocate resources and time
for its use. In the end, those flimsy light-brown assessment pamphlets
with tear-out pages went the way of many other educational innova-
tions and wound up gathering dust in the corners of storage rooms.

But the idea of portfolio assessment did not die in my district,
probably because it continued to be taken seriously by policymakers,
at least through the mid-1990s. In 1991, having changed my assignment from that of an elementary reading specialist to that of a middle
school English teacher, I found myself among a group of reform-
minded English teachers who viewed portfolios as an important and
useful strategy for engaging students and for improving their program. After having studied as a participant-observer the serious, systematic portfolio-assessment project which they implemented in 1994,
I saw more clearly why the commercial portfolio-assessment system
that had arrived as part of the basal series in the 1980s had been
doomed to failure from its conception. In the 1980s, before I had the
chance to learn about portfolios as assessment tools from this faculty, I
might have agreed that portfolios could and should be separated from
external assessment. Now, it makes no sense to me to talk about portfolios as an instructional strategy apart from external assessment, just
as it makes no sense to talk about *any* instructional strategy apart from
assessment.

I have come to think of portfolio assessment as less an oxymoron
than a paradox. No progress can be made, I have decided, if we set in
irreconcilable opposition all that is romantic, magical, and joyful about
language arts pedagogy against all that is cold, hard, and analytical—
and then force teachers to choose sides. There is ample precedent for
thinking that such a tension in language arts exists more broadly. Peter
Elbow taught us about the tension between our creative and our judg-
mental writing muscles when he taught us about freewriting. Joseph
MacDonald, a theorist who became important to the California Center
for School Restructuring during the early 1990s, taught us to look at
student work through three progressive lenses—first a warm lens, then
a cool lens, and finally a hard lens. The warm lens is essentially value-
free, deeply appreciative, intensely local. The cool lens begins to raise
questions, to compare, to analyze. The hard lens introduces public criteria and must yield valid and reliable judgments. Leave out any lens
and you've left out either the love or the learning. Look through the
hard lens first and you've destroyed everything.

This book provides readers with an examination of a portfolio-assessment project that set out to be warm, cool, and hard. Because the study looks at portfolios as a teaching and learning tool in classrooms, it examines close up the lives of teachers and students in their classrooms and investigates how the system felt and what it meant to them. Because it looks at portfolios as a researchable strategy with implications for other schools and districts, it raises questions about how the system fit within other school and district initiatives. Because it looks at assessment as an essential and serious aspect of teaching and learning in public schools, and as the site where public criteria about good and bad enter the school, it examines the historical and political circumstances which gave rise to the values inherent in the system.

If readers of this study see portfolios warmly as a way to enhance student ownership and engagement, one which assessment distorts beyond recognition, then the early chapters of this book, which analyze historical influences and political pressures external to the classroom, will be interpreted as irrelevant, even harmful, to portfolios. On the other hand, if readers look hard at portfolio assessment as a method by which political bodies like states (e.g., Kentucky) hold schools accountable through the reliable examination of valid evidence of achievement, with ambiguous regard for student and teacher ownership, then the later chapters of this book will be interpreted as tangentially relevant at best, perhaps interesting in a novelistic sense, but hardly enlightening.

If, however, readers can conceive of portfolio assessment as the ground upon which public agreements can be made among teachers and students in classrooms, as well as among external stakeholders, about what it means to teach and learn reading and writing—agreements which are then honored in those semiprivate classrooms just as student intentions and interests are honored; if portfolio assessment is taken seriously as a potentially useful instructional tool for motivating and engaging and empowering students; if portfolio assessment can be seen as a link between the institution's social and legal obligation to evaluate and its pedagogical aim to instill a love of learning, then this study stands a chance of making sense. Portfolio assessment becomes a broad pedagogical-cultural practice with roots in the institution and its larger context and blossoms in the classroom—a broad practice in need of ethnographic examination at a variety of levels.

Schools are not cultural islands—nor are classrooms. This study attempts to explicate the origins and consequences of a portfolio-assessment system at a middle school, seen as a set of agreements that tried to accommodate those whose lives were most immediately impacted (that is, teachers and students) and those with intense legitimate interest in the students (principals, parents, superintendents, legislators, the public at large). In a macroethnographic educational case study such as this, cultural and historical influences are seemingly infinite and could defeat the most persistent researcher. Guba and Lincoln (1989) spoke of the "multiple simultaneous shapers" of any complex phenomenon involving people; indeed, to explicate all of them in finite text would daunt not just the writer, but the reader.

So this book tells a story with many gaps. The story is set within the broader context of state assessment initiatives begun a decade earlier after legislation was enacted to reform what was perceived to be California's unresponsive and ineffective set of institutions—institutions unresponsive to changes in societal needs and ineffective in preparing children for adulthood. The plot is about how, for almost fifteen years, assessment drove instruction across the state, often in unexamined and contradictory ways, but always in powerful ways. The plot is complicated somewhat by a mid-level network of political authority called the District, a seemingly invisible web of power relationships stretched between the School and the State, which the State apparently ignored in its quest for institutional reformation, at least in California. The book traces the ebb and flow of a variety of assessment philosophies located in living rooms, classrooms, principals' offices, district headquarters, and downtown Sacramento—a variety of philosophies coming and going which left behind sedimented, imbricated histories of conflict in classrooms.

From what I can tell, this story has parallels in the recent history of schools all across the United States.

Acknowledgments

I deeply appreciate the support and guidance given to me by my dissertation committee, a group of dedicated and wise teachers who inspired me to do the best research I could through their example and their thoughtful engagement: Sandra Murphy, my major professor; Carlton Spring, of the University of California at Davis; and P. David Pearson, of Michigan State University. Additionally, I owe a debt of special thanks to Karen Watson-Gegeo and Michele Foster, both professors at Davis during my time there, who together gave me new eyes to see through as an ethnographer.

I also thank my colleagues with whom I have worked during the past decade or so on large-scale assessment projects and in the Area III Writing Project: Mary Barr, Sheridan Blau, Lynda Chittenden, Charles Cooper, Mel Grubb, Jim Hahn, Sally Hampton, Kristi Kraemer, Miles Myers, Linda Peddy, Liz Spalding, Laura Stokes, and Darby Williams. Each of these individuals has contributed in important ways to my growth. For her truly magical thinking, I am especially grateful to Fran Claggett, poet and teacher, test maker par excellence, who is the white crow.

My personal and professional gratitude goes to the principal at Charles Ruff Middle School who encouraged and supported my research because he wanted to contribute not just to Charles Ruff, but to the larger school community; to the three portfolio-assessment teachers who worked so hard and thought so deeply about their practices and their students and who generously and fearlessly let me in on their work and thinking; and to the examination teachers who gave of themselves to the project even while they carried on with their own full load of teaching duties. I also thank all of the students who allowed me to talk with them during the course of the school year and who freely shared their frustrations, their accomplishments, and their criticisms.

I wish to thank several anonymous reviewers from NCTE who carefully read and critiqued early drafts of this work. Their thoughtful analyses and suggestions helped me to see possibilities in the work which I had not seen before. I am especially grateful to Michael Greer, senior editor at NCTE, for his help in re-seeing the arrangement of ideas in the text, for his encouragement and support, and for his belief in the worthiness of this study.

Finally, I am grateful to my wife, Joanne, for her encouragement and her understanding and her willingness to give me the gift of time to do this work—even while she was giving me the greatest gift of all, our daughter Karen.

I am grateful to my colleagues, teachers, friends, and family for all of their contributions to this work, but I am solely responsible for its final shape.

1 Washers, Dryers, and School Reformers

Background

This study of portfolios was conducted in an urban, ethnically and linguistically diverse, lower-socioeconomic institution. Located on the outskirts of a city on the West Coast of the United States, Charles Ruff Middle School (a pseudonym) enrolled 1,633 seventh- and eighth-grade Asian American (20.3%), African American (17.2%), Hispanic (14.3%), Filipino and Pacific Islander (8.2%), American Indian (1.7%), and Euramerican (38.3%) students, according to available data, during the year in which this study was conducted. Five hundred nine (509) students qualified for federal Chapter 1, now Title I, services in reading, according to a standardized test of reading comprehension.

To qualify for Title I services, Ruff students placed at or below the 35th percentile nationally. The whole-school, national, median percentile rank for reading was 42. Median percentile ranks for mathematics were 48 for seventh grade and 50 for eighth grade. Of three commonly used poverty indicators (AFDC rates, free/reduced lunch rates, and census data), the district recorded both AFDC and free/reduced lunch-rate data. Thirty-nine percent of the adolescents attending Charles Ruff came from households on AFDC, while a somewhat higher percentage of the students ate at a free or reduced-price lunch. According to an estimate from the school counselors, more than half of the students came from single-parent households.

The following table, published in a major local newspaper in the mid-1990s, summarizes real estate data for the neighborhood in which the school was located:

Average square footage	1,245
Average year built	1965
Average # bedrooms/baths	3/1.6
Average sale price	$87,000
High sales price	$125,000
Low sales price	$43,000
Owner occupied	75%

(The median sales price for homes in this city at the time was approximately $121,000.) But these data do not tell the entire story, for most Charles Ruff students live in outlying areas and ride a bus to school. Although these outlying neighborhoods represented the same general socioeconomic level suggested by the preceding real estate data, some were worse off, while others were better off. A drive through the territory within Ruff's attendance boundaries revealed scattered, large apartment complexes, many of them battered and run-down, with a smattering of rural homes in the outback, a few of which were set up to keep horses.

Situated within the economic and political reality of California in the mid-1990s, Charles Ruff Middle School operated on a limited budget, as did most of the families who sent their children to the school. According to a quote in one of California's metropolitan newspapers (May 1995) attributed to Delaine Eastin, then newly elected state superintendent of public instruction, "California has the most crowded classrooms in the nation."

In the same article, Senator Leroy Greene, then chairperson of the California Senate Education Committee, described discussions of reducing class size as "an absurdity." (Of course, as anyone who knows anything about the California of the late 1990s is aware, absurdities do happen. Class-size reduction in the primary grades has come to pass in the state. Middle schools, however, continue to schedule quite large numbers of students into each period of the day.)

Assemblywoman Deidre Alpert, then chairwoman of the Assembly Education Committee, speculated that California would need "16 new classrooms [built] . . . every day, including weekends and holidays for the next six years just to accommodate increased enrollment. And at the end of that time we would be in the same fix. . . . Classrooms would be just as crowded as they are today." Classrooms at Charles Ruff, including the portfolio classrooms under study here, were no exception to the rule: Most teachers at Ruff saw between thirty and thirty-five students per period on the average (physical education teachers sometimes saw as many as forty-five students per period).

Charles Ruff students faced the full panoply of urban problems all too familiar in newspapers and on TV in America in the 1990s. For example, one Friday afternoon during the fall of the year in which this study occurred, I happened to enter the administration office and saw Ruff's principal huddled with his secretary, studying a large map of the surrounding streets which had been hung on a wall, talking heatedly, trying to locate a particular intersection. A parent had called the school just minutes earlier to report that there had been a shooting at the intersection less than a mile away, that a helicopter had landed in a nearby parking lot, and that police on foot, on motorcycles, in cars, and in vans were scouring the area. This parent requested that the principal not allow her son to walk down that street.

Within seconds a vice principal had arrived in the office, a tall African American male doing a hard job, and he and the principal began devising a plan for a safe dismissal, including mapping out a route to avoid the commotion. (Later that evening, a TV news reporter told the story of a high school student who had been shot in the head and killed at a stop light south of Ruff, by a former Charles Ruff student who had used a gun to steal a bottle of liquor from a grocery store earlier in the day.)

There were only two incidents of students' being shot in the vicinity of Ruff that year, but at least once or twice each week something occurred to test the mettle of the children and adults at the school. After school one day, for example, a Mexican American paraprofessional female, who worked in the office and also headed the Maya club for Hispanic students, stood at the desk in the principal's office to tell the principal about a family with children whose mother had just died.

"There is no father," she said, "and there's no other family in the vicinity. Everyone is back in Mexico."

The county had balked at giving the mother what could be considered a decent funeral because there was no money to cover expenses. Though the loss of dignity was infuriating to this paraprofessional, it wasn't the central issue. What made this a problem for Charles Ruff was that the oldest child in the family, at the time a freshman in high school, had been a Ruff student the previous year and a member of the Maya club. He was taking care of the "three or four younger children" in the family, with no money for food.

According to one of Ruff's counselors, also a Mexican American female who tried to keep close tabs on the Hispanic students at Ruff, the landlord wanted to move the children out of the house as soon as possible so that he could find paying tenants. The paraprofessional was taking donations so that she could take groceries to the children; she was reluctant to turn the money over to the county because she believed "it would never make it to the kids." I watched the principal pull his checkbook out of his back pocket, write a check for $20, and hand it to her.

Just as the character of the real estate varied across Ruff's attendance area, these examples of shooting and death do not faithfully characterize the lives led by all of Ruff's students. Some of them, though certainly a small proportion of the population, went home after school to intact families with parents who worked at jobs that paid relatively well. In recent years, for example, one seventh-grade female student who had practiced gymnastics since she was a toddler became a national competitor. Her parents and her Ruff teachers worked together to see to it that this student achieved in school, even though she would miss classes for a week or two at a time while she attended gymnastic events.

And many of the problems faced by school administrators were much less demanding and defeating than were those cited above. For example, one morning the daily "Charles Ruff Teacher Bulletin" greeted teachers with this message:

RUBBER BAND EPIDEMIC

We have a rubber band epidemic. Students all over campus are shooting each other in the face during class, on the campus, on the bus, and at lunch. Please monitor this behavior with strict enforcement of referral directed to VP.

[On the daily bulletin for students, this message was written:]

REPORT AND TURN IN THE RUBBER BAND SHOOTER

Report or turn in the rubber band shooter; or anyone in possession of rubber bands. Many students have reported being shot in the face by rubber bands or other objects. Students in possession of or shooting rubber bands will be sent to the VP and receive an automatic suspension.

Despite the challenges, the faculty at Charles Ruff remained hopeful, if willingness to seek supplemental grants to improve the school constitutes a measure of hope. Since 1989, staff members had written grant proposals for, and had won, well over a million dollars cumulatively in state funding to develop innovative curriculum and to restructure their school. In fact, the portfolio project that sits at the heart of this book was conceived and funded as part of the school's effort to improve its services. But as the literature on school change suggests (Fullan, 1991), the change process is difficult, and Charles Ruff was no exception to this rule.

Change at Charles Ruff was riddled with contradictions. This school's twelve brick buildings with Ruff's American and California Bear flags flying out front, its gymnasium, and its multipurpose room were just over a quarter of a century old at the time of this study, and many of the school's approximately eighty-five teachers had taught in those buildings for fifteen or more years. Just as the staff was made up of teachers who had never taught anywhere else and teachers who had taught at a variety of schools, a curious mixture of tradition and innovation pervaded Ruff's classrooms and its instructional culture. Students walked from one classroom where they had just spent fifty minutes writing individually, in silence, in reaction to lists of literal questions requiring rote memory of facts, to another classroom where they would spend fifty minutes in cooperative groups making paper-mâché sea animals to hang from the ceiling.

The agents of change at Ruff functioned quite successfully in a perceived political atmosphere that required them to mute the old ways and to celebrate innovation in their documents in order to win the approval of state committees. Official documents, such as the one submitted in a quest for a state award, for example, presented Ruff as being on the cutting edge of innovation. According to this document, Ruff's students "learn to think like mathematicians by solving complex and authentic problems in cooperative groups using the tools of technology; they learn to think like scientists in hands-on, minds-on classrooms where science comes alive under constructivist pedagogy—also using technological tools." The audience is invited to get the impression that technology pervaded the curriculum.

Observation on site, however, painted a different picture. Using grant funds, the administration had released an English/social studies teacher from his instructional duties to serve as the site "technology coordinator," charged with bringing the school into the twenty-first century—just as another English/reading teacher (me) had been released from instructional duties to help restructure assessment practices on site. If you had visited Charles Ruff during the year in question and had asked to meet with the technology coordinator, however, you would have gotten a somewhat different impression regarding the role of technology on site than that depicted in the official document submitted to win an award.

You would have found this technology coordinator tucked away in a small "office" between a science classroom on one side and a drama classroom on the other. This "office" had a door on either side, one to the science classroom and one to the drama classroom, an arrangement which forced the technology coordinator to enter through one or the other classroom even when students were in class.

"Office" furniture? Against the back wall were a washer and dryer used by the Physical Education Department. Hanging from the ceiling was a large metal box that housed the transformer for the building, which constantly hummed. Noise from both classrooms filtered into this "office." At the rear of the room, in the ceiling, was a return vent; when the classrooms were being heated, the "office" got cold air. When the classrooms were being cooled, the "office" got hot air.

"Just look at this!" the technology coordinator said during an interview with me one day, as he sat in an old kitchen-style chair at a large, rusty, metal desk. He waved a frustrated hand at his brand-new Macintosh computer station, fully equipped with a CD-Rom, state-of-the-art at the time. "You know, this is probably the worst place I could think of to put computer equipment. The two worst enemies of a computer are moisture and dust."

He continued, waving his hands: "And guess what? This thing [he waves toward the washer] produces enough moisture to fog up the room, and this thing [he waves toward the dryer] produces enough dust to make you cough."

It wasn't just the moisture and dust. The coordinator was in competition with all of the other secondary sites in the district for limited district resources—such resources as labor and supplies to rewire aging classrooms for Internet access, a dedicated phone line with enough capacity to have twenty-four-hour access, and other niceties which district personnel were doling out to sites that could prove their willingness and readiness to make use of these things. Just as the district had had to dole out available moneys to replace old tile floors with carpet as those moneys became available, the district had to move slowly with expenditures on technology. Who got what first was a district decision.

"The district people came out here to meet with me, and when they saw this room, they went, '*What?* This is a school that supports technology?'" he squawked.

Certainly, this scenario occurred partially because California schools were—and still are—overcrowded. The principal simply did not have any space. He was already storing textbooks in a converted bathroom. Later in the year, when it became clear that something would have to be done about the technology coordinator's quarters if the school's technological capabilities were to improve, a storage room in the library was cleared and painted and made into an office, a telephone line installed, and filing cabinets and other office accessories ordered. A server was purchased to manage an internal e-mail system, and a storage system for software and hardware was devised.

This school background is presented in order to provide some symbols to keep in mind while reading and interpreting the findings regarding the portfolio-assessment project at Charles Ruff. All of these elements—the below-average national percentile rankings on standardized tests; the below-average value of real estate in the immediate neighborhood; the violence of students shooting students at stop lights; the pathos of children losing a mother within a system of social services stretched too thin to help; the vigilant attention to safety characteristic of the administration, whether it was guns or rubber bands; the courage and pride of an adolescent gymnast who takes on challenges to both mind and body and excels with the help of family; the tension between the official mask and the real face of the institution; the contradiction of locating the hub of technological innovation in a PE laundry room; the resourcefulness revealed when a storage room in the library is transformed into a center for growth—all of these elements set the stage for discussion of the portfolio project.

Genesis of the Portfolio Project

California State Senate Bill 1274, enacted in 1990, authorized the Department of Education to allocate grant funds to approximately 200 schools in an effort to "restructure" these schools such that all students would have an opportunity to learn. California's Center for School Restructuring (CCSR), organized in connection with SB 1274 to oversee these efforts, promoted the idea that teachers at restructuring sites ought to "examine student work for what matters most," a motto which legitimized portfolio assessment as a tactic for uncovering what was really happening to children in schools (Jamentz, 1993). In 1993, Charles Ruff Middle School received a grant totaling $1 million over five years under the auspices of the CCSR.

To qualify for the money, the principal and a handful of his teachers wrote and defended a proposal before a committee of representatives of the CCSR, which applied a rubric to the proposals. The concept of "backwards planning" was a central theme of the rubric: In order to be funded, schools had to demonstrate the capacity to begin planning by looking at desired learning outcomes and then by "working backwards" to come up with actions with a demonstrable potential to support student growth toward those outcomes.

A corollary was that schools would be able to assess the degree to which planned actions either constrained, promoted, or had no effect on student growth. This tight linkage between learning outcomes and school plans via analysis of naturally occurring student work processes and products suggested a role for portfolio assessment. When small committees of Ruff teachers attended regional conferences put on by the CCSR, they heard much talk about portfolios and brought this talk back to the site.

Nobody seemed to know exactly how to carry out the careful examination of students' day-to-day work processes and products that was needed to discover which instructional actions were having what effects on students. In the absence of such examination, so the logic went, those in leadership positions in schools could neither pinpoint where in the locally negotiated curriculum the school faced instructional problems nor weigh the worth of proposed solutions to those problems.

Although alternative measures like the CLAS test system in California and the New Standards Project's portfolio-assessment system (New Standards Project [NSP], 1994; M. Myers, 1996) looked at actual student-constructed responses, these systems did not fulfill the needs of backwards planners because they could not assess student work in light of locally established curricular intentions; they could not account for historical changes in individual student work processes and products as shaped by local instructional practices; and they could not be instantly modified or reinvented to accommodate immediate needs for information on a spectrum of constantly arising questions. In short, large-scale assessment systems of any sort were too clumsy. Backwards planning suggested almost an ethnographic stance toward school and classroom culture—an ethnographic analysis of academic life as it was lived by students within an interpretive framework that could explain the "multiple simultaneous shapers" of events (Guba & Lincoln, 1989).

The Ruff leadership thought about using traditional data, like standardized test scores and teachers' issuance of grades for course credit, but found that neither system had the sensitivity, trustworthiness, or comprehensiveness required to do the job. Although district-level administrators relied on test scores to make judgments about school performances, they were of limited local use because overall percentile ranks would fluctuate from year to year, although no one could really say why. Discussions usually rested on quicksand, often shifting from instructional issues to social and economic issues (e.g., test scores seemed to go down one year because students took the tests shortly after the accidental death of a popular student), always shot through with speculation and guesswork.

Ruff students got grades, but scrutiny of these data simply highlighted the perennial pitfalls of most traditional grading systems. Some teachers refused to give"D's" and "F's" while others gave them liberally. Nobody knew what an "A" really meant. Assessment data determined by teachers in isolation without reference to common criteria, it was argued by Charles Ruff's Performance Assessment Committee (PAC), could hardly serve the informational needs of backwards planners who were asking specific questions about the impact of specific actions on precise learning outcomes. The restructuring leadership council at Ruff during 1993–94 ultimately concluded that standardized tests and letter grades were equally incapable of providing the kind of detailed information necessary for backwards planning.

As a result, $52,000 from SB 1274 money was set aside for the 1994–95 school year to experiment with a tool having the potential to produce the high-quality, contextualized, fine-grained information needed for effective instructional monitoring and planning. This experiment, hereafter referred to as the portfolio project, was to involve intensive design and implementation work from six "pilot" teachers during the experimental year, who would then make recommendations to the entire staff about expanding the system during the 1995–96 school year.

These six teachers were to apply for the project; they were to represent a variety of disciplines across the curriculum; and they were expected to report their individual perceptions of the effectiveness of portfolios to the school community at the close of the year. The funding for the project was to go toward releasing each of the six portfolio teachers from one period of teaching in order to complete teacher-research work with respect to the portfolios; to release as many as ten additional teachers at three separate points during the year for four-day portfolio scoring sessions; and to fund a project coordinator who would manage the administrative details involved in setting up the portfolio scoring sessions, support the project teachers in their work, and report back to the school community with respect to the effectiveness of the project as a whole.

The idea behind the portfolio project was to find a way to collect student work and to evaluate it systematically so that local judgments could be made about local classroom practices—the strength would be that everyone would refer to common criteria while anchoring discussion in real student work. The major structural characteristics of the portfolio project were to occur in two areas: (1) instruction was to be carried out by the project teachers in alignment with uniform student learning outcomes across classrooms as articulated on a detailed rubric; and (2) assessment was to be carried out by an external jury of teachers who would examine student portfolios in light of the rubric in order to issue report-card grades.

The portfolio teachers would teach to the rubric, but not evaluate their students; the jury of teachers would do the evaluation through "examining student work for what matters most," as these matters were indexed in the rubric. Although the school community was interested in whether this approach would actually produce useful data, the bottom-line questions were these: Would the students actually do their work in such an assessment system? Would their parents tolerate the change? Would the examination committee be able to judge work reasonably? Would the participants survive the year? Would such a system hold water in middle school practice?

The Charles Ruff school community was divided on the question of the worth of this portfolio project. More than a few teachers found little wrong with the traditional grading system and, in fact, saw great potential harm in changing it. Some thought it was unethical, even immoral, perhaps illegal for the teacher of record not to issue grades. Others did not like grades, agreed that criteria were mushy-to-nonexistent and that teacher judgments were idiosyncratic, but were skeptical about the possibility of finding anything to replace the A-through-F system.

A minority took the perspective that the grading system was, if not corrupt, at least absurd—and possibly harmful to students. Each of the three English portfolio-project teachers, whom we will meet shortly, espoused some version of the absurd theory. Why should the portfolio system be connected with grades at all? Why not eliminate grades entirely and use narrative commentary? Why burden the portfolio system with this baggage? The entire school community seemed curious, at the beginning of the 1994–95 school year, to learn the fate of the teachers in the portfolio classrooms who had agreed to transfer the power of the grade to an external committee and to teach according to common goals and criteria.

Those closest to the project, on the other hand, were most curious to learn the fate of the students in the portfolio classrooms who would be asked to learn in a classroom culture with rules that differed profoundly from those they had internalized since kindergarten—no daily or weekly doses of evaluative feedback in letter or other form, no opportunity to get to know and understand the idiosyncracies of the adult in power, no connection between classroom behavior and report-card grades. In the end, while much benefit could come to the school from an improved assessment system, the critical question was this: Would students respond well?

Or would they shut down?

Researcher as Participant

My hiring at Ruff as a seventh-grade English teacher in 1991 followed a circuitous route. Having worked as a district resource teacher specializing in literacy assessment between 1989 and 1991, I had visited Ruff several times to help with an assessment initiative spearheaded by the Ruff English Department. In the late 1980s, the English Department had convinced district administrators that its seventh-grade English classes ought to be changed from one-period sections to two-period "blocks," a move that increased the number of seventh-grade English teachers and decreased the number of "survey" teachers (art, music, wood shop, drama, etc.) at the site.

My understanding was that district administrators had agreed to this change not because it had come to devalue survey courses, but because standardized reading-test scores had been steadily declining for a number of years across the district, including the scores for Charles Ruff students. Moreover, everyone knew that the state was designing a new open-ended reading test, a situation which had everyone on edge. The winning argument was that a two-period arrangement would let English teachers teach writing for one period and reading for the second period. One widely circulated hypothesis for the decline in reading scores was that instruction had focused too heavily on writing after the state mandated a writing test a few years earlier. Something had to be done to enhance reading instruction on the district's standardized measure without damaging writing performance on the state test.

Shortly after the two-period block change, however, it became clear—or at least the district believed—that many of the seventh-grade teachers had *not* divided up their instruction adequately into a writing period and a reading period. In fact, as I learned firsthand when I visited the campus, these English teachers had attended inservices and workshops for the past several years which urged them to integrate the language arts. Many seventh-grade English teachers saw the expanded time as a way to integrate by giving students more time for collaborative groups, for extended projects, for "grand conversations" and the like. They were not devoting discrete periods in the day to traditional aspects of reading instruction, such as vocabulary development, comprehension, study skills, and reading rate. Concerned that the block scheduling was not likely to have the desired effect on reading test scores if teachers did not use the time to teach reading, district administrators asked the Charles Ruff English faculty to come up with evidence that the block was, indeed, helping students learn to read better.

The then-chair of the English Department, together with the Chapter 1 coordinator and the reading specialist, requested district support in designing such an assessment, and I was it. The English Department and I collaborated to document progress among seventh-grade students. During early exploratory meetings at the district office with the district's staff development coordinator, I liked the Ruff teachers' enthusiasm for their work. Later, during meetings with them in the Ruff teacher's lounge and in the Ruff library, I appreciated the opportunity to develop a local system for assessing reading.

In part because Charles Ruff's principal was, in my eyes, an inspired and inspiring school leader, and in part because Charles Ruff's English Department was largely a committed group of teachers, I decided to seek a position at the school which the English Department chair had told me about, and we scheduled a meeting with the principal during which I was offered and accepted the position. In addition to teaching English classes, my role would be to bring expertise and leadership in assessment to the site. Indeed, it didn't take long before I was being used in that capacity.

During my second year, the principal hired a long-term substitute to cover my classes for two months so that I could examine writing instruction across the curriculum and design and deliver staff inservices. This assignment came about because their state writing-test scores from the previous spring were among the worst in the state (Ruff scored at the eighth percentile relative to others in its socioeconomic band). Although I went back to teach my classes after the two-month release, the following year the principal assigned me to the reading specialist slot at the school, a position then defined as a staff development position, not a teaching position. Again, I was out of the classroom working on assessment and staff development projects.

During the early 1990s, the school applied for and won a rather large grant—$250,000 each year for five years—from the state to "restructure" the school. Part of this restructuring effort meant launching outcomes-based projects in the hope of creating systemic change at the site. When the school's restructuring leadership team approved a proposal to experiment with the portfolio-assessment project discussed throughout this book, I became the school's "performance-assessment coordinator," charged with helping to develop, monitor, and evaluate the effectiveness of the portfolio-assessment system.

Because I was an English teacher on the staff, I knew what it was like to be a teacher in the classrooms at Charles Ruff. Because I had done many inservices for the English faculty, I knew the English faculty's varying philosophical and theoretical perspectives on reading and writing instruction. Because I was studying assessment as part of my doctoral work at a nearby university, I knew something about the technical aspects of assessment which might be useful to other faculty groups interested in assessment projects, such as the Science and Mathematics Departments.

My work with the portfolio project would be funded by the state grant. What is important for the study of portfolios reported in this book is that my status as participant-coordinator included my professional obligation to observe the project unfold, to be the eyes and the ears of the site, so that I could collect both quantitative and qualitative data for the leadership committee to help them make decisions about future directions for assessment.

Beyond my earlier work in the district as a resource teacher, I had had prior experience in large-scale assessment. Beginning in June 1989, the state asked me to serve as a member of a team of teachers chosen by the California State Department of Education to write the state's new reading exam (CLAS). While serving on this team, I participated in the full range of activities necessary for making a statewide, open-ended reading exam, namely, developing a design framework for the exam, selecting test passages, writing test questions, field-testing exam designs, examining student responses to test questions, revising exam designs, developing a rubric to score the exams, selecting exemplars for each score point on the rubric to train scorers, writing commentaries for those exemplars, training scorers to read and score the tests, and revising training protocols to increase reliability in the scorings.

As I went about this work, I worked closely with Ruff's English faculty during workshops; during the development and scoring of their own local, open-ended reading assessment; and during development of curriculum and of common instructional strategies. My participation on the state development team and at the Ruff site helped bridge the gap between the state and the school. Without a doubt, my presence at Charles Ruff influenced the faculty to move in the direction pointed to by the state test.

However, the California performance-based assessment system of the 1980s and early 1990s had a huge influence on schools across the state and would have influenced Charles Ruff whether I had been there or not. Several members of the Ruff English staff had participated in the California Literature Project or the California Writing Project summer institutes and had become thoroughly familiar with the instructional ideology of reading and writing embedded in the new assessments (more on this later). Indeed, the California projects had been woven into the reform legislation of the early 1980s specifically to create changes in the schools. I believe that my personal influence at Ruff was minuscule in comparison with the tidal wave of influence coming from the state generally and from the California projects specifically.

Researcher as Observer

In qualitative studies in which outsiders enter a field, a central problem is obtrusion; that is, the observer's presence can change what is being observed. As Schatzman and Strauss (1973) stated, "The observer is observed" (p. 63). The degree to which obtrusion occurs constitutes one indicator of the degree to which conclusions from the study can be trusted. A classic example of the problem of obtrusion, and of one researcher's solution, is William Corsaro's (1985) study of a preschool entitled *Friendship and Peer Culture in the Early Years*. Corsaro wanted to discover what friendship was all about and what peer culture meant from the perspective of preschoolers, a discovery which could be made only if the observer could be accepted as a genuine part of the culture— an insider.

Despite his physical size and chronological age, through strategy and persistence, Corsaro managed to become accepted by the children. He ate pretend dinner with the children as they role-played family scenes, never once choking on the sand; he was granted the privilege of watching boys transform stick horses into guns, despite this trans-formation's being against the rules set up by adults. He painstakingly *became* an insider—a *participant*-observer, an outsider growing toward the inside.

In my case, I was an insider; I did not have to eat sand to prove myself part of the group. Being an insider, however, carries its own threat to trustworthiness. Schatzman and Strauss (1973) pointed out quite clearly an important problem facing the inside researcher: "[The researcher] is more easily able 'to go native,' adopting one or another position prevalent among his associates . . . because, being trained or experienced in his participatory activity has so unwittingly absorbed certain viewpoints that his participatory activities tend to reinforce those taken for granted to such an extent that he never thinks to chal-lenge them" (p. 61).

A critical characteristic of my peculiar status as an insider, how-ever, somewhat mitigated this concern: My official role as a partici-pant was to observe. In other words, I was an *observer*-participant, an insider growing toward the outside. All of the other insiders in the school culture—the portfolio teachers, their students, and the rest of the school—knew full well and expected that I would collect, analyze, interpret, and evaluate data, that I would study them.

Moreover, the school principal believed that the grant funds which had come to the school ought to be spent in such a manner that the fruits could be shared with other schools which had not gained extra resources. This principal, my immediate supervisor, wrote a letter in support of my research project to the Human Subjects Committee of a local university, in which he stated his hope and belief that the findings of this project would have relevance for an audience beyond the school. In the eyes of my supervisor, then, I was an observer not just for the local community, but for more distant communities as well.

This definition of my role at Charles Ruff mitigates at least partly Schatzman and Strauss's (1973) list of disadvantages for the participant-observer. "The researcher cannot just freely float in space and time but is tied to his work," Schatzman and Strauss (1973, p. 61) wrote. In my case, the work to which I was tied *was* to move freely within the campus in order to learn about the consequences of the portfolio project for teachers and students. "He cannot pretend to be a learner in early stages of the research, for he is presumed knowledgeable," (p. 61) they wrote. In my case, though I was presumed knowledgeable about assessment in general, no one was presumed knowledgeable about the consequences and usefulness of a portfolio-assessment system at Charles Ruff; discovering this knowledge was the intent of the project. "If his participatory activities are especially demanding of energy or time, or both, then the research work will suffer" (p. 61), wrote Schatzman and Strauss. My participatory activities were demanding of both time and energy, but these activities were identical to the observational activities—time and energy devoted to the participant role was simultaneously devoted to the observer's role.

Schatzman and Strauss (1973) outlined several advantages for the participant-observer which, I believe, apply to my case. "Full participation may allow accessibility to certain situations and information— some not always equally accessible, or not so quickly, to an 'outside' researcher" (p. 62), they wrote. In my case, my participation did indeed give me access to situations which I'm certain I would not have had access to if I had visited the school as an outsider. For example, while I observed students in the process of choosing work for their portfolios, I simultaneously talked with them and helped them reflect on their work, and I talked with their teachers and helped them reflect on this process. My participation gave me full rights to help with and to influence the development of history; as a consequence, I knew what it felt like as a teacher to face the prospect of having your students choose work which was destined to be transported outside the classroom for final grading. I did, in fact, "share with other participants in the collective failures and triumph of group endeavors" (Schatzman & Strauss, 1973, p. 62).

I must report here that I entered and left the project with a deeply rooted conviction that standardized multiple-choice tests of literacy are irremediably flawed as measuring instruments and have unwanted, detrimental consequences in that they diminish students' opportunities to learn and therefore their life chances. I do not see that this bias altered my collection and interpretation of data in this study; if anything, this bias made me even more careful in the research. Because I am opposed to the widespread use of standardized multiple-choice tests, I am not automatically in favor of performance-based or portfolio assessments. In fact, the opposite is true. My perspective on multiple-choice tests has made me suspicious of all forms of assessment. *Assessment of any sort is dangerous.*

My conclusion at this point is that every school ought to have on staff an observer-participant whose job it is to collect and interpret data for the local school community with reference to whatever assessment systems are applied at a site. The creation of this position as a routine part of the school would acknowledge the power of assessment and would provide the capacity of the school to understand and mitigate the damage done to children by any assessment system. [Note: For a detailed explanation of the research methodology used in this case study, see the Appendix.]

2 The Portfolio-Assessment System as an Innovation at Charles Ruff

Dear Evaluation Teachers,
I'm very proud of Mary, she is a very hard worker. She loves to experiment,
it's her way of trying new things. She has grown and she has seen the dark-
ness in R. L. Stine's doing. That he is meant for fourth, fifth, and sixth
graders but NOT seventh graders. She has grown so much she understands
Shakespeare and writes so well her poems almost make me cry.

Apprehensions

So begins a letter of recommendation composed in June 1995, by Susan
for Mary, two seventh-grade students who were about to finish a year
of instruction in one of the experimental portfolio classrooms at
Charles Ruff Middle School. Mary submitted this letter as part of her
third-trimester language arts portfolio, to be scored by an external
committee of Ruff English teachers.

Her entire third-quarter grade rested on her portfolio.

For both Mary and Susan, the portfolio-assessment system had
governed the issuance of their course grades during the year. The system had required—some might say rather brutally—that they make
changes in their approach to reading and writing. Like Mary and
Susan, most of the students (and teachers) who were involved in the
portfolio experiment had had some experience with portfolios prior to
their participation in the project, some having "done" a portfolio as a
small part of a classroom grading system, others having "done" a
"showcase" portfolio completely separate, on the surface at least, from
the credit-granting function of schools. According to interview and
survey data, however, none of them had ever experienced a portfolio-
assessment system wherein student portfolios left the classroom to be
graded for the report card.

To be sure, there was more than a little apprehension at the
beginning of the school year about this innovation, as exemplified by
the following excerpt from an interview with two eighth-grade male
portfolio students early in August 1994:

[I ask the two students what their first reactions were when they heard that their portfolio scores would be reported as their grade for the course for each trimester.]

Harry: I didn't like it at first because I don't do good at portfolios, and my whole grade depends on my portfolio.

TU: How do you know you don't do good at portfolios?

Harry: Because I've done portfolios before, and I usually get, like, a C or something on them.

TU: That's interesting. Why is it that you think you don't do good at portfolios but you do good at other ways?

Harry: I don't know.

Thomas: Because you have to write out about why you picked this certain work for your portfolio.

Harry: And there's not much to write about.

TU: What do you mean there's not much to write about?

Harry: Like, why you picked papers, there's not much to write about.

Clearly, these students knew something about portfolios, and they were not alone in their apprehension. In fact, Martha Goldsmith, Maria Madsen, and Jennifer Johnson (all pseudonyms)—three volunteer portfolio English teachers for the 1994–95 portfolio project at Charles Ruff—each expressed their own brand of anxiety as they began their yearlong journey into portfolios. Jennifer, for example, who, unlike Martha and Maria, had been teaching for almost two decades, verbalized what could have, but fortunately did not, become a serious obstacle in the path of the portfolio innovation:

[About three weeks before the first portfolio scoring session in October, I ask Jennifer, who has expressed concerns earlier in the interview that her students are just not doing much work, whether her students have begun to put forth more effort as the scoring date approaches. I ask this within the context of a larger question, namely, what issues are bothering Jennifer?]

Jennifer: Some are, yeah. Some are beginning to ask questions about can I still get this work done and in, and I said "Oh yes! You can do that!" What else is bothering me? Mostly parents, I think, Terry. I'm not worried about the administration or the district office. That really doesn't bother me. I probably, to be real honest, subconsciously, am concerned about my reputation as a teacher. But . . . that's [a]more subconscious-type thing, I think. I'm not worried about what [the principal] thinks or what the district office thinks.

TU: Tell me more specifically—

Jennifer: —about that reputation thing?

TU: Yeah, what you perceive your reputation to be and what you're afraid will happen to it.

Jennifer [makes a face as though she's eaten something sour]: Oooh . . . I knew you were gonna ask that. Um . . .

TU: And you can go ahead and be as honest as—

Jennifer [animated]: Oh, I am! I am! I'm trying to be. I'm having a hard time verbalizing all this, that's all. This is, this is, this is . . . uncomfortable stuff. [laughter] OK. I think that I've built a reputation as being a strong English teacher and having students produce quality work—the majority of students. Granted, there have been a handful of kids who have turned in [garbage] but, um, every teacher has that. With this system and not—which I like, I mean, I'm not saying I don't like this system, but it's just frustrating right now because some kids are still not picking up the ball and getting their work done, and they will not have enough evidence to demonstrate what kind of language art student they are. They won't *have* the stuff to demonstrate their reading and writing *habits*. And it concerns me that I will have more than my usual handful of students that are not doing well.

Perhaps because Martha and Maria had just entered the profession and had barely had time to begin building their reputations, they expressed somewhat different concerns as their students put together their first portfolios for external scoring. Both teachers had the same concern, namely, that the project seemed likely to exact an unfair toll from their students. The following illustration of this concern was taken from an interview with Martha:

[Martha has just commented that she likes the portfolio project, but that her students are paying the price.]

TU: What is the price for them? Their grades mean a lot to them, I know.

Martha: Yeah, and I know that's something we're working on so that grades no longer mean so much, grades no longer mean direction in life or anything like that, but unfortunately they still do. I guess it might be a matter of just toughing it out, and breaking down those barriers through all this stress, and all this, um, just tough stuff, I guess. But right now it just feels as if it's at such a great price.

TU: The kids are paying the price?

Martha: Yeah.

TU: Can you be a little more specific in terms of what it is that they're paying?

Martha: Just that—I just feel like I'm learning so much, and I think all of the teachers are, and it just feels like all this— like, I keep learning how I would have done things differ- ently, and how I'll do things a lot better next year or next trimester, but all this learning that I'm doing and all this figuring things out—figuring out what's really really important—comes out on them. They don't get the benefit of me really really really knowing what I'm doing. [whis- pers] Not that I'll ever really know what I'm doing. [normal voice] But they don't get that benefit, and it comes out in their grades.

The grades the students received on their portfolios did, indeed, hold unusual importance for them: The volunteer portfolio teachers had solemnly agreed that grades as determined by the external com- mittee's examination of student work would constitute report-card grades for each of the three trimesters. One might wonder how these report-card grades could have assumed such significance in the lives of adolescents not yet old enough to drive a car; after all, GPA's count in high school. But as we will see, the semiotic capitalism of the school, and of the elementary Ruff feeder schools, had already begun to build social structures which had transformed the first four—and then the sixth—letters of the alphabet into richly textured symbols representing a spectrum of real consequences for students, ranging from material rewards or punishments to self-worth as a human being.

Confidence in the System

Though teachers and students alike were on shaky ground at the start of the year, by the time the third portfolio scoring dates arrived, the portfolio teachers and their students were old, experienced hands at the process. Returning to Susan's letter of recommendation for Mary which opened this chapter, readers can discern a confidence and a pur- posefulness that Susan hopes will provide a focus on Mary's work for the examination committee. It is almost as if Susan wrote her letter for Mary in order to communicate for sure what might be hard to see amidst the landscape of Mary's portfolio:

> I'm surprised on how well she's followed her goals and, I believe, achieved them all. She takes challenges and wins. She was writing a long story and balancing a poem on her nose at the same time.

On Mary's behalf, Susan made careful use of the language and ideas of the portfolio scoring rubric (see the Appendix) as she argued Mary's case in her letter to the examination committee—Mary "experiments," wrote Susan; Mary "sets goals and achieves them, accepts challenges, writes powerfully." Having spent a considerable amount of class time reading, discussing, and applying the rubric, these students and their peers in this seventh-grade English class had become experts at "rubric talk" by the time that the final portfolios were due. After all, they had passed through two previous scoring sessions during which their report-card grades had also been determined by the examination committee. Susan continued to persuade the examination committee by closing her letter of recommendation for Mary as follows:

> She is so open to opinions, when she wanted a title for her poem, she had me read it and give suggestions. She will also ask questions on spelling and revisions to make her story better. She uses drafts as a place to revise and experiment so her final is perfect. She writes so many drafts her little story packet isn't very little. She reads almost everyday and for long times she has 59 text log entries. That's all I have to say.
>
> Love, Susan

Though this letter directly benefitted Mary, it also demonstrated that Susan had learned well one of the tricks of the Ruff portfolio trade as a consequence of her participation in Charles Ruff's 1994–95 experimental portfolio project. Susan showed that she knew it wasn't enough simply to mouth the words of the rubric; for claims to count in her friend's favor, they had to have evidentiary support within the contents of the portfolio. So she pointed to specifics: fifty-nine text-log entries, Shakespeare versus R. L. Stine, a long story with several drafts.

In her letter, Susan revealed that she had looked at Mary's portfolio through the lens of the rubric. Susan also wrote from the stance of one who knew that a central purpose served by peer letters of recommendation in the Ruff system was to provide the examination committee, who did not sit at a desk next to Mary from day to day, with information about Mary's work habits to help them contextualize Mary's work products. And so she reported that Mary's poems almost made her cry, that Mary asked for help when she was stuck, that Mary engaged others within the community of learners which the teachers hoped the portfolio system would engender.

Mary's teacher, Martha Goldsmith, also submitted a letter as part of Mary's portfolio, as she did for all of her other students (like peer letters of recommendation, teacher letters were a formal part of the portfolio system). Similarly grounded in classroom details, Martha's letter further situated the body of work Mary placed before the examination committee. Here is Martha's letter:

> Mary decided that in the beginning of the quarter that she wanted to try some poetry reading and writing. She began by looking through my college anthology of poetry. Her greatest feat was composing a piece of writing in which she combined poetry and narration in a story written in diary form. I think this was a major experiment for her as well as a risk. She tried something she has not tried before and researched her style by reading poems and becoming more acquainted with the language of poetry.

Martha's letter, like Susan's, was filled with the meanings and words of the rubric. "Mary decided," Martha wrote, and then, "She wanted to try. . . ." Indeed, the language of the Ruff portfolio rubric deemed intentional learning behaviors to be of the highest value; establishing goals, setting up experiments with explanations of purpose and outcome, and being alert to one's own thought processes were qualities for which the examination committee awarded the highest marks.

Martha Goldsmith and her two portfolio colleagues, Maria Madsen and Jennifer Johnson, knew full well that their participation in the Ruff experiment would mean committing themselves to a model of instruction akin to one termed "intentional learning" by Bereiter and Scardamalia (1987). According to these theorists, reading and writing instruction in American schools has traditionally operated within an "exercise" model wherein students are assigned work to do, often in workbooks or on worksheets, and are motivated to complete tasks by extrinsic incentives. They labeled a more recent wave of reform the "knowledge-base" model—one wherein "the main determinant of performance in comprehension or composition is . . . adequacy of world knowledge"; the assumption is that "cognitive skills . . . are either already available or will develop naturally under conditions of high available knowledge" (p. 13). A third wave of reform, however—one which Bereiter and Scardamalia believed had not yet achieved a solid theoretical and empirical foundation in 1987—these theorists called the "intentional-learning" model:

> Within [the knowledge-base model] . . . interests and intentions . . . are mediators of competence. The competence that a student will display depends on interest and intention, and these in turn influence the constructive activity that leads to future development. . . . At any one moment student motives are taken as

givens, [though] they are also thought of as evolving and capable of being stifled or nurtured by the teacher. The same notions apply to the [Intentional Learning model], except that in [this model] *interests and intentions are not just mediators of competence; they are part of a person's competence—something to be developed.* (p. 14; emphasis added)

A major instructional challenge for Martha, Maria, and Jennifer, therefore, was figuring out how they could best help students develop not just their skills in comprehension and composition, but also their interests and intentions. They also had to help students communicate and demonstrate their growth in these areas for an external evaluative body.

In addition to letters from peers, classroom teachers, and parents (if students wished), the portfolio-assessment system asked students to prepare and submit a paper called "Autobiography of Me as a Reader and Writer," a device imported from Pittsburgh which the Ruff teachers had heard about in staff development workshops. Specifically, the Ruff version asked students to explain their goals for each trimester and to describe what they had done to achieve their goals over the term. Here is a portion of Mary's third-trimester autobiography:

> My goals for reading for third trimester were to read about poetry. Here's my goal and I quote "I've never read a poetry book so it's my next target." I accomplished my goal which leads to my story. My goals for writing were to write a story with poetry and I quote "My goal is to write a story with poetry I made up myself." I wrote a wonderful story about poetry with poetry. I really wanted to just make a book of poetry because it would be easier to just write poems and harder to write poetry and write a story. I took the challenge. I was satisfied that I tried my best because if I didn't than I would feel cheated inside. It makes me feel good to know I've done something even though it challenged me to my greatest limits.

Quoting from 3 × 5 index cards that Martha had asked her students to complete during the early portion of the trimester, Mary was able here to articulate quite specifically what her interests and intentions were for the term, and she offered the examination teacher her portfolio as evidence of her process and progress, a portfolio which had been built according to the specifications in the student handbook. Beyond the autobiographical piece and the various letters, students were asked to submit the following entries: best writing of the trimester, text logs, shared readings, and a free-choice entry.

Each of these entries was to be introduced by an entry slip which served to explain to the examination committee why the work was done and what the work represented about the student and his or her growth. Although students made full use of a set of packaged entry slips with several guiding questions for the first trimester scoring, by the time the third scoring session occurred, almost all of the students had abandoned these forms and wrote self-contained essays or letters to explain the role of particular entries. Occasionally, examination committee members at the third-trimester scoring session would come across first-trimester entry slips with their telltale prefabricated questions, but invariably those slips appeared in portfolios constructed by recently transferred students.

Here is a sample of Mary's entry slip for her best writing entry for the third trimester:

> My story turned out great. I never thought I could write so much so fast. I chose to write this story because a lot of kids are asked by friends why their parents are so busy but they don't realize that their parents are just trying to help them. I think that this story shows that kids like my characters should think twice before running away or lieing to their parents. This story was challenging because it had to be put in diary form. That wasn't the most challenging thing, it was that before every diary entry I put a poem. The poem said how my day went. Another reason it was hard is because I had to become 21 years old. I experimented with drafts because I have two drafts not counting the final. But I think that the point that shows experimenting is in my second draft I have two endings because I thinked that they were both great but I decided on the first one because it was more realistic.

This commentary served as a sort of selected reading guide for the examination teachers: They needed simply to look at the evidence and determine whether Mary's claims were good.

The next entry in Mary's portfolio—the entry just past the thick packet of jottings, scribbles, drafts, experiments, and final copy of the writing entry—was her text logs. Ruff portfolio students had a standing homework assignment: to read for a minimum of one half-hour at home in a book of their choice. The following day, upon entering their language arts class, students would use the first five minutes to record what they had read the previous evening, along with their responses to it. Of course, not just anything would do. The rubric specified that top grades would go to those students who read every day for long periods, often for an hour or so; who selected readings that not only entertained but also challenged; who set goals for reading and achieved them; and who "read like a writer." Mary's text logs were full and rich, highlighted in yellow and pink with a key to point out particular entries that she wanted the examination committee to notice for particular purposes. Here is a section of Mary's entry slip for her text-logs entry:

> This is my textlog entry slip. It might be to hard to read all of my 61 entries. So if you want it you can read the highlighted areas which show important areas I want you to see. I read habitually every day for one hour because it is clearly seen in the time place. My reading isn't only for entertainment, it's also for challenge. For example, I decided that this trimester I would try to read some of Shakespeare's poems. For example, in the entry dated "4-14-95," "At first I thought this poem was just about spring but it's not. It's about love." (Most of Shakespeare's poems are about love.) For example, "Cuckoo, cuckoo: O word of fear, unpleasing to a married ear." To me this means that spring is a time for love to people who aren't married.
>
> That shows a lot of things like rereading, using examples from the text, and that I show persistence. Also that I analyze my own processes thoughtfully. All that came from one entry. Just think how many you'll get from 61. In text log "4-13-95" I show that I interpret my readings personally and deeply. See "As I finished 'Death Be Not Proud' I felt so bad at the end because I knew he was going to die but I kind of well, hoped that they would surprize me with a happy ending. But they didn't and with the ending that way I said 'Ohhh' when I got there because it seemed so real I guess it was real for his family." I think that was one of my best entries. Behind this entry slip is a list of new words I've learned with the defenision.

In her shared reading entry, Mary presented a "reflection" on *The Giver*, a novel by Lois Lowry (1993) which Martha Goldsmith had decided to assign as a whole-group text. The intention behind whole-group texts, one which was explained carefully to the students in these classrooms, was to provide them with instruction in strategies that they could transfer to their personal reading materials. To fulfill this intention the teachers selected novels, short stories, poems, and other readings that presented complex and important ideas and themes, complicated characters, challenging language and stylistic devices, and high-quality textual models. Mary decided to include in her portfolio one of several task sheets which Martha had prepared for her students. This task sheet and the work products which Mary included reflect alignment among the criteria articulated in the scoring rubric and characteristics of the task that Martha set out for her students. Here is a portion of that task sheet:

You will be writing a letter to your classmates expressing your thoughts about *The Giver* chapters 1–6. Consider these questions, but do not be limited by them. Explore your own thoughts and issues!!

Be sure to (1) REREAD parts of the book not only to clarify your understanding, but to deepen it (and explain how your understanding deepened), (2) INTERPRET deeply and personally, (3) REVISE your interpretations as you REREAD and explain how and why your original interpretations changed, (4) SUPPORT YOUR THOUGHTS WITH EXAMPLES AND QUOTES FROM THE BOOK.

[Martha included a question on this task sheet that created a link between the text, the class discussions of the text, the portfolio, and the examination committee:]

How do you feel about the class discussions? What stands out in your mind about our discussions? What have you learned from them? Are there any specific comments made by individuals that are sticking with you? Why have these quotes stayed with you?

Here is a portion of Mary's response to this question:

One thing that stands out to me about class discussions is when we talked about freedom of speach. That day I learned that some people can't help but say things that might make them seem cool, but some people don't want to hear bad language, some people do. But when you talk to your parents you don't swear at them so why should you swear at your friends?

Mary rounded out her portfolio with a free-choice entry. This entry, a poem, was about role models. "At first my goal was to get started then we'll see what happens," Mary wrote in her entry slip, "well, I finally got started but I only had a few lines. But it got bigger and bigger as I revised and added more. I took out some ideas but I mostly added in." Included with the final draft was a series of preliminary drafts annotated so that the examination teacher could easily follow Mary's decision-making process as she worked through the composition of the text.

The Examination Committee

The examination committee was made up of four Ruff English teachers who had volunteered for the job of scoring portfolios. Essentially, this job involved preparing plans for substitute teachers to take over their classrooms for three to four days each trimester while the examination teachers read, analyzed, and scored approximately three hundred portfolios at three different scoring sessions (one per trimester). The first scoring session was held in one of the few empty classrooms at Ruff, in a building on the periphery of the campus where few teachers and other staff members ever came. Scoring sessions two and three were held in a conference room in the Ruff library, a conspicuous location which gave most staff members an opportunity to observe the activity of scoring, if only briefly.

Each of the three scoring sessions took longer than the three days which had been allocated, even though several examination teachers took portfolios home with them to score at the end of very long days on site. Moreover, because the task of scoring involved more time than had been anticipated, teachers not originally part of the project but who had available time were invited to score. For example, during the first scoring session, the technology coordinator was able to spend several hours scoring. Another non-tenure-track English teacher on a half-time contract scored during the morning hours for the second scoring session. Similar arrangements were made during the third session with some changes in personnel. Significantly, the portfolio teachers themselves ended up scoring portfolios during the third scoring session, although in no case did a portfolio teacher score her own students' portfolios.

The original plan called for two examination teachers to score each portfolio (one as the primary scorer and one as the validation scorer), but the time factor made double scoring unrealistic. So the portfolio teachers assumed responsibility for signing off as validation scorers for their own students' portfolios. Though not an original part of the design, this arrangement provided an important dependability check. On those rare occasions when the portfolio teachers perceived a discrepancy (the Pearson product-moment correlation between grades portfolio teachers would have given and grades issued by examination teachers ranged from 0.86 to 0.95), the portfolio teacher as validation scorer discussed the portfolio with either the examination teacher or the coordinator of the portfolio project before anyone reported a final grade. (Though grading disagreements between portfolio teachers and examination teachers were infrequent, those disagreements that did occur raised serious and complex issues regarding the limits of both portfolio assessment and classroom teacher observation, issues which will be discussed later.)

The actual scoring of the portfolios involved a number of steps. A few days before the first scoring session, the portfolio and examination teachers met to discuss the upcoming session. This meeting focused on several expected and unexpected issues. Of course, the teachers analyzed the rubric in group discussion to ensure common understanding; the portfolio teachers also explained to the examination teachers how students had been instructed to organize their portfolios and what sorts of entries to expect. But heated debate arose about who would be responsible for answering telephone calls from parents when parents wanted an explanation about a particular grade.

The following, rather lengthy excerpt comes from the transcript of the tape recording of that discussion and involves teachers from the other disciplines who were involved in the portfolio experiment as well as their examination teachers. It is presented in this lengthy and detailed manner so that readers can get a clear sense of the level of nervousness, anxiety, and tension that surrounded this question of who is to be held accountable for a student's grade:

> *Ms. A.* [English examination teacher]: Terry, does that mean that we're going to be the first line, then—right now when progress reports come out, we all get lots of calls—I—are we the first line when these report cards come out? The examination teachers, not the classroom teachers?
>
> *TU:* No, the pilot teachers will be the first line.
>
> *Jennifer:* Oh, absolutely.
>
> *Mr. W.* [science portfolio teacher]: And I would imagine that, for the most part, it shouldn't necessarily have to go that far because we will have already—I mean, if I see a huge aberration in what I think students should be getting, I will have already talked . . . previously . . . I mean, we're gonna have a chance . . . or not? I mean, I thought the original idea was that the classroom teacher would get a chance to kind of look and discuss if there was a question on any grade.
>
> *TU:* Well, we'll cross that bridge when we come to it. I don't know. Jennifer, what are your thoughts on this one?
>
> *Jennifer:* I don't know whether—I have the utmost faith in these guys, but—in what I *think* they're going to see, and I also have a lot of faith in—not to say W. that you don't—
>
> *Mr. W.* [laughs]: Well . . .
>
> [general laughter]
>
> *Jennifer:* Anyway . . .
>
> *Ms. K.* [science examination teacher] [amidst laughter]: *I* don't know what you're talking about. I have a lot of faith in you, W.
>
> *Jennifer:* But in that we've talked so *much* about what's been going on in the department and the kinds of things that

these guys are going to be seeing, I don't anticipate right now—I may be wrong, though—but I don't anticipate them seeing things completely different than what I do.

Mr. W.: But—

Ms. K.: It seems to me you're gonna have some kids, though, that—

Jennifer: Oh, but hopefully that's going to be addressed in my letter of recommendation that will be in the portfolio that [the examination teachers] may see. And also that I will be available, and that W. will be available in case you guys are really having problems and we can scurry over to [the classroom on the margin of the campus] and talk through it on our prep.

Unknown: OK.

Jennifer: Don't you think?

[four seconds]

Ms. K.: Oh, *yeah.*

[general laughter]

Jennifer: W., what do you think?

Mr. W.: I don't anticipate any major problems, but I'm not worried about problems, I just think, you know . . . if it's *way* off, then . . . I mean, honestly, if it's way off, then there should be a question.

Jennifer: Well, yeah.

Ms. K.: If it's way off from what you think, or if it's way off from what the primary and the secondary scorers thought?

TU: Yeah, the question that I have is who's way off?

Jennifer: Yeah.

Mr. W.: Well, either way. I'm not saying if—

Mr. S. [mathematics examination teacher]: Yeah.

Mr. W.: —but the dialogue should have occurred.

[three seconds]

Ms. K.: But when we're scoring—

Mr. W. [excited]: —if, if, if it's way off from what I thought, I'm at least gonna ask. I'm gonna say—

Ms. A. [English examination teacher]: But way off from where your reports that go home have indicated previously or—

Mr. W.: Well, I don't know about the rest of you guys, but *I'm keepin' track* . . . for my own . . .

Mr. S.: Huevos?

Mr. W.: Huevos—I mean, if everything fell apart right now and
they pulled funding and somebody said, "OK, you have to
give a grade," I'd know exactly what grade, I think, based
on the way I've done things before, that the kid should get.
And if it's way different, I mean, I would at least want to
dialogue with the people who scored it. You know, how
come? Why?

While this sort of excited laying down of rules characterized
the first few weeks prior to the first scoring session as well as the
scoring session itself and several days that followed, all of the teachers involved in the project—with one very important exception,
which will be discussed later—discovered the requisite formal and
informal rules and routines that permitted the portfolio teachers to
turn over their students' work to the examination teachers for high-
stakes evaluation.

This process of discovery went on throughout the year, particularly during discussions among the examination teachers while they
were scoring portfolios. The field record is saturated with examples of
exploratory discourse among these teachers. Consider the following,
rather lengthy section from a tape recording made during the second
portfolio scoring session at Ruff. Here, the examination teachers discussed the interplay between the portfolio scoring rubric and instruction. Notice the continuous interweaving of issues of curriculum,
instruction, student learning, and assessment:

Kate: What we're finding—the two of us that have started
working on this—is that they [students] are paying attention to literary and stylistic features because they are called
to that attention in class. They are not necessarily understanding what those features are or interpreting them
beyond a surface level, at least the two we have here. We're
seeing this infusion of different opportunities here for them
to do it, but they're—

Frank: Then we have to define "pays attention" to mean
"understands."

Milly: I think using it on their own—you know, if this were,
maybe, a freewriting activity where they were reflecting on
everything that they had done with "Little Drummer Boy
of Shiloh [*sic*]," then—and they *chose* to bring in some of
these aspects, but I think in the way that we're seeing them
right now, they're just going through the motions of kind of
retelling what they did in class during discussion. So it—I
don't see them using these on their own or making them
their own. They're just kind of going back through what
happened in class.

Frank: What does the entry slip have to say? Does that provide you with any . . .

Kate: Let me read you this. "Some of the strategies to deepen my understanding was open minds, visual imagery, letters to characters, different layout of poems, predictions, prose to poetry. I showed persistence in my shared reading in tracing symbols. I reread and wrote down about blind and sight. When I continued to read I found that sight meant correct and the right thing and blind meant wrong and mistaken."

Milly: See, that's mechanical!

Kate [continues reading]: "Tracing symbols helped me with what the story was about. The hard way may be the easy way out." Tracing a symbol helped her to see, maybe, the hard way out? I guess? What's she talking about here?

Milly: Yeah, because, I mean, obviously they have more than just exposure to shared reading. There is some superficial understanding, but I don't think it's enough to even move up into the B range, is what I'm seeing here.

Kate: Right.

Frank: Unless they do that—some of those different strategies with their text logs, and they've transferred some of those activities with their shared reading, and they try it with their text logs. Then you're talkin' *transfer.*

Milly: Yeah.

Frank: So that's something to keep your eyes open for.

After the third scoring session, Mary, the seventh-grade student whose portfolio we have been following, got her scored portfolio back with two additional elements in it: a copy of the scoring rubric with the criteria met by the work highlighted, and a "comments with final grade" sheet that provided written commentary with a letter grade. Here is what Mary's examination teacher had to say to her:

Mary,

I love how you worked the poetry into your story, into your diary!! Very enjoyable to read. You clearly made some revisions. Your interest in poetry is exciting! I can see you're excited with it as well. Keep experimenting and taking chances with your writing and you will continue to grow and improve.

    Do you see a difference in your text-log responses? (Comparing R. L. Stine and *Death* . . .) The more challenging the text, the better your responses. You connect with *The Giver.* You are involved with the story and though some parts confused you, you pulled deep meaning from the book.

    Great Entry Slips!

The highlighted areas on the rubric were largely within the "A" categories. However, "supports views but may need to explain more thoroughly" and "shows some attention to learning new vocabulary" in the "B" categories for reading were also highlighted. Overall, the portfolio earned a grade of "A," the grade which would be reported on the final report card to Mary's parents.

The original design of the portfolio-assessment system at Ruff included the provision that examination teachers would provide three kinds of feedback to students: (1) written commentary that would explain the judgment, point our strengths, and suggest ways to improve; (2) highlighted criteria on the rubric to provide students with a more standardized and fine-grained data set with which they could refine and extend their work; and (3) a single letter grade that would represent their overall level of performance for the grading period. Most of those who served either as portfolio classroom teachers or as examination teachers agreed that the written commentary served two vital purposes. First, it forced examination teachers to search for coherence and patterns in student portfolios; if scorers were let off the hook in terms of having to offer something useful to the student, they could have easily resorted to a less exhaustive approach to reading the portfolios that isolated portions of the evidence while never considering it in its totality. In Delandshere and Petrosky's (1994) terms, writing commentary or interpretive summaries "assist[s] the judges in formalizing their interpretations . . . so as to provide a fair representation of the patterns of performance" (p. 15). Further, the requirement that commentary be prepared fulfilled the standard of ontological authenticity as articulated by Guba and Lincoln (1989):

> This criterion refers to the extent to which individual respondents' own emic constructions are improved, matured, expanded, and elaborated, in that they now possess more information and have become more sophisticated in its use. It is, literally, "improvement in the individual's (or group's) conscious experiencing of the world" (p. 248).

Consequently, writing the commentary served the dual purpose of enhancing the consistency and validity of the scoring while providing information that could prove useful to the individuals undergoing evaluation.

The foregoing, then, constitutes in outline form the basic principles and parts of the Ruff portfolio-assessment system during the 1994–95 school year. The next chapter presents information about portfolios and portfolio assessment in the larger world from which Ruff's portfolio system emerged.

3 Portfolios in Review

What can be more different than Leonardo's treatment of daylight, and Velasquez'? Light is pretty much the same in Italy and Spain—southern light. Each man painted what he got out of light—what it did to him.

Willa Cather, *Willa Cather on Writing* (1949)

The Ruff decision to allocate funds for a portfolio project was not made in a vacuum. Most of the teachers at Charles Ruff were fluent speakers of educationese, and educationese could not exist without reification. Terms like "intelligence" and "learning disability" and "attention-deficit disorder," for example, must be uttered with the same assurance of concrete understanding that terms like "chair" and "table" are—or else participants in educational speech acts could not use them to make consequential decisions about the lives of children: to direct placement in programs, say, or to write prescriptions for Ritalin. We have to assume that "intelligence," like light, must be fairly much the same everywhere. Perhaps part of the difficulty we have with a term like "portfolios" stems from its not having been around long enough in the mouths of the powerful to have acquired its reality. It casts no shadow on the walls of the cave.

Murphy (1994) called the term a "chameleon," a metaphor which aptly captures not just the instability of the set of assumptions individuals may or may not hold regarding portfolios, but also the uncanny capacity of portfolios to change colors in the face of danger from the Right or the Left. Jordan and Purves (1996) examined talk about portfolios from the mouths of teachers nationwide and developed a set of metaphors which capture the array of meanings for the term: portfolio as agenda, as portrait, as mirror; portfolio as museum, as title, as testimony. Indeed, Graves (1992) warned us to step softly around portfolios lest they die an early and somewhat pathetic death:

> Portfolios are simply too good an idea. . . . We need to explore the many uses of portfolios for at least another five years, and perhaps indefinitely. Without careful exploration, portfolio use is doomed to failure. They will be too quickly tried, found wanting, and just as quickly abandoned. (p. 1)

There are few statements one can make to characterize the notion of "portfolio" with any hope of consensus. One, perhaps, is that portfolio as a useful tool in language arts instruction came to us, in part, by way of analogy with the arts as a means for improving literacy opportunities for children. Wolf (1987/88) explained the connection as follows:

> [T]he arts . . . have some unique properties . . . that make them a provocative context for rethinking how we assess student learning. First, in the arts, the ability to find interesting problems is . . . as important as being able to answer someone else's questions. In music, visual art, or creative writing, individuality and invention are at least as essential as mastering technique or knowledge. Second, learning in the arts often occurs in very large chunks spread out over a long period of time. . . . Third, it is essential for young artists . . . to develop a keen sense of standards and critical judgment. Consequently, in the arts, assessment cannot be restricted to highly structured problems or just to finished products. (pp. 26–27)

Early advocates for portfolios as assessment tools, Wolf and other members of Project Zero, a research institute at Harvard, joined forces in the late 1980s with the Educational Testing Service (ETS) and the Pittsburgh Public Schools to explore the possibility of portfolios under the auspices of the Rockefeller Foundation. Based upon the central roles played by problem finding, long time periods for learning, and self-evaluation in instruction and assessment, this project had a profound impact not just on Pittsburgh teachers, but on the field's emerging sense of the construct "portfolio" (Camp, 1992; Freedman, 1993; Zessoules & Gardner, 1991).

A second statement with almost universal application to the notion of "portfolio" is this: Portfolios involve samples of student work created over time in a natural classroom environment—not responses to "highly structured problems or just . . . finished products" (Wolf, 1987/88, p. 27). Although Flood and Lapp (1989) argued for the inclusion of multiple-choice, norm-referenced test scores in student portfolios, and although Cooper and Brown (1992) asked students to include at least one sample of a timed piece of writing, the notion of portfolios seems to have emerged in opposition to what have been considered more narrow and restrictive assessment techniques like standardized "bubble" tests and "on-demand" essay tests. Belanoff and Elbow (1986), portfolio pioneers at the State University of New York, Stony Brook, explained that "herd[ing] . . . students into large lecture halls for a two-hour [writing proficiency] exam" (p. 28) seemed to contradict an instructional program committed to collaboration and community:

> We were instinctively troubled . . . by a testing procedure that worked at cross purposes to our teaching—a proficiency exam

that said to students, "Your real writing, your writing that counts, is writing you do alone, with no time for real revision, without discuss[ion] . . . with others, without sharing drafts, without getting feedback, and without in any sense communicating with real readers." Because it's a . . . tough battle to change such individualistic attitudes, we sought a testing process that reinforces collaboration—that rewards students for . . . get[ting] help from others on their writing. (p. 29)

Of course, Elbow (1994) has commented more recently on the danger of a huge assessment "dystopia" engendered by portfolios, wherein students face the possibility of assessment with every scribbled word and scrap of thought; such a possibility sends shudders down the spines of teachers who privilege learning behaviors such as risktaking, tolerance of confusion and ambiguity, and willingness to entertain multiple interpretations. Other theorists, particularly those who seek the Grail of Pure Reliability and Validity, likewise problematize the relationship between portfolio assessment and classroom culture, but for different reasons. Gearhart, Herman, Baker, and Whittaker (1993), for example, studied the work processes of students as they prepared products that eventually made their way into scored portfolios, only to find, lo and behold, that some students get more help than others and that their portfolio scores vary accordingly. Nonetheless, from these early efforts to shift the focus of assessment from on-demand, uniform events to classroom work which unfolds over time, a spectrum of portfolio projects has emerged to explore this educational terrain across whole states, ranging from Vermont (Koretz, Stecher, Klein, McCaffrey, & Deibert, 1993) to Kentucky to California (see Freedman, 1993, for discussion; also Calfee & Perfumo, 1996). All that is wanting is a national portfolio-assessment system.

Portfolios in Response to the Limitations of On-Demand Tests

The roots of portfolio assessment can be traced to the mid-1980s, when a number of theorists and practitioners, such as Belanoff and Elbow (1986), began to voice concerns about distortions in writing instruction shaped by single-session, on-demand essay exams that had been designed in accordance with assumptions of writing as a unitary, isolated process, and that valued first-draft efforts above the work of revision. Of interest is that the modern use of on-demand writing tests themselves grew out of a concern that multiple-choice tests of writing were doing damage to writing instruction. Greenberg (1992) traced the origins of on-demand essay tests to 1916, when the College Board added an hour-long essay exam to its Comprehensive Examination in English. Such exams continued to be administered routinely until the 1960s, when the board commissioned a study that found a high correlation between multiple-choice tests of editing and usage skills and written essay exam scores; for the next few decades, the board relied on multiple-choice tests. According to Greenberg, the pendulum began swinging back toward essay exams in 1978, when Rexford Brown, coordinator of the first National Assessment of Educational Progress (NAEP), began to argue forcefully against the use of multiple-choice tests because of their stultifying influences on writing instruction.

Throughout the 1980s, on-demand writing tests proliferated. Late in the decade, just as California unveiled its state-of-the-art, on-demand, essay-examination system with a multidimensional approach to writing tasks (see Cooper & Breneman, 1989; Mitchell, 1992a), Lucas (1988a, 1988b) published a well-received argument calling for an end to "Phase Three" testing, that is, assessment systems like California's intended to provide teachers with "tests worth teaching to." According to California's reasoning, "teaching to the test" was not the problem—teachers always taught to a test whether they liked it or not (WYTIWYG—"what you test is what you get"—became a real word in California). Teaching to a *bad* test was the problem. On the contrary, argued Lucas, teaching to *any* test compromises both teachers and students: "Even when many kinds of writing are practiced in the classroom, if each is tightly constrained to prepare students for test questions, students are not encouraged to practice 'authoring' text as opposed to merely 'crafting to given forms'" (Lucas, 1988b, p. 6).

Lucas's "Phase Four" teachers—and students—would be shielded from the stultifying impact of even a conceptually well-designed test; instead, student writers would be encouraged to write for real audiences. Here is how Carini (1994), another powerful and foundational voice in the portfolio-assessment literature, put it:

> This is how I understand our responsibilities as teachers and evaluators of works (including writing) and the making of works. Our primary responsibility, our first moral obligation as educators, is not to shrink or deflate or contain the voice and hand of the maker (writer). Primary value, in carrying out that obligation, must be given to the recognition and development, not the stripping away, of contexts that expand the possibilities for works to be made (written) and understood and the possibilities of the person to be a maker of works—for example, a writer. Centering thought and activity on that obligation would,

I believe, reframe the discussion of standards and assessment in productive ways and turn our attention as educators to new and refreshing horizons of thought. (p. 64)

Beyond this concern that on-demand writing tests tend to narrow students' opportunities to learn to "author" and thereby diminish their capacity for achievement, in practical as well as theoretical realms dissatisfaction with the direct writing-assessment model (uniform writing prompts, uniform writing times, uniform respect for the norm of isolation) is widespread for a second reason: The model doesn't assess writing as writers in the real world actually write, a somewhat cruel irony considering that this model had only recently come into its own—after more than twenty years of scholarly attention (M. Myers, 1980)—as a psychometrically legitimate practice. Single-session, prompted writing-assessment methodology has been challenged in Wisconsin, for example, where an effort to implement an alternative assessment model called the "curriculum-event" design occurred. Witte (1992), consulting architect for the Wisconsin effort, described his view of single-session writing assessment as follows: "'On-demand' performance assessments . . . are no more capable of achieving authenticity with regard to either classroom or nonclassroom practice of the language arts than is a paper-and-pencil test of swimming" (p. 6).

In addition to Witte's charge of ecological invalidity, criticisms of one-shot, prompted writing assessments range from inadequate procedures for prompt development (Murphy & Ruth, 1993), to untrustworthy, even theoretically untenable, scoring practices (Cherry & Meyer, 1993), wherein scoring session leaders can't decide whether to follow a blind-scoring procedure or to allow the exchange of information when resolving a "split," that is, a test paper scored differently by two independent readers. Developing effective prompts may, in fact, prove to be impossible in light of constructivist reading theory, wherein even texts like writing prompts are filtered through the reader/writer's prior knowledge in ways that prompt composers might never predict (see Murphy & Ruth, 1993). The curriculum-event design described by Witte, an alternative to single-session tasks, gives students opportunities to read and talk about a common topic or theme for up to a week as they plan and before they create pieces of writing to be scored (see Sutherland, 1993, for a description of a similar assessment design implemented in Sweden in 1985).

Variations on this design have been turning up in places besides Wisconsin during the past few years. The New Standards Project (NSP), for example, has field-tested and scored student essays at the elementary, middle, and secondary school levels written as culminating activities after considerable student-student and student-teacher interactions with readings, viewings, and discussions (see M. Myers, 1996). In one NSP writing task, after reading and talking and viewing videos about Gandhi's theory of nonviolence and its connections to Martin Luther King Jr. and the Civil Rights movement, students learned about the Rodney King incident during which violence and destruction reigned in south-central Los Angeles; students then wrote essays for an imaginary audience made up of teenagers who live in south-central L.A. to let those teenagers know about the theory of nonviolence (NSP, 1993a). Pearson commented that this sort of design defines social acts of interpretation as the new norm and aims to assess "individual performance[s] in everyday social learning or problem-solving situations" instead of "individual perform[ances] in a completely isolated environment devoid of any human or material resources" (Pearson, 1994, p. 220). These curriculum-event–like writing assessments do open the aperture considerably in that they introduce invention, arrangement, and revision within a social context into the test. They are, nonetheless, somewhat artificial; they do not represent writing as it is done in a locally negotiated classroom curriculum and therefore, while they may supplement portfolios, cannot supplant them.

A third problem with on-demand writing tests is perhaps more disturbing than any mentioned thus far. After conducting a series of empirical studies of the relationship between scores on on-demand writing tests and the socioeconomic status of students, Simmons (1992) condemned the traditional model: "Timed writing tests are worse than shallow. Most students who score the lowest on timed writing tasks do significantly better when classroom writing is [rated], while most average and above-average scorers do not" (p. 111). Simmons found that socioeconomic status predicted on-demand writing-test scores for low-socioeconomic students far better than it predicted portfolio scores for the same students. These findings uncover at least two thorny questions: (1) Does the nature of on-demand writing assessment mirror sociolinguistic features of middle-class, mainstream culture in a construct-irrelevant fashion that advantages mainstream students? (2) Are scores for on-demand writing exams reflective of window dressing as opposed to substance, a condition which melts away when low-socioeconomic students are given greater opportunities to shape pieces of writing in a natural context? The notorious NAEP writing test of the late 1980s, for example, was truly an "on-demand" assessment in which, one might speculate, middle-class, mainstream children more accustomed to generating well-tailored language "on demand" might do better than nonmainstream children lacking practice in such "display" discourse patterns. On this NAEP test, eighth and twelfth graders responded in forty-five minutes with three essays, and fourth graders produced up to four essays during a thirty-minute test in a sort of writing frenzy unlikely to occur in any natural writing context (Freedman, 1993). And as Pearson (personal communication) pointed out, no one did well!

The history of reading assessment has not paralleled the history of writing assessment in that only recently has the reading analogue to the direct writing-assessment model been explored. For most of this century, large-scale assessment of reading has been accomplished by means of multiple-choice tests (Resnick & Resnick, 1992) with relatively little concern for the impact such assessment might have on instruction. Despite the credibility multiple-choice tests have in the public eye as objective and reliable measurement tools, reading theorists have long believed that general reading tests of this type provide only limited information about the degree to which readers can interpret written messages (e.g., Artley, 1975; Peters, 1975). Such tests do not provide information about a number of important aspects of reading, e.g., whether readers go about reading texts efficiently (Miholic, 1994), whether readers successfully interpret texts across a variety of genres and disciplines (Peters, 1975), or how readers fare within social contexts involving texts (Au et al., 1990). Although multiple-choice reading scores are arguably useful (Bennett, 1993; Valencia, McGinley, & Pearson, 1989) and have even been nominated for inclusion in student portfolios (Flood & Lapp, 1989), much work has been done recently to develop alternative reading-assessment methods, namely, open-ended, on-demand–like examinations asking for constructed responses and portfolio systems that broaden the scope of information routinely available about readers and their reading processes (Au et al., 1990; Au, 1994; Blau, 1994; California Assessment Program's English–Language Arts Development Team [CAP], 1992; Dias, 1989; McKenna & Kear, 1990; NAEP, 1990; NSP, 1993a, 1993b, 1994; Pearson, 1994; Purves, 1989; Valencia et al., 1989; Weiss, 1994).

Though writing theorists had the better part of this century to pursue "on-demand" writing exams, the "on-demand" aspect of reading assessment has unfolded only within the past few years primarily, as with writing, in response to perceived limitations of multiple-choice reading tests. Differing theoretical perspectives of assessors on what it means to read "well" have caused the nature of test questions found on multiple-choice versus open-ended exams to differ accordingly. The kinds of questions asked on traditional tests range from those probing "knowledge of the meaning of specific words . . . to finding main ideas for brief passages to determining the literal meaning of figurative expressions" (Valencia et al., 1989, pp. 4–5). By implication, reading "well" means knowing the meanings of esoteric vocabulary items and showing that the core concepts in a short passage have not been confused during the reading act. In contrast, alternative reading assessments often ask open-ended questions requiring constructed responses as opposed to selection, reordering, or completion tasks (Bennett, 1993); theoretically, such open-ended questions "reflect attention to reading comprehension as an holistic understanding of the major ideas and conceptions in a text" (Valencia et al., 1989, p. 5) and often ask readers to go beyond basic understanding.

Two recent examples of on-demand reading examinations using open-ended questions are the CLAS tests in California and the portfolio anchor tasks developed by the New Standards Project (CAP, 1992; NSP, 1993a, 1993b). The CLAS tests require students to read independently one complete story or other genre of literature (or paired literary passages) during one session. This test does not require students to write a summary of the passage as a more traditional test might; instead, students are asked to make notes in the margins while they read in isolation, to write down initial responses upon completing the reading, to answer questions about their interpretation of the passage, and to include "anything else" that might help another person understand how the test taker interpreted the passage (see Pearson, 1994; Weiss, 1994). Test activities and questions are aimed primarily at getting readers to reveal their unique interpretations and processes. Scorers trained to apply the criteria of a rubric then rate student responses on a scale of 1–6 with score point 1 as the low score. According to this scale, students who demonstrate a basic understanding of the "gist" of the passage(s) score at score point 3. To earn a higher score, readers must move beyond the basic plot or main ideas expressed in the passage; they must show evidence of "thoughtfulness" or "insightfulness" (CAP, 1992).

The New Standards Project's portfolio anchor tasks, like Witte's "curriculum-event" exams, present students with test passages within a naturalistic classroom context in which discussion and instruction occur. These tasks usually ask students to read several different passages of some length over several different class periods; often, students view videos related to the readings and participate in related discussions (e.g., NSP, 1993a). Like the CLAS test, the NSP exam asks students to compose responses to open-ended questions, but the NSP questions often invite students to synthesize ideas across texts, including verbal and video texts. Again, like the CLAS test, the NSP exam calls for demonstration of a basic understanding of textual ideas to score above the lowest score point; however, basic understanding is not enough to qualify a performance for the higher score points (NSP, 1994). Arguably, reading "well" requires greater astute cognitive activity on these alternative tests than it requires on multiple-choice tests. An important dimension of the NSP scoring system is that, to score well, readers are required to demonstrate intertextuality; that is, to score at the higher end of the four-point scale, readers must demonstrate "complexity," or the ability to see relationships not just among important ideas within one text, but across texts and among prior knowledge, ideas presented in videos and other information sources, and points made during class discussions.

While designers of traditional multiple-choice reading tests have recognized little if any distinction between the kind of reading one does to process a poem and the kind of reading one does to process a telephone book, the designers of open-ended reading assessments have become concerned with differences in reading performances as determined by the stances readers take toward reading events as they approach, move through, and step out of texts (Langer, 1989). Drawing on Rosenblatt's (1938/1983; 1978; 1983; 1991; see also Dias & Hayhoe, 1988; Langer, 1985, 1987, 1989; Loban, 1987) theory of the aesthetic and efferent reading stances, designers of several statewide and national reading tests (e.g., CAP, 1992; NSP, 1993a, 1993b; NAEP, 1990) have begun to incorporate into their exams the notion that texts are not unitary in function, do not raise uniform expectations among all readers, and therefore do not evoke uniform cognitive actions. Rosenblatt (1978, pp. 16–17) adopted the term "transaction" from John Dewey to describe the kind of negotiation that goes on between readers and texts; the roles of readers during "transactions" vary depending upon the expectations readers bring with them to reading events, and it is a serious mistake to approach the reading of art as though it were the reading of information. "A poem," wrote Rosenblatt (1978, pp. 20–21), "should not be thought of as an object, . . . but rather as an active process lived through during the relationship between a reader and a text."

During such aesthetic reading events, readers "weave 'a web of feelings, sensations, images and ideas' between themselves and the text" (Rosenblatt as cited by Claggett, 1994, p. 4); assessing this kind of transaction suggests a much different approach than that used by multiple-choice test designers interested in finding out whether readers simply comprehend texts. In fact, as Dias (1989) wrote in connection with a large-scale assessment he worked on in Canada, "[H]ow . . . we create, within examination contexts, the conditions that allow students to respond truly and fully to literary texts . . ." (p. 45), knowing that "such testing can easily be damaging to the delicate network of feelings and motives that energize aesthetic reading" (p. 44), poses a substantial challenge to reading-assessment theory. Of course, portfolio advocates might extend Dias's comment beyond the assessment of aesthetic reading; they might ask how assessors hope to create "examination contexts . . . that allow students to respond truly and fully" to anything—not just literary texts. The problem might rest not in the difficulties inherent in assessing this particular type of reading, but in the limitations inherent in the examination context, which is contrived and artificial—the context which portfolio-assessment theory came on the scene to replace.

Rosenblatt (1978) identified a second main stance, the efferent stance, wherein "'the reader's attention is . . . focused on what will remain as the residue after the reading'" (Rosenblatt cited in Claggett, 1994, p. 5). Of interest is that some theorists have interpreted Rosenblatt's notion of efferent reading to be compatible with multiple-choice testing. Anderson and Rubano (1991), for example, commented that "SQ3R and many other reading strategies are really aimed at the efferent stance in reading; what the student remembers for reiteration on a test of 'story or informational recall' becomes the aim of instruction" (p. 2). Indeed, the multiple-choice format may well serve assessment of the efferent reading stance *if* the aim is to test recall of what Sheridan Blau refers to as "brute signifiers."

The New Standards Project's portfolio anchor exams, however, were not developed from the perspective that efferent reading—reading for the residue—implies rote memory and correct answers. Reading for information requires sophisticated and complex thinking that is impossible to capture fully with the multiple-choice format. *Man and His Message* (NSP, 1993a), the example noted earlier, asks students to read a series of informational texts discussing topics like Mahatma Gandhi's theory of nonviolence and its connection to Martin Luther King Jr., King's role during the Civil Rights era of the 1950s and 1960s, and the Rodney King incident in south-central Los Angeles in the early 1990s. Although the task includes questions about information expressed in single texts, questions which might have been developed in a multiple-choice format, the larger purpose of the task is to give the assessor a view of how students read and use information presented in multiple texts situated within a social learning event—not just whether students can read and recall main ideas or details from single texts processed in isolation. Clearly, reading-assessment theorists are on the brink of the same divide between on-demand and portfolio approaches that writing assessment theorists discovered several years ago.

Incidentally, there is theoretical and empirical justification for taking the position that efferent reading involves just as much transactional work (or two-way negotiation between reader and text, to use Rosenblatt's terms) as does aesthetic reading. Spivey (1989), for example, wrote in her occasional paper "Construing Constructivism" that "constructivism portrays the reader as actively building a mental representation by combining new information from text with previously acquired knowledge . . . by *organizing* content . . . , by *selecting* content . . . , and by *connecting* content" (p. 4). Later in the paper, Spivey characterized standardized multiple-choice tests as being "clearly inadequate when one examines the tasks and the texts from a constructivist perspective" (p. 9), a logical conclusion if one wishes to see how readers combine new information with old knowledge, why readers select certain ideas, and how readers connect content, not simply to gather evidence that they do and then rank them.

Further, Langer (1989) analyzed think-aloud protocols from readers as they processed texts that signaled both literary and nonliterary reading stances. Not surprisingly, she found differences in their cognitions depending upon the nature of the stance cued by the texts, but the important point here is that she found complexity even during efferent reading:

> They [readers with science and social studies texts] began their reading trying to gain a notion of the topic, at least in some broad sense. This done, throughout the reading they built local envisionments by trying to understand and clarify what the particular idea they were focusing on meant in terms of its relationship to the topic, also using it to contribute toward their growing understanding of the topic. There was no distant horizon [as there was during aesthetic reading], no questioning of how the whole might evolve. Instead, their envisionments contained few ambiguities as they narrowed the possibilities of meaning and built a growing web of understanding, all related to the topic which served as their point of reference. (p. 18)

Here again is Rosenblatt's metaphor, the "web"—not made of strands of feelings or images connecting the reader and the text as in literary reading, but made of strands of ideas connecting narrowed possibilities of meaning to a topic. In both kinds of reading, readers—not authors—spin webs, a rich metaphor that suggests both fragility and strength, subtlety and simplicity. In neither kind of reading is meaning handed over neatly shaped to fit in slots in passive minds.

There is a middle ground somewhere between seeing the task of readers as one of memorizing words as if they come wrapped in godlike purity, representing in pristine fashion the "author's intention" (Hirsch, 1967, 1988), and seeing the task of readers as one of deconstructing the text to "look for places . . . where a writer's language mis-speaks her, where she loses control of her intention, where she says what she did not 'mean' to say" (Crowley, 1989). In the case of efferent reading, perhaps the best readers are vigilant against remaining at one or the other of these extremes while they shift along the continuum as the reading act progresses in its context. Constructed-response exams, such as the NSP portfolio anchor tasks, afford opportunities to see such shifts—just as the CLAS literary tasks afford opportunities to see readers build whole imaginary worlds. Neither type of exam, however, affords glimpses into how readers read art and information over time in their historical contexts; that domain is left to portfolios, and there is much, much work to do before portfolios will be understood in this regard.

Perhaps because more has been done in the elementary grades with reference to reading and portfolios than has been done in the secondary grades, I ask the reader's permission to swerve for a few paragraphs from the focus of this study, which is the secondary level. For example, many portfolio-assessment designers suggest that decoding ability is far too important for beginning readers to relegate it to a silent, visual test of recognition of phonological, orthographic, and morphographemic knowledge like traditional multiple-choice tests at the primary level. Many alternative elementary-level portfolio systems provide techniques for systematically capturing and analyzing oral reading performance data in the regular classroom. The PLAS portfolio system, for instance, provides teachers with an explanation and example of the "running reading record," a strategy which enables teachers to document and analyze the types of cues particular readers use to figure out words (Ash et al., 1994). Similar techniques form part of the design of a number of other portfolio systems, such as Project KEEP (Au et al., 1990), the New Standards Project's system for elementary schools (NSP, 1994), and the Primary Language Record (PLR) developed in England and modified for California (Barr, Ellis, Hester, & Thomas, 1990).

These techniques reflect Clay's (1979) conception that successful word identification involves all of the subsystems of language, i.e., phonology, orthography, syntax and grammar, and semantics; and that productive assessment ought to describe how children use these sub-systems to make the print-to-speech match. "Reading running records" hold real promise for improved instruction through careful, on-going classroom assessment of word-identification processes, especially in the early grades, and make assessment information serve both immediate instructional needs as well as long-term reporting needs (see Barr et al., 1990; Barr and Hallam, 1996). It is somewhat ironic that voices in the literature insist that "the current movement . . . is a movement away from skills" (Cunningham, 1989, p. 3) such as phonics, and that students are not being taught to decode. The fact is that almost all large-scale elementary portfolio systems encourage the implementation of running records to inform instruction and to document growth; it is the *old* testing approach that de-emphasizes word identification through its silent, visual format.

A number of elementary systems have tried to raise the stakes in reading portfolio assessment above decoding. The Project KEEP assessment system in Hawaii assesses reading at the third-grade level, not just by asking students to read a story independently and then to demonstrate comprehension by writing a summary of it, but also by asking them to take questionnaires and keep reading logs to provide data over time that is useful in assessing levels of student "ownership" of their literacy processes and their amounts of voluntary reading (Au et al., 1990), developmental aspects of reading which have received considerable attention (e.g., Morrow & Weinstein, 1986). Similarly, the PLR system assesses not just knowledge and understanding of print, but also important developmental aspects such as confidence and independence, use of strategies, range of reading experiences, and reflectiveness (Barr et al., 1990). In a recent ethnographic study of more than ten schools (a study that deserves careful attention among theorists who are interested in the reciprocal relationship between assessment and instruction), Johnston, Afflerbach, and Weiss (1993) demonstrated that an emphasis on such naturalistic data descriptive of more personal aspects of reading development can have positive effects on teachers' conceptions of what to pay attention to when teaching youngsters to read, and can thereby strengthen instruction aimed at aspects of literacy, such as ownership and attitude in addition to skill.

Because of a desire for assessment that supports and represents individual performance in ordinary social learning situations in contrast to artificial examination contexts, portfolio assessment has become a central developmental focus for those charged with constructing methods for evaluating students as readers and as writers. According to Lucas (1992), portfolios began in the 1980s as a grass-roots classroom innovation intended to "heighten intrinsic motivation by releasing teachers and students from the defensive stance of test takers, substituting an informed self-evaluation" (p. 3). Portfolios grew amidst a cluster of instructional values that included empowerment of student writers (Cooper & Brown, 1992; Round Table, 1989), student reflective analysis and self-assessment (Ballard, 1992; Rief, 1990; and Schwartz, 1991), and student ownership (Valencia et al., 1990). But pressure to produce reliable individual student scores has, in some instances, brought about examples of compromises of these classroom values when writing portfolios have been tried on a large scale. The 1990 NAEP portfolio field trials wherein students selected "best essays" were an improvement on the older, frenzied, on-demand methods, but teachers were still given only a few days notice to assemble the portfolios, an intrusive policy at best (Freedman, 1993), and scoring rubrics looked much like the old rubrics which "cause[d] students and teachers alike to aim for the formulaic" (Wiggins, 1994, p. 132).

Of interest is that despite the fact that the 1990 NAEP pilot did not adequately reflect classroom instructional practices, one big concern arising afterward had little to do with grass-roots instructional values like student empowerment, ownership, and reflection and focused instead on familiar assessment values such as uniformity, reliability, and predictability: "It is difficult to create the controls necessary to ensure a fair and valid basis of comparison," Gentile (1992) wrote in an ETS report (cited in Freedman, 1993, p. 47). Along this same line, Gearhart et al. (1993) turned the goal of student empowerment on its head with their study which focused on the question "Whose work is it anyway?" Interested in "portfolio assessments . . . to be used to rank [and] make serious decisions about students, schools, or districts" (p. 8), these researchers found the fact that teachers actually *help* students—some teachers more than others—problematizes the harvesting of pure scores. As Murphy (1994) noted, educators who are interested in portfolio assessment, like the Cheshire cat, had better first decide which direction they want to take before they go much further in their journey.

Portfolios and Classroom Cultures

Advocates for portfolio systems claim that portfolios nurture the seeds of change in language arts classrooms' instructional cultures. According to Murphy and Smith (1992), portfolios change the relationship between teachers and students and give teachers (i.e., "us") "a new role" within the dramaturgy of instruction:

> Portfolios give us a new role. No longer are we simply a "teacher-as-examiner," as Britton (1975) describes it. In a situation where we and our students make the examination of portfolios a *collaborative* venture, portfolios offer us the opportunity to be researchers with a range of data that might tell us what we have accomplished and what we might do next. (p. 58; emphasis in original)

This shift in teacher stance from "examiner" to "researcher" suggests perhaps a deeper shift in the nature of classroom events which teachers choreograph for children. Deyhle (1987) studied the dynamics of the classroom event that we label a "test" and found that Navajo children attending a school on a reservation and Anglo children attending a middle-class, mainstream school learned in the early elementary grades the connection between failure and tests; most of the children "[felt] sort of nervous" and "[shook] a little" and felt "scared, because maybe I won't have a hundred" (p. 103) when they talked with the researcher about their feelings during testing events. Clearly, the traditional notion of a "test" or an "examination" involves children in a limited-duration display of knowledge or competence and reserves for the teacher the power to pass judgment. Although Murphy and Smith (1992) did not recommend a precise balance of power between teacher and student to replace the traditional vertical relationship, their use of the term "collaborative" suggests that portfolio systems are designed to diminish student trepidation and enhance student willingness to work *with* instead of *for* their teachers.

Language arts instruction prior to the process revolution of the 1980s seems to have been consonant with the traditional notion of a "test." Emig (1971) characterized the teaching of composition as an activity in which teachers "[made] statements and [gave] directives about how to write" (p. 1). Students were then assigned discrete, self-contained composition tasks to complete and submit for teacher evaluation. In 1981, Applebee reported that the average time teachers spent getting ready for writing tasks ran approximately three minutes and that most writing assignments called for students to supply a word, perhaps a sentence, at the most a paragraph (cited in Hillocks, 1987). While students might have stored finished products in a binder or folder, such work was kept primarily as evidence that a particular task was, indeed, completed or had, in fact, received a particular grade—just in case the teacher lost the grade book or neglected to record some information. Blau (1993) maintained that literary instruction in the language arts classroom could still be characterized by an approach more congruent with the old notion of the "test":

> Whatever professional progress we may have witnessed during
> the past decade in the teaching of writing, the teaching of litera-
> ture appears to remain largely text-centered rather than student-
> centered, competitive rather than collaborative, and product-
> oriented rather than process-centered (see James Marshall's
> 1989 study of secondary school literature teachers, and Don
> Zancanella's related 1991 study of junior high teachers). (p. 1)

In the main, it appears that prior to portfolio theory, students were
rarely directed to look back—or ahead—or to evaluate their own work
processes and products; such craning of the neck was for the teacher to
do. Doing the work and turning it in for credit were the jobs of the student; judging the work and keeping track of the credit were the jobs of
the teacher (see Everhart, 1983, for an ethnography of this "quota" system in a junior high school).

To greater or lesser degrees, one could argue that portfolios,
where they have been tried, have both shaped and supported a
process-oriented instructional culture for many teachers and students
in language arts classrooms—or at least have stimulated a lot of questions (Calfee & Perfumo, 1996). At a baseline level, teachers who "do
portfolios" make a conscious effort to have students save their work
products, often even samples of their work processes, not to prove an
argument in case of a technical mistake, but to improve learning. With
portfolios, students have more to show for their efforts at the end of a
term than a simple letter grade on a report; they have a collection of
work which they can look at or show to others, thereby enhancing their
sense of ownership and pride and perhaps influencing their future attitude toward learning and school.

A variant on this baseline level are teachers who build expectations into their instruction that students do something with their
saved work from time to time. For example, even though individual
work products may have received separate grades, and even though
the teacher may have a series of marks in a grade book to tally up for
a final grade, some teachers ask students to look over their completed
work to select their best effort, or their most interesting effort, or the
piece of writing they would most like to rewrite. This kind of looking
back for purposes of student self-evaluation is an important difference
introduced by portfolios; it attempts to stimulate students—and
teachers—to understand relationships among acts of learning, perhaps to catch a glimpse of larger lessons about what it means to
improve as a reader and writer than one might get from limiting the
view to a series of single assignments. Still other teachers and groups

of teachers have developed an entire approach to grading based almost exclusively on portfolios in contrast to an aggregate of scores on individual tasks (e.g., Belanoff & Elbow, 1986; Thelin, 1994).

Whether teachers grade students on the basis of either discrete assignments or collections of work which have been self-assessed, one might argue that in some fundamental sense, nothing has really changed in terms of classroom cultures. The power relationship between teacher and student remains the same when the teacher retains the authority to certify; students still are "examined," ranked, and moved on by socially sanctioned authority, a condition which, it could be argued, plasticizes student ownership of their literacy processes. Drawing on Foucault's brand of postmodernism, Faigley (1992) explains how the nature of the "examination" remains the same, regardless of how the evidence is gathered:

> One of the most effective devices of power is the examination, a "tiny operational schema" as Foucault refers to it, which . . . [is] a means of constituting individuals within the discourses of institutions. Individuals are transcribed onto a grid of features established in the examination, then categorized and transmitted to a central body. These procedures make every individual into a "case," one that can be compared, measured, and judged in relation to others. (p. 144)

Accordingly, the degree to which students personally value portfolios that have been constructed for and indexed on an institutional grid could constitute the degree to which students have internalized Habermas's "false consciousness." Indeed, Elbow's (1994) argument (citing Barbara Herrnstein Smith) against the privileging of inter-rater reliability within scoring sessions has a broader application against the nature of examination itself:

> "[W]henever we have widespread inter-rater reliability [or widespread student ownership of work which was constructed primarily to comply with characteristics spelled out on an institutional grid], we have reason to suspect that difference has been suppressed and homogeneity imposed—almost always at the expense of certain groups" (p. 189).

Other theorists of large-scale portfolio-assessment practices have acknowledged that "the contents of a portfolio reflect the direction toward which the institution leans" (Black et al., 1994, p. 244), but argue that institutions can lean in benevolent directions. Berlin (1994) analyzed the fit between postmodern theory and portfolio assessment, and concluded that portfolios can serve noble goals to the degree that institutions come to regard students "not as 'human capital' that can enhance corporate profits but as human beings who deserve to be the beneficiaries of history" (p. 67). How did Berlin explain the paradox that portfolios could be a means for liberating students from capitalist oppression, when portfolio assessment "credits" students for assuming subject positions as inscribed by the powerful within institutions—and "discredits" them to the degree that they fail to construct ideologically acceptable textual-cue systems?

> The portfolio can encourage students to explore in an unthreatening situation the intersections of private behavior and larger economic and social categories in a way that enables both women and men to construct and, in the same moment, critique the spoken subject that is appropriate to discourses of power. Creating the subject position, the voice, of the powerful can be fruitfully studied from the perspective of rhetoric, of the textual devices that construct this voice. In its insistence on the creation of diverse texts and extensive reflection on the differences in these texts as they unfold over time, the portfolio is well suited to this effort. Such activities simultaneously demystify discourses of power and enable writers typically excluded to enter their circle, a position from which the discourses can be effectively resisted and reformed. (p. 67)

In essence, portfolios function paradoxically. On the one hand, portfolio systems define acceptable discourse structures and require students to construct them. On the other, they leverage students to a position from which students can penetrate official ideologies. What students own, therefore, are not simply written utterances they have created, but templates of the keys to power which they can use or not as they decide, being the "beneficiaries of history."

Berlin's contention that portfolios can liberate students, however, assumes the presence of a highly implausible condition, i.e., that portfolios exist in unthreatening situations. Unthreatening situations may be rare for students in classrooms where teachers hold institutionalized power over futures. Thelin (1994), for example, studied a portfolio system in a freshman composition course which was fashioned in light of all of the lauded characteristics of exemplary portfolio practice—postponing grading until the end of the term, lots of experimental drafting followed by student selection of a few pieces to "polish," discursive instructional responses which engaged students in exploration of ideas prior to revision and selection of pieces to publish, etc. Thelin studied four composition students and discovered that they learned to write not in an unthreatening setting which "demystified discourses of power" (as Berlin wrote), but in one which encouraged a predictable variation on an old theme:

> Ms. Green [the instructor] wanted the students to make judgments in regards to revision, but she also wanted to determine the boundaries of those judgments by introducing her political and social agendas. In other words, if the student had disagreed with or challenged Ms. Green's responses, in which direction were they to go? What choices were there to make once they had chosen to reject her position on the subject at hand? (p. 123)

The portfolio system simply masked the teacher's power temporarily. Although Ms. Green and many other teachers might assume that putting off the exercise of their power until later somehow changes their relationship with students, it seems clear, at least in this case, that students did not share the pretense. Like Deyhle's (1987) elementary schoolchildren who learned fear and trembling as part of the culture of "testing," Ms. Greene's students felt "confusion and anxiety . . . [as] a result of the impending final grade" (Thelin, 1994, p. 123). In fact, students might legitimately feel less threatened in a classroom where the role of power is explicit, the "teacher-as-examiner" is straightforward, not indirect and reserved, and there is little focus on underlying selves.

Black et al. (1994) described one version of the writing instructor's role in terms that clarify how Ms. Green could delude herself and that raise knotty problems for theorists who define situations as "unthreatening" for students before looking at the situations through the students' eyes:

> Those who teach writing are as much concerned with the writer as they are with the writing. When we describe good writing, for example, we share terminology with psychologists; we talk about maturity and development. As Peter Elbow has pointed out, we "embody" the writing, speaking of its voice, how it "touches" us. . . . *The substance of the writing becomes inseparable from the substance of the writer.* (p. 236; emphasis added)

This perspective on writing instruction, it seems to me, negates the benefit of portfolios as spelled out by Berlin. No longer do portfolios give students the chance to demystify the rhetorical devices used to construct the voices of power. Instead, the constructed voices in the portfolio are read by the powerful (i.e., teachers) as the *true* voices of students, a reading which suggests to students that the voices of the powerful are not represented by textual cues, but are somehow *naturally part of* texts (the substance of the writing is inseparable from the substance of the writer). The opportunity to learn "the distinction between the subject who composes the text and the subject who is presented in the text" (Berlin, 1994, p. 63) is lost. And we lose the leverage offered by portfolios to make students the masters, not the slaves, of discourse patterns used by the powerful, if we agree on the assumption that access to the power code is a good and desirable and morally defensible goal. Faigley (1989) commented wisely on the limits of our capacity to empower students, as follows:

> No matter how well we teach our students, we cannot confer power as an essential quality of their makeup. We can, however, teach our students to analyze cultural definitions of the self, to understand how historically these definitions are created in discourse, and to recognize how definitions of the self are involved in the configurations of the relations of power. (p. 411)

Before leaving this question of students' understanding of voice as a rhetorical construction on one hand, or as an honest revelation of a deeper inner self on the other, let me return to a topic mentioned earlier, namely, voluntary reading, and connect it to the issue of portfolio assessment of aesthetic reading and the pedagogy of disclosure. Clearly, no one-shot reading tests have ever taken into account the gathering of information about whether or how much or what students read voluntarily—the diary of a "reading voice." In recent years, however, motivating students to read voluntarily has become an important instructional goal for many language arts teachers (Glass & Gottsman, 1987) and has generated professional literature designed to help teachers and administrators instill in children a "love of reading" (O'Masta & Wolf, 1991; Spiegel, 1981). But even this goal is complicated by the fact that teachers of literature are concerned not simply with motivating students to read on their own, but with motivating students to read works of *substance* on their own. Nell (1988), who studied "ludic readers," i.e., readers who read "trash" compulsively to the degree that their ordinary lives are sometimes negatively impacted by their "habit," noted that English teachers have definite views about what constitutes "trash" and what constitutes "literature," and likewise have a long history of denigrating the reading of "trash." Writing instructors believe that the substance of the writing is the substance of the writer; literature instructors assume that the substance of reading *becomes* the substance of the reader (see Rosenblatt, 1938/1983). This transfer of self to and from text seems to me to oversimplify both the nature of text and the nature of self.

There is an intriguing relationship between literacy and notions of the self that never arises as a topic when literacy instruction and assessment are viewed traditionally as a series of exercises designed to raise students' "skill" levels. Getting the main idea, focusing on a topic, rearranging sentences in a paragraph to improve cohesion, or learning to use the colon do not necessarily involve the "substance" of the self. Instructional issues such as suitable distance from an audience, personal connections with a short story, or emotional engagement with poetry, however, create a problem for portfolio-assessment theorists, who must finally come to clarity about the role of "voice" in reading and writing classrooms, not just for assessment purposes, but also and more important, for instructional purposes. The assumption of a coherent, unified self (see Faigley, 1992) seems to underlie much of the current emphasis on "voice," in writing instruction particularly (see Faigley, 1989; Black et al., 1994), and obscures what is arguably a central insight of postmodernism, i.e., that individuals consist of multiple selves constituted historically and culturally via semiotic systems. Do textual "voices" correspond to authors' stable, inner selves? Or do textual cues guide readers to construct "voices" that present stability for what are really authors' unstable, situated selves? Do texts construct readers, or do readers construct texts (e.g., Dias, 1989)?

In fact, the unified, stable-self theory seems to serve the assessment purposes of those who would argue for on-demand assessment. If this theory were true, all one would have to do is give a "self" a chance to speak and see if readers with ears can hear its "voice"; provide uniform opportunities for all "selves" to speak and see which "voices" are clearer, more convincing, more "authentic." But if the self is multiple, unstable, a rhetorical configuration, if utterances are always linked to past voices speaking social dialects, as Bakhtin suggested, then single-session examinations could never get at how individuals go about presenting voices in texts composed over time for different audiences in different situations, and the degree of correspondence between the speaking subject (author's "self") and the subject as spoken (textual "voice") becomes irrelevant. Letting go of the romantic notion that the substance of writing is the substance of the writer opens the possibility of a much more complex relationship between writing and writers, the complex territory which portfolios might map. Such a letting go might provide students with the chance to explore—in unthreatening situations, in Berlin's (1994) words—"the intersections of private behavior and larger economic and social categories" (p. 67). Of course, in a world where unthreatening situations are the norm, disconnecting the writer and the writing might permit an even greater imposition of authority into writing classrooms.

Portfolios and Achievement Motivation

The kinds of assessment practices teachers use in classrooms—and the kinds of tests required of students—have a well-documented impact on students' motivational patterns (see Crooks, 1988, for an extensive review of the literature). Students can be motivated to employ either rote memorization or deep-processing strategies on the basis of their expectations regarding how they will be evaluated (e.g., Butler & Nisan, 1986). It follows, then, that changes in assessment routines suggested by portfolios could have important consequences for students' motivational patterns. Indeed, a persistent theme in the literature on portfolio assessment is that portfolios influence students to approach classroom work with a heightened, more global awareness of learning processes and an increased willingness to experiment with and to revise their thinking (e.g., Camp, 1992). This section will develop aspects of achievement-motivation theory from a psychological perspective which might help to explain how portfolios could be thought to bring about such improvements, a claim which was tested empirically in the case study I am reporting.

Goal-orientation theory, a fairly new perspective in the long history of theorizing about achievement motivation, seems to offer a fruitful approach to research on the motivational effects of portfolio practices (Ames, 1984; Diener & Dweck, 1978; Dweck & Leggett, 1988; Hayamizu & Weiner, 1991; Nicholls, et al., 1989; Nicholls, et al., 1990). According to this theory, students who put forth effort in school tasks have an identifiable goal orientation; that is, they work because they anticipate a personally desirable outcome. Nicholls et al. (1989, 1990) and Dweck and Leggett (1988), principal voices in the literature of goal theory, describe two primary goal orientations: (1) an ego or performance orientation wherein students work to gain approval or extrinsic rewards or to prove themselves better than others; and (2) a task or mastery orientation wherein students work to improve their abilities or to derive internal satisfaction.

Because the grass-roots values of portfolios focus students on their own learning processes and the empowerment that comes from self-improvement, one might hypothesize that portfolios strengthen task orientation, arguably a good thing to do. High scores on ego-orientation measures have been associated with a litany of negative characteristics, including high levels of self-consciousness in achievement settings; strong concerns about scoring well on tests; choice of easy assessment tasks when competence is being assessed; reduced persistence on difficult tasks when told that most students do well at it; heightened persistence on any task when told that few do well on it; less tendency to practice a task during free time; less spontaneous use of effortful deep-processing strategies when reading; and less tolerance for ambiguity, complexity, and thoughtfulness. Conversely, "it seems that task orientation . . . support[s] effortful strategies that would increase understanding and lead individuals to seek complex, ambiguous situations that might demand cognitive restructuring as well as higher levels of divergent thinking" (Nicholls et al., 1989, pp. 200–201). With the exception of Hayamizu and Weiner (1991), who argued that Dweck and Leggett (1988) had oversimplified the ego or performance orientation and consequently had ignored its positive contribution to students' achievement motivation, many theorists seem to concur that educators would do well to reshape school and classroom cultures to reduce ego orientations while encouraging task orientations among schoolchildren (see Anderman & Maehr, 1994; Covington, 1992; Midgley, 1993).

However, as Midgley (1993) noted, the typical secondary school setting seems designed to stimulate ego orientations through its emphasis on academic performance and standing (not improvement), standardized test scores that rank students, extrinsic reward systems, and an instructional approach still heavily based upon recitation and memorization (see Alpert, 1991; Mehan, 1979). Changing instructional practices such that students come to privilege self-improvement (task orientation) more than performance relative to others (ego orientation) may require not just a change from on-demand to portfolio assessment, but a fundamental redefinition of academic success. To change this, students will need to learn, first, to perceive their own progress as users of literacy through reflective analysis, an instructional challenge in itself, and second, to recognize this progress as worthwhile. Covington (1992) commented that schools must fundamentally change the goal of *"efficient learning"* to the goal of *"effective thinking"* (p. 250) if achievement motivation is to improve. It is possible that portfolios in the language arts classroom could influence students to become more task oriented and less ego oriented even without radical changes in the larger school culture. This issue will become important to the study of the particular portfolio-assessment project profiled in this book.

Portfolios in Practice

In addition to the evidence reviewed by Crooks (1988) suggesting a relationship between assessment practices and student motivation to learn, there is an abundance of evidence that suggests the existence of a reciprocal shaping relationship between assessment practices and curriculum and instruction (see Johnston, Afflerbach, & Weiss, 1993). Au et al. (1990), for example, explained a conceptual framework for a portfolio system within a whole language curriculum with "benefi[ts] to students, teachers, and administrators alike" (p. 81). Wolf (1989) reported on a portfolio-development project in the Pittsburgh schools and claimed that portfolios "offer a humane, useful, and generative portrait of development—one that . . . a student can learn from long after the isolated moment of assessment" (p. 39). Vavrus (1990) offered a template for implementing portfolios which hesitant teachers might follow and concluded with a quote attributed to a fourth-grade teacher who was relieved that "we are finally coming around to documenting and evaluating the growth that I just know is happening in my class-room" (p. 53).

There is, however, an ensemble of voices in the literature that warns of dangerous complexities and tensions inherent in portfolios which must be accounted for if portfolios are to succeed. Elbow (1994) has positioned himself as a clear supporter of portfolio assessment in the English classroom, but he has also pointed out a potentially devastating intellectual consequence of its use:

> Portfolio evaluation, in a horribly perverse manifestation of its very virtues, opens the door to the ultimate assessment dystopia: where students feel that *everything* they write—the tiniest scrap of exploratory writing, private journal writing, or feedback to a buddy—might find its way into their portfolio and be fodder for assessment. Thus every occasion for engaging in writing of any sort is an occasion for being assessed. (p. 50)

Gomez, Graue, and Bloch (1991) paint a portrait of portfolio assessment that, while affirming all of the positive qualities for schools, teachers, and students that one finds throughout the literature, nonetheless sounds a sour note, concluding as follows: "The reality of portfolio assessment . . . tells us that the responsibility of this restruc-

tured assessment work falls squarely on the shoulders of already bur-
dened teachers" (p. 628).

Beyond these dilemmas of implementation, several researchers
and theorists question the psychometric soundness and import of portfolio assessment (e.g., Herman, Gearhart, & Aschbacher, 1996). The
construct validity of portfolios as assessments of student performances
in English classes, for example, is problematic. Whereas some theorists
claim that portfolios provide the most valid look at students' literacy
development of any assessment approach yet devised—because portfolios provide multiple opportunities for assessors to judge student
work produced in a natural context across a range of genres and tasks
(e.g., Elbow, 1994)—others disagree. Gearhart et al. (1993), for example,
asked the question "Whose work is it anyway?" that assessors see
when they open the covers of a student portfolio; their study of students at work in natural contexts found great variation in instructional
and other support as students completed products which made their
way into portfolios for external assessors:

> In our study, the quality of work appeared to be a function of
> substantial and uncontrolled support as well as student compe-
> tence. Thus the validity of inferences we can draw about student
> competence based solely on portfolio work becomes suspect.
> While this is not a grave concern for classroom assessment
> where teachers can judge performances with knowledge of their
> context, the problem is troubling indeed for large-scale assess-
> ment purposes where comparability of data is an issue. (p. 7)

From this perspective, the fact that there is uncontrolled variance in
opportunities to learn diminishes the assessment value of portfolios.

Others argue that traditional notions of construct and face validity, such as those held by Gearhart et al. (1993), are overly concerned
with ranking students in a distribution for use by individuals hierar-
chically superior to the students—principals and superintendents who
use such data to enhance perceptions of their job performances, real
estate agents who use such data to sell homes, admissions officers who
use such data to make cuts, etc. The ultimate purpose of educational
evaluation in a democratic society, it is argued, is to foster improvement of both teaching and learning for children, not to rank children
on a list for economic or political use by adults. The most important
type of validity is, therefore, related to the degree to which use of an
assessment technique actually improves teaching and learning
(Frederickson & Collins, 1989; Guba & Lincoln, 1989; Johnston, 1989;
Moss, 1994a, 1994b). Indeed, in demonstrating that instructional context shows up in student performances as seen in portfolios, data from

Gearhart et al. (1993) also demonstrate that opportunity to learn varies widely. Instead of arguing that portfolios produce invalid and therefore unreliable individual scores and are thus suspect, Gearhart et al. could have argued that portfolios are valid and reliable measures of differences in opportunity to learn across classrooms and schools and might be used as a way to allocate staff development and administrative resources for improving schools. Assessment in the service of improved instruction seems arguably more useful to educators than does assessment in the service of reliable prediction of individual performance or of placement in a distribution.

The second pillar of traditional psychometric evaluation, reliability, is also problematic when it comes to portfolio assessment in English classrooms. In the late 1980s, for example, the state of Vermont undertook the development of a statewide portfolio-assessment program in both composition and mathematics which was implemented in 1991–92 (see Koretz et al., 1993, for a detailed description of the portfolio system). Introduced with high hopes and great enthusiasm, the system ultimately took somewhat of a nose dive because inter-rater reliability, defined as blind agreement between two raters on a numerical score, was dismal according to traditional standards. It is interesting to note that Vermont students also took an on-demand writing test to supplement their portfolio score, called a "Uniform Test," which was scored with relatively high inter-rater agreement (correlation coefficients in the 0.80s). Koretz et al. (1993) explained the difference between the Uniform Test reliability and the portfolio reliability (far below the 0.80s) as follows:

> High agreement rates can only be obtained when all students respond to the same or similar prompts or when they all produce works that fall within certain well-defined genres [but see LeMahieu & Eresh, 1994], for instance, each portfolio contains one poem, one short story, etc. That did not happen in Vermont. . . . As a result, portfolio raters were asked to assess whether one student's response to one task was better than another student's response to a totally different task. This job would challenge even the most conscientious and skilled grader, and given the results discussed above, we now have begun to question whether it can be done with an adequate level of consistency in an operational program. (p. 51)

Like disagreements over validity, which often hinge on political beliefs, there are fundamental disagreements over reliability, especially in relation to portfolio assessment. On the surface, one can sympathize with Koretz et al. (1993) as they discuss the challenge facing "conscientious scorers" when asked to assess chess players against hockey players, but Moss (1994b) refocused the discussion on issues more germane to students' learning in classrooms where everyone *is* her own unique game. Moss pointed out that as scores are made visible and consequential, instruction tends to focus on what is assessed, and this tends to drive out other important values that cannot be so reliably assessed in standardized fashion: (1) students finding their own purposes for reading and writing; (2) teachers making instructional decisions consistent with the needs of individual students; (3) students and teachers developing their own criteria collaboratively. Indeed, if the effect of traditional reliability requirements is to erase thoughtfulness, responsiveness, and sensitivity from instruction in the name of uniformity, then ethical questions become paramount. Reliability, often conceived of as a measure of what is just and fair, becomes paradoxically unjust and unfair in its own right. In a system that is truly fair and just, no test would ever be employed if it limits opportunities to learn.

Summing Up

Though the term "portfolio" is slippery, it has a clear theoretical history which has been sketched in this chapter. Within the growing body of literature that has been published during the past decade, the notion of portfolios involves samples of student work created in locally negotiated classroom settings over time. It seems clear that interest in using portfolios within assessment systems emerged as a reaction to the perceived limitations of on-demand tests, and that portfolio advocates believe that portfolios support process-oriented literacy instruction in ways that traditional assessment approaches do not. Despite the rather romantic claim that portfolios offer students the opportunity to develop authentic and sincere voices as readers and writers in safe and comparatively free environments, there seems to be no reason inherent in portfolios to compel one to accept the argument that portfolios alter fundamentally the power relationships traditionally played out between teachers and students in classrooms. There is some logic to the proposition, I believe, that portfolio systems which emphasize reflective analysis hold the promise of influencing a shift in goal orientations among students from ego to task orientations, a shift which might arguably lead to greater achievement. While this promise may be real, a number of theorists, both advocates and skeptics, have pointed out serious obstacles in the path of those who would implement portfolio assessment sooner rather than later, not the least of which are the intellectual challenges to be faced in sorting out what can be salvaged in traditional conceptions of reliability and validity and in inventing and discovering what must be newly formed or found.

Portfolios are, to say the least, in their infancy. And from all indications, they are not likely to have an easy childhood (see Calfee & Perfumo, 1996). If the yearlong portfolio-assessment project at Charles Ruff described hereafter is representative at all of what happens when portfolios intersect with institutional power, the road ahead is certainly long, and like the song, with many a winding turn.

4 The Seeds of Change in California, 1983–1994

California State Senate Bill 813

The seeds of change were planted deep in the California soil of 1983 by the legislature and by then-Superintendent of Public Instruction Bill Honig (Chrispeels, 1997; Honig, 1987). During that year the state legislature passed Senate Bill 813, an omnibus school-reform bill aimed at reshaping academic instruction from the ground up. According to Chrispeels (1997), SB 813 mandated that minimum high school graduation standards be raised, that the school year be extended, and that the State Department of Education create model curriculum standards to align with official curricular-framework documents. Further, SB 813 established the California School Leadership Academy, with twelve regional centers at county offices of education, designed to enhance the skills of current and prospective administrators. SB 813 also laid the groundwork for the legislation that was to follow during the next decade, including Senate Bill 1274 in 1990, the school restructuring legislation which made funds available to Charles Ruff Middle School for the portfolio-assessment project under study here.

Also important was that SB 813 required the state assessment system to shift the focus of measurement from how well students acquire facts to how thoughtfully students apply knowledge, think critically, and analyze skillfully. The tests themselves were to be catalysts for deeper instructional changes. Superintendent Honig made clear his perspective on assessment: "We want to make sure . . . tests give curriculum messages—this is what to teach," Honig wrote (1987, p. 5). He called test questions "power items," and he believed that political authority ought to self-consciously use them as reform tools. Test coaching was a euphemism for "teaching to the test," an instructional behavior then viewed as unprofessional, even unethical. Honig, however, capitalized on the common tendency to do such coaching and argued that requiring teachers to teach to his power items "look[ed] more like curriculum reform than [it looked like] test coaching" (p. 4).

The curriculum reforms Honig sought were officially articulated through what he termed a "consensus process," which was begun in 1984 when the State Department of Education assembled committees

with statewide representation ranging from teachers to district superintendents. The charge of these committees was to revise subject-matter
framework documents, which in final form advocated instructional
goals often characterized as progressive (see Shannon, 1990), such as
understanding, not memorization; application, not recitation; constructing meaning, not receiving it. However, unlike other states with
the centralized authority to appoint local school officials who could
enforce the new frameworks (see Apple, 1993), the state of California
had no legal mechanism to mandate implementation. But assessments
could provide the engine for change. Honig's power items could be used
as "friendly persuaders" (McDonnell, 1994).

It is interesting to note that policymakers in California had long
ago recognized the persuasive power of statewide tests; the difference
was that this power had always before been viewed largely as
unfriendly. In fact, in 1961, when the first state test bill (Assembly Bill
340), carried by Assemblyman Gordon Winton, was enacted as one
response to the launching of Sputnik, the use of this power to influence
schools was carefully constrained. In his opening remarks to the 1961
legislature, then-Governor Edmund G. Brown, father of Jerry Brown,
cautioned the legislature as follows: "As we develop these tests, we
must provide safeguards to ensure that they do not result in unhealthy
competition among our schools or geographic areas. Even more important, we must be certain that they do not encourage our teachers to
'teach to the tests' rather than the curriculum" (cited in Kennedy, 1985,
p. 58). Indeed, Education Code Section 12820 stated that "No results
which identify the school or district shall be made public without the
written consent of the governing board of the district" (Kennedy, 1985,
p. 59). By 1966, however, the legislature had found a way around the
code and published scores describing more than 100 districts without
their permission. The door to a future of high-stakes, high-pressure
assessment was opened.

California's Writing-Assessment Program (CAP)

California English teachers resisted the state's multiple-choice test of
written expression almost from the beginning in the 1960s and 1970s.
According to an e-mail from Beth Breneman, who began working in the
assessment unit for the Department of Education in 1975, "No matter
how hard we tried, no one in the language arts community ever was
really happy with what was produced in the realm of multiple choice.
Whenever there was a meeting with teachers, there was always tension

and testiness (forgive pun) in the air—like what are you going to do to us next and how can we beat the system." Beth recalled several attempts during the 1970s and the early 1980s to fashion multiple-choice versions of writing tests based upon samples from actual student-written essays. In 1974, for example, a full-blown direct writing assessment was conducted in order to cull student essays to correlate with multiple-choice items in an effort to enhance the validity of the test. James Gray, a founder of the Bay Area Writing Project, worked alongside Dale Carlson, the state's head of the assessment unit, to develop defensible approaches to writing assessment that would nonetheless retain the multiple-choice format. Teachers in general, however, were never pleased with these efforts.

By 1987, Honig's department had done away with the multiple-choice test of written expression and had created California's direct writing-assessment system, a system which indeed had a great impact on instruction (Loofbourrow, 1994). Momentum began building for additional assessments to change other aspects of the curriculum as the California Assessment Program (CAP) writing-assessment system had changed writing instruction (Blau, 1994; Claggett, 1994; Cooper & Brown, 1992). Mary Barr, one of the test-development consultants representing the University of California, commented at a state test-development meeting around 1990, "You can almost hear the drumbeat growing louder and louder." Teachers from San Diego to Humboldt County had begun to teach writing, even in the elementary grades, in response to the state test, and they were very interested in teaching reading through literature, just as the language arts framework suggested. A new reading assessment would legitimize such instruction.

Among many California teachers, particularly those who had participated in the California Writing Project and/or the California Literature Project—two staff-development organizations funded through the State Department of Education as an outgrowth of SB 813 (cf. Blau, 1993)—the writing-assessment system was highly regarded for a number of reasons (see Mitchell, 1992a). First, *teachers* had created the writing tests, not commercial test publishers. As Honig (1987) had argued, tests should provide teachers with models of good instruction, and who else could be expected to create such tests if not teachers? Second, although the system still included multiple-choice tests, the writing test asked students to construct their own texts to express their own thoughts in their own words. Many California English teachers, like English teachers in other places and at other times (cf. Greenberg, 1992), welcomed the political sanction to teach—and test—not just editing, but also composition, which the writing assessment brought with it.

Though many teachers viewed the CAP system as a good way to organize composition instruction, not everyone knowledgeable about composition welcomed it with open arms. Lucas (1988a; 1988b), for example, argued that the system was not "ecologically sound" in that it did not promote "authoring," but instead privileged "crafting forms." Lucas argued that the system "encourage[d] highly constrained writing assignments . . . [wherein] the restrictions on an assignment [were] derived [not] from the goals of instruction, [but from] the limitations of testing technology" (pp. 6–7). She maintained that "[good instruction] helps students discover how to navigate through the earliest stages of task representation, rather than taking the helm only when the vessel is safely underway (p. 7)."

The CAP types, unfortunately, robbed students of the opportunity to represent tasks for themselves, as authors do in real-world writing events, because the instructional machinery constructed by the assessment system was explicitly designed to teach task representations for each of the task types. The job of students was to learn to read the official writing prompts such that they could recognize clues in the prompts that would lead them to represent the writing task as the test developer had intended it. Essentially, Lucas articulated a concern held by many others at the time (Pearson, personal communication) that CAP and other such systems could lead to formulaic teaching and learning. Perhaps because of such criticisms, the California State Department of Education began issuing statements as early as 1986 (pp. 3–4) and again in 1989 (p. 60) warning teachers to guard against formulaic teaching and curriculum constraints as a consequence of the writing assessment.

Superintendent Honig and his Department of Education did not stop at the simple act of putting together a set of power-assessment items intended to drive curriculum and instruction. In September of 1986, the Department of Education composed and published a handbook with suggestions for teaching the CAP writing types, entitled *Writing Assessment Handbook: Grade 8*, which included a question-and-answer insert explicitly proclaiming the assessment system to be a force for the reform of instruction. "The present indirect, multiple-choice approach to writing assessment has proven successful at testing knowledge of writing skills," stated the unidentified author of this document, "but has tended to de-emphasize writing instruction in favor of instruction in writing-related skills. . . . The addition of a direct writing assessment to the California Assessment Program (CAP) is expected to reinforce the importance of writing in the curriculum [and] stimulate more instruction and student practice in writing . . ." (p. 1).

To accomplish this goal, the handbook included separate instructional guides for each writing type. Each guide explained and illustrated the rhetorical features of the particular writing type; suggested classroom writing assignments, including prewriting and revision activities, specific to each type; and gave examples of student writing to "remind us that there are no formulas for a particular type of writing." The eight writing types explained in the version of the handbook circulated at Charles Ruff in 1986 were (1) Report of Information, (2) Evaluation, (3) Problem Solution, (4) Autobiographical Incident, (5) Firsthand Biography—Sketch, (6) Eyewitness Memoir, (7) Story, and (8) Analysis—Speculation about Effects. There were almost a dozen types of writing in the high school handbook, but the assessment-system design team had not yet completed its work with respect to the elementary grades.

To provide a flavor of the kind of instruction called for in these guides, I will summarize and quote from the guide entitled "Firsthand Biography—Sketch." Consisting of ten pages clearly written for an audience of teachers, the guide opens with a general definition (e.g., "Firsthand Biography—Sketch is one of several types of personal writing. It is closely related to Autobiographical Incident . . . and Memoir"). Next, the guide discusses the importance of the writing type (this type gave students "the opportunity to bring their imagination and creative powers into play to highlight the subject's most significant characteristics") and the characteristics of the type ("incidents and descriptions"; "Many strategies are available; the best will not be determined by a prescribed assignment, but by students' understanding of their subject"). Then the guide provides seven examples of "classroom writing assignments" (A Favorite Relative, Friends, A Person I Admire, A Bully in the Elementary School, Adults Lacking Understanding, Student of the Year, An Adult's Help) offered in the form of California-style writing prompts (i.e., an introductory section called "Writing Situation" and an instructional section called "Directions for Writing").

The next section lists and defines the "main features" of the type:

- Beginning ("Writers should be encouraged not to begin with 'The person I have chosen to write about is' or a similar construction");
- Significance;
- Details;
- Specific Narrative Action ("Writers strive to create a living character on the page");

- Expression of Feelings;
- Focus;
- Coherence;
- Ending.

(California State Department of Education, 1986)

A student revision guide appears next, which directs peer responders to read the partner's essay two times: the first time "just to learn about the person described in the sketch," the second to respond to "one or two of the following [questions]." This is followed by a list of exactly twenty questions organized around the "main features" of the type, which direct peer responders to consider such aspects of the student text as "characterization and relationship," "details," "writer's feelings," and "ending." The guide finishes up with several sample student essays with commentary, pointing out how the sample matches the type, an "example of a published firsthand biography sketch," and a "reading list." This list ends with the following comment:

> Many of these works will seem sophisticated for eighth graders, but might provide teachers with examples. Students may be encouraged to find examples from their own reading of popular young adult fiction.

The particular guide which I've referred to in developing this aspect of the field record had been stored for almost a decade in a filing cabinet in the office of the Ruff English Department. Its pages were well worn, and there were scribbled notes in the margins. In one of the guides, the word "expository," which had been used several times in the original typeset version of the document, had been neatly crossed out, and the word "persuasive" had been penciled in in the white spaces between the lines, suggesting that an official definition of the power item had been revised and that the Ruff staff had been apprised of the change. Guides sent out to schools after the initial binder had arrived had been inserted into the handbook. Surrounding the handbook in this particular drawer of the filing cabinet were folders containing worksheets and exercises developed locally and labeled "autobiographical incident," etc. Generally, these artifacts suggested that considerable activity involving the CAP materials had gone on at Ruff since 1986, an interpretation reinforced by language and routines deeply embedded in the Ruff instructional culture as I observed it during the 1994–95 school year and involving teachers who had arrived at Ruff long after the state department's handbook had already begun to gather dust.

California's Reading Test (CLAS)

During the spring of 1989, the State Department of Education began to put together a design team of elementary school teachers to complement the original and separate design team for the writing test, which had been constituted of secondary teachers. As stated earlier, I was a member of this elementary team, which met for the first time in June at ETS headquarters in Oakland. During that and subsequent weekend meetings that summer and fall, the elementary team received a heavy dose of training in a particular model of reading—a model made up of elements of Judith Langer's (1987) envisionment-building perspective and of Louise Rosenblatt's (1978) transactional perspective. Members of the English Language Arts Advisory Committee (ELAAC) had, we were told, been steeped in these perspectives before the elementary team was ever convened. Fran Claggett's primary responsibility during this early period was to help the elementary team members come to understand the official state model and to try out some preliminary test designs. The basic idea was to develop an integrated language arts test by inventing a constructed-response reading-test design to fit with the writing-assessment system that was already in place.

During the next three years the elementary and secondary design teams collaborated and eventually merged. Out of this work came the CLAS Integrated Language Arts examination system, complete with an array of three-day prompts for fourth, eighth, and tenth grade levels; a scoring rubric for the reading portion of the test; and type-specific scoring guides for the writing portion of the test. According to the design, during day one students would read a literary passage (sometimes paired passages), make notes in the margin while reading, and then write or draw responses to open-ended questions following the reading. During day two students would meet in small groups of four to discuss the passage and their responses to it using a prepared discussion guide. During day three students would write to a prompt which had been designed to have either a topical, thematic, or generic tie to the passage and to the discussion of the passage. Written responses to the reading done during day one would be scored for reading. Essays written in response to the prompts during day three would be scored for writing. Day two, the transition day of talk, was not to be scored.

The following quote, taken from the state scoring guide for the reading test, explains in part what sorts of evidence readers had to provide in order to receive a score of "6," the highest possible score on the reading rubric (California State Department of Education, 1994b):

> Readers performing at level six challenge the text. They carry on
> a dialogue with the writer, raising questions, taking exception,
> agreeing or disagreeing, appreciating or criticizing text features.
> They may sometimes suggest ways of rewriting the text. They
> may test the validity of the author's ideas or information, by
> considering the authority of the author and the nature and qual-
> ity of evidence presented. They may speculate about the ideol-
> ogy or cultural or historical biases that seem to inform a text,
> sometimes recognizing and embracing and sometimes resisting
> the position that a text seems to construct for its reader. (p. 3)

The values embedded in the CLAS reading test pushed an agenda that
moved the definition of the "good" reader beyond T. S. Eliot's "agile"
reader (Bartine, 1989) to Blau's (1993) "resistant" reader. Indeed,
Sheridan Blau served as a university consultant to the English language arts test-design team and left his unmistakable thumbprint on
the rubric.

The definition of the "good" reader suggested by the CLAS reading test, in my view, differs in important ways from the definition suggested by the California English–Language Arts Framework document
prepared several years earlier. The framework document emphasized
the role of core literature in the schools. Although some theorists maintained at the time that the use of a core literature list to organize
instruction in English classrooms was really nothing new (e.g., James
Moffett), Superintendent Honig seemed to perceive such a list to be an
educational innovation and to believe that the titles on core literature
lists could parallel the writing types as power items in the struggle to
reform the schools. Honig believed, as did Hirsch (1967, 1988), that literature could conserve culture, a belief evidenced by the following
quote attributed to Honig in an interview (Brandt, 1989). Here, Honig
spoke about the general mood at the publication in 1986 of the
"Recommended Readings," a state-sanctioned list of titles appropriate
for classroom use:

> There was a little controversy at the start about [the statewide
> list of recommended readings] because some people, mostly
> from the universities, were skittish about saying, "Here are 1,000
> books that are part of the repository of our culture." They didn't
> like that idea; they liked what you said a few minutes ago about
> tailoring book selection to individual interests. But there are
> ideas about the world in some of these books that you don't find
> in any other place. Now, we're not dictating that a student has
> to read all 1,000 books, but we are saying that a student . . .
> should have read a substantial portion. . . . The main idea is that
> reading . . . is not just a set of skills; it's a content area. . . . (p. 11)

Honig's belief that students should master the content of literary texts was echoed in the state framework's call for helping students to develop "a common background of core works that speak to all of us in the American society" (Glass & Gottsman, 1987, p. 6). According to Bartine (1989), this idea was not new. The notion of cultural conservation had been promoted in England and in the United States in the first half of the twentieth century by T. S. Eliot and I. A. Richards. Eliot, in particular, had concluded that for "culture" to be preserved, members of the dominant class must accept the responsibility to keep it alive by passing it on. Honig seemed to have taken a similar position, although he appeared to have broadened the scope of the inheritance to include all social classes as well as the cultural elite.

It is interesting to note that Honig's cultural conservationist position ignored troublesome questions about the relationship among readers, literary texts, and authors. Studying literary texts, according to Honig, was tantamount to studying a "repository of culture," i.e., storage containers for ideas created in earlier times. Viewing texts as repositories, however, ran counter to the views of texts espoused by many influential twentieth-century literary theorists. The New Critics, for example, who emerged in the 1940s and 1950s (see Blau, 1993) had rejected the approach to literary instruction that included study of the life of an author in his or her historical context as a backdrop for interpreting a text. In fact, the New Critics considered the author's intentions irrelevant, even untrustworthy, and introduced the term "intentional fallacy" as a way to exclude interpretive claims about texts which were grounded in knowledge of an author's personal history or of what an author said or thought he or she meant to say. Mistrusting any interpretation not linked directly to text, the New Critics further excluded propositions about the meaning of literary texts grounded in readers' personal responses to text; such personal responses were deemed faulty by the criterion of the "affective fallacy." In essence, the New Critics disallowed authors and readers the privilege of using a text as a simple bridge between the past and present, the primary use to which the state framework put literary texts. Further, the New Critics wanted not to permit readers to change the inner workings of a text by mistaking their own inner experiences of that text for its objective meaning.

In viewing literary texts as "repositories," the superintendent ignored not just the New Critics, but the entire panoply of theorists who came after them and rejected them as he developed his conservationist perspective. Beginning in the 1960s, a range of literary theories sprang up in opposition to the New Critical perspective (see Anderson & Rubano, 1991; Blau, 1993; Crowley, 1989; Dias & Hayhoe, 1988). Although most of these theories argued against the New Critical glorification of text as object, almost none of them returned to the simpler days when authorial intention reigned—almost none, that is, except for E. D. Hirsch (1967), who argued that any interpretation worthy of the descriptor "valid" must be rooted in the author's intention. Again, in 1988, Hirsch argued for cultural conservation in his plea for development of cultural literacy.

While Hirsch—and Superintendent Honig—returned to the past, other theorists staked out new territory. Rosenblatt (1978), for example, argued against the New Critics' notion of affective fallacy and authorized the reader to attend to his or her subjective responses: "A poem," wrote Rosenblatt (1978), "should not be thought of as an object, . . . but rather as an active process lived through during the relationship between a reader and a text" (pp. 20–21). Still other theorists, notably deconstructionists, argued against the cultural conservationists like Hirsch, the reader-response theorists like Rosenblatt, and the text-as-object position of the New Critics. As Crowley (1989) explained it, "[deconstructive] read[ers] look for places in the text where a writer's language mis-speaks her, where she loses control of her intention, where she says what she did not 'mean' to say" (p. 7). The deconstructive reader is more interested in what a text does not say than it what it says.

The model of literary instruction developed in the state framework and again in Honig's interview with Brandt (1989) stipulated that a work of literature on the approved list in California was to be treated not as an object to be skillfully interpreted with internal consistency apart from the historical context in which it was composed; not as a part of a transaction in which readers negotiate meanings and thereby gain literary experience; not as a reverse image of the author's conscious intentions. In California, a work of literature was to be viewed as a cultural artifact with preserved determinate meanings, generated intentionally and consciously in the past, available to anyone who can read the words.

If text preserves determinate meanings for posterity, then, it would seem logical that the standard for judging the quality of a reader's understanding of a text should rest within the intentions of the author, the generator of the meaning. Language itself should be treated as transparent, its words simply vessels carrying the same meaning to all. If the state's reading-test system had been developed according to such conservationist principles, such a testing system might have resembled the one which served as the College Entrance

Examination Board's 1929 examination in English before the birth of the New Criticism, a portion of which is cited here (Faigley, 1989):

> 1. It has been said that literature helps readers better understand life. Express your opinion of this statement, using specific illustrations from at least four works you have read. (p. 398)

As Faigley pointed out through his analysis of this testing approach, raters in 1929 easily got a glimpse of the reading habits of the examinee; the board had little trouble distinguishing students who had routinely read the officially sanctioned list from those who had habitually read less prestigious works. Using this approach, the state of California in the 1990s could have checked on California students to see if they could name and discuss four works from the state list—not all of the titles on the list by any means, but then the superintendent had not argued that students should read all of the titles, just a portion of them. This sort of test in the hands of a well-trained scorer could assess not only whether a student had read the "right" texts, but also whether those texts had had the "right" influence.

Somehow, when the state assembled the elementary design team in June of 1989 at ETS Headquarters in Oakland, no one mentioned E. D. Hirsch. Instead, the state's advisory board (ELAAC) had formally subscribed to theoretical models which privileged the reader's response. Its members had relied on the work of Rosenblatt (1978) and Langer (1989) to form the theoretical basis for the CLAS reading test, despite the fact that the conservationist principles promoted in the rhetoric of the superintendent and the framework document ran counter to this theoretical basis.

This misalignment between the official emphasis on core literature and the actual design of the CLAS reading test, in my view, explains in part why the CLAS reading test had a much different impact on reading instruction at Charles Ruff and elsewhere than the CAP writing test had on writing instruction. Where the CAP writing test asked students to package language in predetermined containers (repositories?), the CLAS reading test, which by rights should have asked students to display their knowledge of literature as a content area, instead asked students to interpret language in original ways—to "resist" textually constructed, mainstream cultural norms.

At least one version of the rationale for the CLAS reading test circulated publicly in 1992–93 (California State Department of Education, 1992) directly contradicted, in my view, the conservationist rhetoric of the state superintendent. Consider the following excerpt from this test rationale:

> English–language arts teachers . . . have long recognized that students use language actively, interactively, strategically, and fluently as they construct and communicate meaning. Students can grow in their ability to use language as they explore the universe of discourse through their reading, writing, and thinking. Authors of the *California's English–Language Arts Framework* envisioned a literature-based English–language arts program that actively engaged students in . . . a wide range of significant literary works and human experiences. *At the heart of the framework is a paradigm shift in which "constructing meaning" replaced "gaining knowledge" as the primary goal.* (p. I-1; emphasis added)

On the surface, it would seem that teachers could subscribe both to the superintendent's and the framework's conservationist position and to the position staked out by this rationale simply by agreeing to teach students to "use language actively, interactively, strategically, and fluently," while students read the titles on a core list of texts deemed suitable for providing the knowledge required to build "a common background [for] all of us in the American society" (Glass & Gottsman, 1987, p. 6). But the statement of rationale for the test explicitly demotes "'gaining knowledge' as the primary goal"; the instructional emphasis instead focuses squarely on helping students to use language to construct meaning—*any* meaning, not a common meaning shared by citizens of the democracy.

Taken to its logical end, the view of instruction implied by the test's rationale compels no student to read any particular text, and the earlier official state emphasis on core literature is muted. Furthermore, Honig, as superintendent, had implicitly located the standard for judging the quality of a reading within authorial intention; certainly, the state framework writers would have contradicted themselves if they had agreed that literary works could mean different things to different Americans. If literary works could be resisted and deconstructed, how then could anyone argue for "a common [American] background"? Indeed, the rationale for the test shifted in the direction of reader-response theory, wherein the reader is at least co-author of meaning, a shift which became even more apparent when the test scoring guide was finally composed.

In fact, the CLAS reading test, when finally implemented, was clearly not designed to measure the degree to which students had acquired "a common background of core works that speak to all of us in the American society" (Glass & Gottsman, 1987, p. 6). The CLAS reading test had nothing to do with the assessment of literature as a "content area." To be sure, the CLAS test focused on the reading of literary passages as opposed to functional or informative documents, but nothing in the scoring guide which test raters applied to individual student reading performances privileged evidence that a student had read a sufficient portion of the titles listed in the state's directory above the evidence that a student had read other titles. Ultimately, the CLAS system was praised by scholars for its incorporation of social learning theory (Pearson, 1994) and for its fidelity to currently accepted theories of literary reading instruction (Blau, 1994; Dias, 1988; Rosenblatt, 1978). It was never discussed as a political tool intended to pass on a literary cultural heritage in the manner proposed by T. S. Eliot and Superintendent Honig.

The conservationist ideology of the framework had constructed a profile of the ideal reader as thorough, conformist, careful. That the state superintendent and the state's legislative body should have opted for the conservationist ideology to be communicated in the sanctioned discourse of political and educational institutions should not be surprising; for as Apple (1993) explained, the State in America has long been in the business of legitimizing bodies of knowledge that are appropriate as "official knowledge" for transmission to young people in schools. Apple's own words are useful here:

> One of the most interesting historical dynamics has been the extension . . . of the direct or indirect State authority over the field of symbolic control. Education has become a crucial set of institutions through which the State attempts to "produce, reproduce, distribute, and change" the symbolic resources, the very consciousness of society. (pp. 66–67)

What should truly have been surprising, then, was the invitation to intellectual give-and-take in the symbolic field expressed in the CLAS scoring guide.

Meltdown

When the ill-fated CLAS test finally made its way to large-scale implementation in California, it generated a firestorm of controversy. The system had begun to unravel in the early 1990s, however, long before the Rutherford Institute of Virginia and other fundamentalist forces attacked it. Honig's forceful, if not completely coherent, presence at the core of the movement was lost when he became entangled in legal charges which ultimately caused him to resign his elected post and to leave the Department of Education. Fueled by organized conservative fundamentalists who believed that the California assessment system was a political tool engineered to stimulate unwelcome changes in students' values (Marzano, 1992), public sentiment even among ordinary citizens turned against the new tests, particularly the reading test, and parents across the state pressured district administrators to boycott their administration (Wilgoren, 1994)

Not surprisingly, in late September 1994, Governor Pete Wilson vetoed legislation (SB 1273) which would have extended the completed CLAS assessment system through 1999. Three days later, Maureen DiMarco, Wilson's education advisor, characterized the name associated with this test (i.e., "CLAS") as "almost radioactive" (Carlos Alcala, *Sacramento Bee*, October 1, 1994). As of this writing, California still has no official state test system, despite the fact that Governor Wilson threatened to hold up the 1998 state budget if legislators did not agree to mandate the use of a norm-referenced, off-the-shelf, commercially made standardized test in grades 2 through 11.

Theoretical and Political Schizophrenia

All of this background—the early development and implementation of the task-driven CAP writing test; the California English–Language Arts Framework's call for core literature in classrooms dedicated to cultural conservation; the CLAS test's contradictory rejection of authorial intention as the standard against which to judge the quality of a reading performance; the surrealistic firestorm and ultimate meltdown of the CLAS test itself; the horrific backlash and the return to a multiple-choice frame of reference—is important to this study of portfolios because it underscores the theoretical and political schizophrenia with respect to literacy assessment and instruction that developed in California after the 1983 reform, the formative years of the portfolio project at Charles Ruff.

The CAP writing test and the framework's agenda of core literature affected the literacy curriculum in districts across the state in identifiable ways, e.g., the presence of district core literature lists and district requirements that students have opportunities to write in all of the CAP "domains" (Cooper & Brown, 1992; Loofbourrow, 1994). The impact of the CLAS reading test, however, was much less monolithic, much more subtle, for two reasons. First, the CLAS test was designed to privilege divergent thinking. It honored the reader's response and privileged the reader's resistance. Such values were difficult to translate into materials acquisition or assignment specifications. To be sure, the test-development team heard stories about the "open-mind" strategy, a CLAS reading-test item type which asked students to create symbols to represent a character's thoughts and feelings at a particular moment, being imported into classrooms in a variety of forms. But we also heard stories about the "empty-head" strategy being ridiculed for its intellectual softness. There was no straight and easy path from the CLAS reading test to teachers' lesson plans.

Second, the influence of the CLAS reading test seemed to run together with the influence of Nancy Atwell's book *In the Middle* (1987). Hardly an official document, Atwell's book was extremely influential (and continues to be influential) in California during the late 1980s and early 1990s, partly because of the interest it generated among teachers who had participated in the California Writing Project and/or the California Literature Project. Of interest is that Atwell's description of a literacy classroom built upon the foundation of student self-selection of texts and topics—the very notion that Superintendent Honig rejected in the Brandt (1989) interview when he claimed that "university people" were opposed to "core literature" because "they liked what you said a few minutes ago about tailoring book selection to individual interests" (p. 11)—seemed somehow compatible with a core literature approach. Because the state's CLAS reading test did not measure the kind of reading instruction called for by the former superintendent and by the framework document, i.e., literature as a content area, the CLAS reading-test design fit well with Atwell's design and likely helped people squeeze core literature into the mold. Surprisingly, few people seemed to notice the conflict between the writing assessment and the reading assessment—at least I did not hear this conflict ever discussed in any public forum, nor did I read any documents going to this issue.

Following the demise of the CLAS system in 1994, most people whom I knew came to believe that California's CLAS test would probably never be implemented again in the form in which it had been constructed. Given the mood in California, it seemed unlikely that an official initiative to construct "irreverent" readers would come again soon. Delaine Eastin, California's new superintendent of public instruction, proclaimed publicly to the media that the California English–Language Arts Framework, spearheaded by Bill Honig in the 1980s, had been a mistake. Indeed, Bill Honig himself began proclaiming that the framework had been a mistake. Eastin assembled a committee to revise the document and was being pressured to make sure that California did not simply put old wine in a new bottle. The following language was excerpted from a document dated April 27, 1995, and entitled "An Open Letter to Superintendent Delaine Eastin," circulated on the letterhead of the Assembly California Legislature and written by Steve Baldwin, a legislative leader of the Assembly Education Committee:

> I appreciate your efforts to re-evaluate how we teach reading
> and mathematics in California schools. . . . However, the panels
> you have established to re-evaluate our reading and mathemat-
> ics curricula cause me some concern. If there is a problem with
> the status quo, as you have suggested in recent media state-
> ments, I would think you would appoint more people with
> approaches that differ from the status quo.

California State Senate Bill 1274

While this tumultuous public debate had been going on around
California's mandated public assessment system, however,
California's Center for School Restructuring (CCSR) was more quietly
overseeing a five-year state grant program (California State Senate Bill
1274 of 1990) which encouraged faculties at schools undergoing
"restructuring" to "examine student work for what matters most."
Through its professional conferences and public discourse, the CCSR
for a time legitimized portfolio assessment as a reform tactic in
California. Indeed, portfolio projects proliferated in the shadows of the
CCSR across the state during the early 1990s, funded in part by
California taxpayers (Jamentz, 1993).

In many ways, the CCSR was at odds with other California
reform tactics of the era. Because the CCSR urged schools to establish
their own documents stipulating local student learning outcomes, the
CCSR was in conflict with Honig's edict that schools ought to organize
instruction around the outcomes specified in the state frameworks.
Because the CCSR urged schools to develop their own local assessment
systems tied to their own local outcomes, the CCSR was again in conflict with a state assessment system that had legal authority to make
moot any locally collected data. Indeed, one wonders whether the
leaders in California during this time period talked to one another.

All of these California reform tactics—use of the framework
document to encourage the construction of a core literature list, use of
the high-profile external assessment system to mandate change in the
glare of media lights, and use of state grant funds to nurture change
through the internal assessment system—had profound influences
over time in the group activities of the Ruff English Department. By
1991, in a single action combining elements of all three tactics, and
before the official state reading test had been unveiled, the Ruff
English Department had already administered a homemade, local,
open-ended reading test patterned after early releases of the CLAS
reading exam. Two sets of pretests and post-tests were developed, one

for seventh grade and one for eighth, each set based on short stories selected by a subcommittee of Ruff English teachers. Selection criteria from CLAS's early development work were used: Passages should (1) represent high-quality literature (as per the framework), (2) engage students in complex thinking, (3) require just one class period (fifty minutes), and (4) systematically advantage no group of students. Particularly important were the requirements that texts represent good literature rich enough in theme, language, and structure to stimulate complex thinking.

The school had also won its grant in 1993 from the California Center for School Restructuring through SB 1274. The CCSR's emphasis on "examining student work for what matters most" became a mantra at Charles Ruff, as we will see in the remaining chapters. At this point in the history of Charles Ruff, the English teachers were teaching students to become good citizens in our democracy through teaching a list of core works of literature. They were also teaching students to become irreverent, resistant readers through the use of a locally designed CLAS-compatible reading test. And they were embracing the invitation to establish their own literacy-learning outcomes as the CCSR had encouraged them to do. Added to this mix was the influence of the district administration, which had, as we will see in the next chapter, its own set of pressure points on the school.

5 Ruff Unified School District

Managing the Sky That Fell

In 1983, when the California legislature was busy enacting SB 813, a political piece of work with enormous implications for schooling in the state, the Ruff Unified School District served fewer than 10,000 largely Euramerican students. A decade later, when Governor Pete Wilson was busy undoing legislation from that earlier time, the Ruff Unified School District had grown to serve close to 30,000 multiethnic students. According to interviews with teachers who had worked in the district since the 1960s, the district had transformed itself from a decentralized, slow-moving, personality-driven organizational structure to a highly centralized, fast-paced, and well-managed one.

Virtually everyone in the district took great pride, and rightfully so, in the quality of the campuses with respect to maintenance, cleanliness, landscaping, athletic facilities, and the like—all of which were centrally managed at district headquarters. By the mid-1990s, the district had replaced its old, run-down headquarters with a modern, efficient, technologically well-equipped building dedicated to staying in front of a rapidly growing population while maintaining high-quality curriculum and instruction for all.

A unit designated "Office of Research and Evaluation" had been developed within the administrative hierarchy during this growth period. Several staff members had been hired to work in this office whose main task was the analysis of quantitative data collected by way of the state tests as well as district-adopted standardized tests; by way of locally developed surveys of parents, students, teachers, and anyone else who might have an opinion on some aspect of Ruff schooling; and by way of school reporting systems, such as attendance monitoring, enrollment, etc. With respect to visibility in the schools, this office existed to oversee the district's standardized testing program. In fact, when the head of the office appeared in schools to speak to faculties, his talk invariably focused on some aspect of test scores.

The Office of Research and Evaluation prepared numerous reports each year—some routine, some special projects—based upon the full range of data it collected. Reports involving the analysis of test data

were routinely presented to the superintendent and to the superintendent's cabinet, a cadre of associate and assistant superintendents, and to
the local board of education. The reports then moved to the level of site
administrators. For several years in the late 1980s and early 1990s, each
teacher in each elementary school was required to provide the site
administrator with an "action plan" that outlined precisely what pages
of what materials that teacher was going to use with students in order to
bolster a "weakness" identified by the standardized tests.

Of all of the tests in the battery, reading seemed to draw the most
administrative attention, especially near the end of the 1980s and
beyond. Ruff district officials used a variety of strategies to communicate the importance of standardized tests to Ruff teachers. Two examples of such strategies collected during this study illustrate how deeply
ingrained standardized test practices had become in the life of the district and its schools as a consequence of the district's long-standing
commitment to them. The first example involves tile floors, new carpet, and cooperative learning.

New Carpet

The Charles Ruff campus was composed of several large brick buildings, each of which housed classrooms representing particular disciplines. One building, for example, housed science classrooms, another
English, another history, etc. When these buildings were first constructed in the late 1960s, before the installation of numerous portable
classrooms around the perimeter of the site, all of the classrooms had
tile floors.

According to a Ruff teacher who was among the original crew
that opened the school, around the time that cooperative learning
activities became popular a decade or so ago, district administrators
realized that tile floors created noise when students rearranged classroom furniture to get into groups. Teachers who couldn't stand the
noise didn't use groups. During the period of the mid-1980s, there
were rumors across the land that the state would soon develop an
assessment system which included a way to examine student performances during cooperative group work, a system which indeed came
on line in the 1990s in the form of CLAS. As a consequence, district officials began to authorize funds to put carpet in buildings as they could
afford to do so over the years.

Gradually, as funds allowed, many buildings were carpeted, but
many were not. Ruff's history building happened not to have been

carpeted. Unfortunately, at some point before the history complex appeared on the carpet list, the district's concern either with carpet or with cooperative learning diminished because the wholesale substitution of carpet for tile stopped. It is interesting to note that the district adopted the new position that a building which currently had carpet could have the carpet replaced if needed. But buildings with other flooring materials in good shape, such as tile floors, could not get carpet.

Needless to say, the Ruff History Department, which had waited patiently over the years for its carpet, was appalled by the new policy. These teachers had watched the English building and the mathematics building get carpet. They watched even as the library got its second carpet after the first one wore out. Year after year, the History Department chair raised the issue of carpet to the principal and to the district administration—to no avail.

As things turned out, while this struggle to carpet the history building was going on, CAT-5 test scores in reading comprehension continually dropped year after year until the district administration came to see the situation as an emergency. At Charles Ruff, the principal decided to develop a content-area reading program in the history classrooms as an important part of the school's response to the district's call for increased and improved reading instruction. As expected, the history teachers were at first reluctant to take on this additional burden, but soon they embraced the task and devoted much of their department meeting time as well as staff-development time to learning about content-area reading instruction.

In January 1995, just over two years after the history teachers began their work in content-area reading, a district administrator in curriculum and instruction sent a memo to another district administrator in facilities and maintenance—composed on district office letterhead with the names of each board of education member near the top and the name of the curriculum and instruction administrator in the right-hand corner—and a copy of this memo was sent to Ruff's principal, who circulated the document among the history teachers. The following language from this memo was recorded in the field record:

> Jan. 4, 1995
>
> TO: [Assistant Superintendent in charge of operations]
>
> FROM: [Assistant Superintendent in charge of instruction]
>
> DATE: December 7, 1994
>
> SUBJECT: Carpeting for B Complex—[Charles Ruff] Middle School

COPY TO: [Charles Ruff Principal]

I would like to put carpeting in B Complex at [Charles Ruff] Middle School on the one-time money list. This is a high priority to me since the teachers have assisted [the principal] in his efforts to improve reading.

Needless to say, the history teachers were quite pleased when workers arrived to renovate their complex.

The story of how the History Department finally got carpet for its building illustrates quite vividly the connection between test scores and power in the institution. In this case, district officials reacted to low reading-test scores by pressuring their principals to pressure teachers to change instructional practices in such a way that standardized test scores in reading would improve. Although Charles Ruff's principal happened to believe for his own reasons that reading instruction needed to be improved, he told me that the district office was putting great pressure on all of the site administrators in the district, and he felt forced to look around his school to find a spot where pressure could be applied publicly. History was it.

Throughout the two-year effort to teach reading in history classrooms before the reward in the form of carpet came about, the principal had been diligent about sending handouts, summaries of meetings, sample reading lessons—whatever documentation he could gather together regarding the history reading program—to the district office so that the administrators there knew about the effort. He knew that this barrage of materials from Charles Ruff would probably not be scrutinized, but he did not intend that. His goal was simply to keep his supervisors on alert that he and his staff were "doing something" about the problem, and doing something ultimately meant new carpet.

Taking It Back

District administrators had other, less pleasant means of persuasion. As reported earlier, Charles Ruff Middle School served roughly 700 students whose family income qualified them for free or reduced lunches. Schools serving populations such as this were often entitled, depending upon district-established formulas, to Chapter 1 funds (now Title I). Charles Ruff had been receiving in the neighborhood of $100,000 per year from these federal funds to pay for special programs aimed at giving these poverty-level children a somewhat better chance at school success.

Each year this money had gone toward hiring instructional personnel to work with the lowest-scoring students in small-group reading instruction. Shortly after the district declared war on low reading-comprehension standardized test scores, however, the district administrator who supervised this federal program sent a memo to the Charles Ruff principal which read, in part, as follows:

> Because your student performance in 1994 was much lower than anticipated, a district decision has been made that Title I funds will be provided for your school only for the next two years. Significant improvement in overall student performance will be necessary to extend Title I funds beyond 1995–96 and 1996–97.

In essence, the principal and the school were being threatened with loss of resources if CAT-5 reading-test scores did not rise.

Yet the standardized test system driving the institution gave the principal no help with improving his understanding of his own instructional role; it gave him no help with improving his understanding of and support for his teachers; it gave him no help with stimulating appropriate instructional action; and it gave him no help with developing a logical course of action. He conceded these points during an interview. The test was a weapon, a tool of intimidation, designed not to provide insight, but to instill fear. I argued that those who would suffer most as a consequence of the ever-decreasing standardized-test mean score in the district would be the students who scored the lowest.

Some months later, after the principal had read a draft of this book, he met with me to discuss his views on these and other incidents reported herein. Among the most interesting revelations was his setting me straight about what had really happened with the new carpet. He had asked the district official to stage the reward of carpet for his history teachers—though he had not revealed this information to the History Department or to me. He had *requested* that the assistant superintendent send a memo linking the carpet to reading instruction so that he could photocopy and disseminate the memo. The carpet would, in all probability, have been forthcoming regardless of this linkage. As principal, he had few tools powerful enough to influence an entire department of teachers, particularly not a department made up largely of teachers who had been teaching at Ruff for years and years. He took advantage of the opportunity to show them that when they cooperate, they get good things.

He also told me—lectured me, more aptly described—that I did not have the slightest idea of the intense pressures district officials faced with respect to test scores. He voiced his opinion that I, myself, would not have had the capacity to withstand the stress they lived with daily, that I would likely not last a week as the assistant superintendent in charge of instruction, and that until I proved myself capable of withstanding the unrelenting pressure from the community on district office personnel, I should withhold judgment. He argued that carpet was needed in the history complex, that the history teachers had cooperated, and that this was the way things get done. He further argued that the Title I administrator was under an obligation to make sure that the federal moneys were effectively and appropriately spent; it was legitimate for this official to withdraw funding from sites that demonstrated little capacity to deliver.

He argued that everyone with responsibility for large groups of children—from principals to state superintendents to federal Chapter 1 officials—relied on standardized test scores. What else could they rely on for information? Hadn't I already proven in my own study that there are no stable sources of information except for standardized tests? When was I going to wake up and realize that this situation was not going to change? No amount of idealism was going to make things even the slightest bit different.

Implementing the State's Framework

This profound and deep emphasis on standardized test scores was an important factor in the district's rather schizophrenic approach to the implementation of the state's English–Language Arts Framework. Although the state did not yet have a reading test in the mid-1980s, it had implemented a writing test, and no one doubted that a reading test was coming. Further, the rhetoric of the State Department of Education spoke clearly of a reading test in alignment with the framework. When the California framework had first circulated in the Ruff district, district administrators in the staff-development office scrutinized the document carefully and used it as a blueprint for establishing guidelines for schools to follow in developing their yearly written school plans, presented in hourlong sessions each spring to the instructional cabinet.

The role of teachers as reading instructors was not spelled out in detail in the framework, but there was enough said to make clear what the intent was. Consider the following excerpt from a section of this document titled "Empowering Ourselves to Implement the Framework":

> Teachers must see the act of teaching as a dynamic one that
> allows students to grow in language use through encounters
> with literature and human experiences. Piecework and frag-
> mented work sheets isolating a single skill must give way to
> activities and assignments designed to involve the student in
> active thinking, responding, exploring, and shaping of ideas.
> Besides using a wide range of literary materials and teaching
> strategies, teachers must develop creative educational uses of
> media and technology that are so integral a part of the student's
> world and workplace. (1987, p. 38)

According to an interview with a teacher who worked in the English
Department before the advent of the framework, Ruff's English Department, like all of the other English departments in the district, was
almost totally dependent upon "worksheets isolating a single skill" and
exercises presented in the anthology. Something had to change.

The preframework English teachers were then using what were
called "LAPS"—essentially, bundles of worksheets written in the manner of programmed learning which students completed in sequence in
order to advance through the curriculum. Just as the English teachers
responded to the call to teach the CAP writing types, the Ruff English
teachers took steps to clear out their filing cabinets brimming with
"LAPS" and to replace them with assignments that involved "core literature" books when the call came.

The notion of "core literature" became central to reading instruction at Charles Ruff and across the district for a number of years during this historical period, and how to use works of core literature in
classrooms constituted an important learning curve for teachers. Here
is the language of the framework regarding core literature which
guided decision makers in the mid-1980s:

> The core literary works identified by a school or district offer all
> students a common cultural background from which they can
> learn about their humanity, their values, and their society. As
> students study such works as the Odyssey and the Book of Job
> and the writings of such authors as William Shakespeare,
> Aesop, and Hans Christian Anderson, the rich fabric of the soci-
> ety in which we live comes alive because the insights of great
> writers into the human condition transcend the limits of cen-
> turies and continents. (1987, p. 7)

The framework and its supporting documents directed local districts
and/or schools to develop lists of core books to include "those selections that are to be taught in the classroom, are given close reading and
intensive consideration, and are likely to be an important stimulus for
writing and discussion" (Honig, 1986, p. ix).

The district wasted no time in putting together committees to develop grade-level lists of titles, in ordering sufficient copies of each title such that each school would have at least one class set per title, and in mandating forcefully that each teacher at each grade level would use the core literature books in his or her instruction regardless of any previous plans. The district's warehouse personnel went on double shifts trying to get the materials inventoried and distributed, and reading resource teachers in all of the schools learned to assemble shelves and prepare storage rooms. For a time there was a veritable literary frenzy in all corners of the district.

How were these literary works to be taught? The following rather lengthy excerpt from the state framework is quoted in its entirety because it captures an important part of the reading instruction that was occurring at Ruff:

> **An Example of an Integrated Language Arts Lesson, Grades 6 through 9**
>
> After discussing their feelings about handicapped or outcast people, students begin the study of a core work like Helen Keller's *The Story of My Life* or Elizabeth Speare's *The Witch of Blackbird Pond*. To relate to the Keller text in sensory ways, they try blocking out sight and sound for an hour during the weekend before they begin the reading. Students also develop a visual representation of the main character in a mandala or chart the relationships between characters, events of the story, and circumstance. After reading the book and seeing their teacher model good questioning and listening skills, they form cooperative learning groups to discuss with each other their thoughts about the story. After discussion, the students write about prejudice and, in small groups or individually, create the front page of a newspaper incorporating the setting and events of the book, with articles, interviews, and advertisements, all reflecting their background and insights into the book. Postwriting activities include preparing a display in the classroom or school lobby of the newspapers students have created. (1987, p. 37)

It is important to note that in this suggested plan, several specific suggestions define what students might do before (discuss their feelings, block out sight and sound) and after (discuss their thoughts, write about prejudice, create a newspaper) they read the text. There is precious little, however, that suggests instructional acts that might occur during the reading beyond "develop[ing] a visual representation." At the risk of oversimplifying a complex notion, this plan generally characterizes what was termed the "Into, Through, and Beyond" approach to instruction in literary reading, an approach which was promoted through the California Literature Project, a state-sponsored staff-development effort that had enrolled almost all of the Ruff English teachers between 1987 and 1994.

During this period the district reassigned a large number of classroom English teachers to positions as resource teachers. The basement of the district office was converted into offices for them. These teachers began going to meetings with real administrators, and the complex, shifting role of the "pseudo-administrator" began to evolve. Their charge was to facilitate the change from a skills-driven, worksheet-driven instructional format to a core literature format, and they did it well. In concert with committees of teachers released from teaching duties for several days at a time, they developed thick binders of activities to go with each of the titles on the core list. They provided inservice after inservice at all of the district schools. And they kept abreast of all that was going on at the state level with respect to test development.

On Not Letting Go

Through all of this literary frenzy, however, the importance of standardized reading-test scores did not diminish. This importance is revealed in the care with which school personnel administered the tests. Each year at Charles Ruff, a site administrator developed and monitored a calendar so that students took only one portion of the test battery on any given day. During the testing window, which lasted two to three weeks, the particular subject area undergoing tests received special care. Posters were placed on classroom doors with the words "DO NOT DISTURB: TESTING IN PROGRESS." Special rules governing the use of the intercom were enforced. A "Parent Handbook," organized and published by the district office, contained a section entitled "Achievement Tests," which directed parents to take special measures on behalf of their children when testing time rolled around. The following quote taken from this handbook illustrates the special efforts to which district administrators went to communicate the importance of standardized tests:

> Helping Your Child Prepare
>
> - Working hard in class and completing homework on a regular basis are the best means of preparing for standardized tests.
>
> - If your child is having trouble in a particular subject, ask the teacher for help well before the test if possible.

- Without making your child feel stressed, discuss upcoming tests and mention that it is important for the child to do his or her best.

- Make sure your child gets a good night's sleep and eats a nutritious breakfast on the day of the test.

The test scores themselves had little directly to do with the majority of students' actual day-to-day experiences at Charles Ruff. In earlier years, the school had grouped students by ability on the basis of test scores, but such tracking practices had been eliminated at Ruff over five years before the portfolio assessment project began—eliminated, that is, except for special education and Chapter 1 students, who continued to gain entrance to "special" programs by virtue of their test scores. So for the very low and very high ends of the distribution, scores had practical meaning. In the main, however, the school's clients—parents and their children—had few practical reasons for going to bed earlier than usual or eating an especially nutritious breakfast on test days.

There were, however, other practical reasons for parents to take an interest in standardized test scores. For one thing, local newspapers sometimes published the results of standardized tests as an indicator of the quality of schooling in a given district or at a given site. The clear implication was that test scores could be taken as good indicators of whether or not schools were doing their job. In the "Saturday Homes" section of the local newspaper devoted to real estate transactions, moreover, references appeared over the course of the year of this study to the quality of the schools in given neighborhoods as revealed by standardized tests—that is, such information appeared if the scores were good. Tests scores, in short, were used in real estate advertisements.

District personnel, particularly individuals serving in district-level administrative positions, understood the messages that test scores carried to parents and to the public in general. These individuals seemed to have quite clear practical and professional reasons for caring how children scored on the tests. The following incident reveals how positive test scores were at least tangentially associated with positive career trajectories for administrators in the district:

> Yesterday in the late afternoon, I was sitting in a conference room with [the technology coordinator], [the English Department chair], and [a site administrator], talking about how we might present information to the State Department of Education regarding our use of grant money for restructuring purposes. The telephone rang, and [the site administrator] went behind a partition to answer it.

The three of us—me, the chair, and the coordinator—sat in silence, each trying to make sense of the telephone conversation from what we could hear [the site administrator] saying. All we could hear were "uh huh's" and "great's" and "OK's."

When [the site administrator] returned to [his/her] seat at the table, [he/she] was smiling broadly.

"That was [a district-level administrator]," [the site administrator] said. "[He/she] was calling from [his/her] car phone. [He/she] was giddy! [He/she] actually had to pull [his/her] car off the road to talk, [he/she] was that excited."

"Well, what's happened?" [the technology coordinator] asked. "Is somebody getting married or what?"

"The new [test] scores are in," [the site administrator] said. "[The district-level administrator] just picked 'em up, and [he/she] was looking them over, and our scores were high, very high."

"Great!" we said, smiling.

"I can just see [the district-level administrator] adding this to [his/her] résumé right now," [the site administrator] said with a grin. Everyone laughed.

Humor is a slippery discourse to interpret. To build too tight a case suggesting a direct link between district-level administrators' chances of promotion and the district's publishing of suggestions that parents put their children to sleep earlier than usual or feed them a hearty breakfast on the day of the test is perhaps pushing the point too far. Nonetheless, something—altruism, love of children, ambition, membership in T. S. Eliot's cultural elite—motivated district-level administrators in charge of Charles Ruff and its sister schools to take standardized test scores, particularly reading-test scores, quite seriously, to insist year after year that teachers gear their instruction toward objectives measured by the achievement tests, and to solicit the cooperation of parents in their efforts to increase the number of correct items bubbled in by students as they took their standardized tests.

In the late 1980s, the individual charged with supervising the Office of Research and Evaluation for the district prepared and published a report with respect to districtwide reading-test scores from 1983 forward. Unfortunately, reading-comprehension scores districtwide revealed a slow but steady decline year after year. Graphs depicting a rather steep ski slope were flashed on overhead-projector screens at faculty meetings over and over again during this time. The district's students had gone from scoring near the top of the national distribution (75th percentile) in 1983 to scoring near the bottom of the distribution (35th percentile) in 1993. Personnel in the curriculum and instruction unit of the district office as well as more front-line administrators started referring to reading as a "problem," and task forces were organized to address the "problem." Nobody did much official talking about the impact of growth and changing demographics on test scores.

These task forces were charged with devising plans that might solve the reading problem. Chaired by a district administrator or by a proxy for an administrator, each of the task forces prepared documents that mapped direct links between classroom instruction and item types as stated in the standardized test manual. Essentially, the task forces were translating the testing manual into a curriculum guide. The following language was taken from notes made by Charles Ruff's principal at a 1994 meeting with other principals in the district office. It suggests something of the urgency with which site-level administrators were being directed to link instruction and standardized test objectives:

> [Wayne] and [Eastwood] [pseudonyms for schools in the district]—analysis of CAT-5 item analysis to track teams—attempting to translate info to teaching strategies—[Eastwood] pushing for rubrics to enhance evenness of program in L.A.
>
> [Pillsbury]—what do we teach from CAT-5? items which are now weak?/what about strengths? will be translated to SIP (School Improvement Plan) for 95–96, grammar added to lang arts as recc of dept members, parent education program, id kids who qualify for reading options program
>
> Thought—clearly all secondary principals are marching to CAT-5 data as the driving force behind instructional program development

Operationally, what this emphasis on standardized test scores was intended to mean for English teachers in the classrooms was clear—even more clear, and more forceful, after the veto of CLAS legislation in September 1994. No one even had to pretend to like "literature-based" instruction any longer. District-level administrators called for teachers to provide "direct instruction in the skills," particularly in those "skills" tested on the standardized tests. To be sure, elementary teachers had been asked in the 1980s to write "action plans" indexed to test-item analyses. What distinguished the district's initiative in the 1990s was its global character. The district's leadership was not talking about teaching to specific item types that had been perceived as weaknesses. This time the focus was on the whole curriculum from top to bottom.

Willard Daggett, Technical Reading, and the Twenty-First Century

To add further weight to this skills-centered stance, several high-level district administrators had begun circulating copies of articles written by Willard Daggett. Billed as a "futurist" who could lead public education into the "21st century," Daggett (1993, 1994) argued that schools ought to teach "technical reading" rather than "reading for personal response," and that such instruction ought to take place in the content areas and not in English classes. Here are Daggett's own words with respect to the role that English teachers ought to assume in the ultra-modern American public school:

> What's left for the English teacher? Literature, of course, which—like the fine arts—is an important part of any child's educational experience. But a literature-based English program is no place to teach students the kind of reading and communications skills they will need for the 21st century. As schools in Europe and Asia have found, the focus of language arts programs has to change. In fact, schools in Europe and Asia are in the process of making the change already by making the language arts program an elective program . . . (Daggett, 1994, p. 20).

In another article, Daggett presented evidence that "reading and writing for personal response" rarely occurs in the workplace, but that "reading and writing for information" occurs almost every day. From this evidence Daggett further argued that instruction in literary reading should be curtailed. Again, here are Daggett's own words on this matter:

> [There is a] need for considerable emphasis on Reading for Information and the Reading for Critical Analysis and Evaluation as requisite for entry-level employment. Although Reading for Personal Response (enjoyment) is a valuable adult skill, it is considered unimportant in the work world. . . . Findings indicate that Writing for Personal Expression is seldom used on the job, while Writing for Information and to a lesser extent Writing for Critical Analysis are important job components. (Daggett, 1993, p. 7)

After having circulated several of Daggett's articles, the district administration brought "key players" from every school site to hear Willard Daggett speak before a large group of members from the business roundtable. In this December presentation, given to people from across the entire county, Daggett suggested that if English teachers didn't like the idea of making English class an elective, if content-area teachers didn't like the idea of incorporating technical reading instruction into their curriculum, then English teachers might modify a typical assignment as follows: Instead of assigning students the task of writing an essay comparing two novels, the teacher could assign them the task of writing an essay comparing the inner workings of two different word-processing programs. Presumably they could compose their essays using one or the other word processors.

Within the upper echelons of the district's administration, a suspicion had been growing for years that the kind of instruction in literature called for in the framework and promoted by the California Literature Project was fundamentally flawed. The California Literature Project—and the California Writing Project as well—were described in meetings I attended as being "elitist," and many wondered whether this sort of high-brow education was all that necessary for the population served by the Ruff district. After Governor Wilson eliminated the alternative assessment system in the fall of 1994, there was much less need even to discuss the relative importance of literature in the curriculum. Although a fear lingered that CLAS might be resurrected or something like it might develop, in the main the district administration expressed the belief that the era of emphasis on literature was over.

After CLAS, the real job, at least as the district leadership perceived it, was to reassert the primacy of the standardized test system and to make teachers understand that the reading problem was their problem, too. The following excerpt was taken from a document prepared as the summary of a brainstorming session of the instructional cabinet. The document was entitled "Secondary Response to Improving Student Performance on the CAT/5":

The Problem

A. There is not enough of a sense of urgency or ownership of the problem by teachers.

B. Secondary curriculum, as taught, does not have enough alignment with CAT/5 objectives.

C. Language instruction does not have enough balance between direct instruction of skills and whole language instructional strategies.

. . .

E. There is little evidence of content benchmarks being assessed frequently in the classroom.

F. Teachers are evaluated mostly on classroom control and instructional strategies rather than student progress and curricular content.

Despite this administrative fomentation, during the 1994–95 instructional year the Ruff English teachers at both the seventh- and eighth-grade levels were still under a formal mandate to teach each of the core literature titles on the district list in accordance with the general lesson plan as exemplified above—despite the fact that the State Department of Education's reading and writing assessment system had been shut down, that the state framework had suffered damage from almost every possible political wind (indeed, even Bill Honig, whose signature is on an introductory page of the framework, was reported to have commented in the spring of 1995 that the framework "had gone too far"), and that the district administration had all but embraced the philosophy of Willard Daggett.

The district had long ago developed binders of activities for teachers to employ in connection with each title on the core literature list. Composed by resource teachers and other teachers working on development committees, these binders represented large outlays of capital; when taken together with the expenditures required to supply each grade level at each school in the district with class sets of trade books, there is evidence of a firm resolve early on among the district leadership to climb aboard the framework train, a resolve which in 1994 was sorely tested by the firestorm that flared up around the CLAS test controversy.

So what was the district's official position after the CLAS melt-down?

As we have seen, the district had never relaxed its commitment to its own standardized test system. As pointed out previously, the "Into, Through, and Beyond" approach from the California Literature Project appeared not to provide students with instruction regarding just what they should do *while* reading—and, unfortunately, the norm-referenced tests in use in the district weren't designed to measure what students did before and after they read. These tests looked at students' reading in isolation and purported to measure the "during" portion of the reading process (e.g., Do students infer when they read? Do they recognize main ideas?). And these tests, particularly the reading-test scores, had been declining slowly but surely every year since 1983. Each year as the test scores declined, the district administrators turned up the heat a bit higher on their principals, who in turn were expected to turn up the heat a bit higher on their teachers.

The depth of the district administration's commitment to its own local standardized-test program was made clear to me in the early fall of 1994. I had just discovered an article by Johnson, Afflerbach, and Weiss (1993) which discussed the influence of standardized tests on the perceptions teachers have of their students. Teachers in "high-control" districts with a heavy emphasis on norm-referenced test scores tended to talk about students in terms of grade equivalents and percentile ranks when asked to discuss their students' reading performance. Teachers in "low-control" districts with little or no emphasis on test scores, however, tended to talk about students in terms of their favorite authors, the books they had read, and other more personal pieces of information when asked to discuss their students' reading performance.

Excited about the prospect of presenting empirical evidence suggesting that too heavy of an influence from standardized tests can actually prevent teachers from seeing students clearly, I copied the article, asked my site administrator to read it, and asked him to send a copy to the district superintendent. Here is his response to my request after he had read the article:

> You don't want to send this to [the superintendent]. Why would you want to do that? You know what he'd say? He'd say, "Yes, these guys are absolutely right." He'd say, "That's our problem. We've been a low control district for far too long now. When you talk to our teachers about kids and their reading, they tell you about the books the kids are reading. We want them talking about test scores." Why would you want to give him any more ammunition than he already has?

The district had long ago established a "Language Arts Steering Committee" composed of teachers and administrators. In fact, it was this steering committee that had made recommendations regarding which titles should go on the core literature list. Lately, however, the steering committee, composed largely of English teachers, was having trouble making its voice heard. According to Ruff's representative to this committee, Jennifer Johnson (a pseudonym), the committee would make a recommendation or write a policy statement, the language of the recommendation or statement would go "upstairs," and the language would be returned to the committee "changed."

Jennifer expressed her concerns that the voice of the steering committee was being ignored during a taped interview in January 1995, the day after she had attended a meeting. In this excerpt from that interview, Jennifer discussed the role played by Bella Bigelow (pseudonym), contractually a teacher who nonetheless worked in the district office, in silencing those whose views diverged from the district's official direction:

> *TU:* What happened in the meeting yesterday?
>
> *Jennifer:* Oh, [expletive]! [more loudly] Oh, [expletive]!!!
> Nothing. It was a *[expletive]* meeting. I *don't* like Bella
> Bigelow.
>
> *TU:* Why?
>
> *Jennifer:* Why? She's controlling.

> *TU:* Give me an example.
>
> *Jennifer:* An example. Um . . . every time we came up with
> ideas that *we* felt were important, she managed to put
> in what I perceive as what the district office or powers
> above us feel is important. Skills—um, teaching of
> skills—teaching of *phonics*—and [a principal] was
> there, too, so we had that perspective, also.

Bella Bigelow did not hold administrative rank in the district,
but she held considerable power. Just as the district had released a
number of regular classroom teachers from teaching duties in the mid-
1980s to become resource personnel—whose role was to support the
implementation of ideas expressed in the state framework—Bella had
been released from teaching duties to serve as the district's "lead reading teacher." Of interest is that a massive turnover had occurred
among the resource teachers. Very few of the resource teachers from
the "decade of reform in the name of literature-based instruction"
remained in the basement of the district office. The interview with
Jennifer Johnson continued:

> *TU:* Did she talk at all about Willard Daggett or technical
> reading?
>
> *Jennifer* [eyes wide, voice raspy, intense]: *Yes!! Yes!!!* Technical
> reading was brought up, and I said under my breath—we
> had rules we had to follow during brainstorming: No judg-
> ments—so under my breath I said, "There goes Daggett."
> No one else knows. *No one else knows!* They're clueless.
>
> *TU:* About Daggett?
>
> *Jennifer:* Yes. I don't think so because no one else said any-
> thing, but we're all supposed to be nonjudgmental in
> brainstorming.

Jennifer's perception that "no one else kn[ew]!" about the influence which the English-as-an-elective thinking of Willard Daggett was
having on the district administration was somewhat shocking to the
Ruff English Department leadership. The Ruff teachers had read
Daggett's articles with interest, had discussed them at department
meetings. However, such was apparently not the case across the district. That the steering committee was not being attended to when its
messages were sent "upstairs" was mirrored by the steering committee's inattention to documents circulated by the administration. The
interview continued:

> *TU:* So Daggett came up in brainstorming.
>
> *Jennifer:* Well, no, technical *reading* came up.

TU: Who brought it up? A teacher or . . .

Jennifer [whispers to herself]: Was it Bella? Or was it [the principal]?

TU: Oh, but it was an administrator—or a pseudo-administrator.

Jennifer: Yes, a pseudo-administrator. And . . . I was pretty quiet because we were given these rules to follow. We were making this needs assessment, and I made a comment, and Bella—we were supposed to be nonjudgmental?—she literally put down my question that I was brainstorming out loud. She said . . . not "That's stupid," but that's what I perceived, that's the way I internalized it. It's unnecessary, or it's irrelevant to the task we have to do. Something along those lines.

TU: What was the question?

Jennifer: Oh, my question was "How happy are you with the current program that we have in place?" And we were supposed to do a sliding scale.

TU: [That was your question?]

Jennifer: That was my question to put on the needs assessment that we're sending out to all language arts teachers.

TU: OK. And she said that that was irrelevant.

Jennifer: Yes.

TU: Why would it be irrelevant? Did she elaborate?

Jennifer: Oh, no, she—they changed it all around, which was fine, but I don't like the way she operates.

When Governor Wilson vetoed the CLAS legislation, an important constituency was silenced in the power struggle to define the "good" reader. In light of this development, the question of whether teachers liked or disliked the current reading program was, in fact, irrelevant—irrelevant at least in the Ruff district. But during 1993–94, the year that the portfolio-assessment system at Ruff was being designed, CLAS legislation was still on the books. The values embedded in its scoring guide, which privileged irreverent, original, provocative interpretations of texts, had made a mark on the Charles Ruff English faculty as evidenced by its own enactment of a local direct-reading test. So it was quite understandable that these values found their way into the portfolio scoring guide despite the district's long-standing privileging of its standardized test system.

In 1987, literary texts were officially conservationist repositories of culture, according to the district. The goal was to teach students the content of common works of literature as though literature were a content area like biology or chemistry. By 1991, literary texts were both conservationist repositories of culture *and* sites for symbolic transactions engendering personal response and change—invitations to challenge, to probe, to resist, to transform one's life world. By 1994, literary texts were a luxury, a frill, an extra—nice, but not necessary. The goal was to teach students to comprehend VCR and computer manuals so that they might find employment in the marketplace.

Clearly, the state's ambiguous view of literary reading was much less stable and coherent than was the view promoted by Willard Daggett and by the standardized test system. Moreover, the state's view of reading had had much less time to become entrenched in the district's culture than did the state's view of writing. To a great degree, in the arena of writing the district had acquiesced to the state, largely because the district had never developed its own tests of writing achievement. In the arena of reading, however, the district grudgingly acquiesced early on, but then the district reasserted its local perspective when it became clear that the state's system was "radioactive."

The Good and the True

Local resistance to the state reading-test system derived, in my view, from the fact that the district leadership, in the form of the superintendent and his cabinet as well as the local board of education, had learned over many years to value standardized tests of reading achievement—and these reading tests measured neither the degree to which students had mastered works of core literature, nor the logic and sophistication with which they could develop original interpretations of texts. These reading tests measured whether students could get the main idea, draw inferences, recognize prefixes and suffixes, select the best title for a passage, and the like. Because district administrators saw their standardized tests as the gold standard, and because the definition of the "good" reader instantiated in these tests differed in important ways from the definition spelled out by the state on CLAS and adopted by the English teachers at Ruff, it was inevitable that there would be some friction between the district office and the portfolio-assessment system.

And, as we will see, there was.

6 Inside the Middle (School)

For Whom the Bells Toll

As we have seen, California as a state took on school reform voluntarily during the 1980s and 1990s with assessment as a tool, a weapon, an enticement. The Ruff district, on the other hand, had no choice but to transform itself during the same time frame—transform without disaster from a small, semirural district to a large, urban one. However, despite the enormous political and economic pressures of the era that derived from both the state and the district office, Charles Ruff Middle School managed to keep essentially to the path cut for it when it had opened its doors in the 1960s. At Ruff, the more things changed, the more they stayed the same.

A good example of this phenomenon is the school's bells. The Ruff day had always been carved into six equal periods. The beginning and ending of each academic period had always been signaled by loud bells; between bells, students had a five-minute passing period. For years, many of the teachers had complained about the bells. "When are you going to do something about those stupid bells?" I heard any number of teachers ask the principal time and time again.

"It's insulting to have to suffer those damn bells every fifty minutes," one teacher said to me one day. "What does he think—that we don't know enough to look at our watches? That the school is going to fall apart if we don't have those bells ringing like a fire engine in our ears?"

Finally, something was done. The principal ordered the bells replaced by an electronic chime system that produced soft, pleasing tones like those heard in a modern airport. And the teachers appreciated the change—those loud, clangy, nerve-wracking bells were gone. "Ah, Terry, it's amazing what little things will make people happy," the principal said to me around the time of the great change, as we talked in his office one afternoon. "Let this experience be a lesson to you."

A surprisingly large number of teachers had taught their entire careers on the Ruff campus, with perhaps more than a little hearing loss attributable to the bells, and they lent the school both an institutional memory and a brake on change. An excursion through the Ruff yearbooks, stored in the school library year after year since the mid-1960s, made clear that hair styles, fashions, certainly the ethnic composition of the student population had changed. But the librarian, several of the history, math, and PE teachers, a few science teachers, and several support staff members documented their journeys from early adulthood to late middle age in the photos of the Ruff yearbooks. More than a few marriages were forged among Ruff teachers over the years.

This contingent of teachers had witnessed the school work its way through wave after wave of innovation and seemed to know that the school was bigger than any individual or group of individuals. Principals, plans, and promises would come and go, but the six-period day would remain as a solid network of slots for holding the traditional curriculum. (Of interest is that in order to provide "common planning time" for the track teams, a committee of teachers dedicated to restructuring the school in accordance with SB 1274 did manage to whittle down the students' passing period from five to four minutes. The extra minutes, accumulated over a week's time, gave the teachers a common period.)

Many of the "old-timers" on the faculty met and talked together in the central office of the library at lunch each day. They talked endlessly about the current folly being concocted at district headquarters. They reminisced about the long roster of principals who had occupied the front office in the school administration building at one time or another. They analyzed past and present superintendents and other district personnel, usually focusing on those whom they had watched make the long climb from the classroom through a principalship to the palace downtown. They talked together about a horrific epoch in the not-too-distant past when teachers wouldn't park their cars in the front parking lot because they were afraid that someone—a student or someone else—might put a bullet through a car window or door. That epoch, they asserted, was the result of a combination of factors, including poor administration, the influx of undesirable elements in the neighborhoods, and inadequate campus supervision. The new principal cleaned things up.

Going Year-Round

Although much remained the same at Charles Ruff over the years, some things had changed. The first big change occurred in the late 1980s. Rising enrollments as well as state economic incentives forced the school to change from a traditional calendar year, with three months' vacation in the summer, to a year-round calendar. The new calendar meant that teachers and students were "on track" for three months and then "off track" for one. It also meant that this large faculty and student body were divided into several smaller organizational units.

This division of the participants in the school's life had important implications for the socio-academic organization of the school. Eight sets of teachers (four seventh-grade sets, four eighth-grade sets) taught the same 200+ students, vacationed during the same months, and attended the same meetings. These sets of teachers became known as "track teams," and the school began to perceive itself as having eight "families," eight intact social groups, each with its own identity and purpose. Of necessity, these teams were interdisciplinary; at least one member from each department had to serve on each track team. As a consequence, Ruff teachers had two loyalties: one to their department, one to their track team. This arrangement did, in fact, result in the implementation of some rather elaborate interdisciplinary instructional units on some of the tracks.

Doing Away with Tracking—Sort of

Another huge change which instigated ongoing debate also happened in the late 1980s. The school changed from an academic placement system based upon ability as evidenced by test scores to one based upon managed luck. Students of the past had been grouped for coursework by ability into homogeneous classes. Students of the 1990s were grouped together according to placement by counselors, who scheduled students in order to achieve equitable balances on each track with respect to ethnicity, gender, and achievement (using standardized test scores).

There were two exceptions to this method. First, parents with more than one child attending the school could request that all of their children enroll on the same track. This development was serendipitous in that only two sets of teachers, though at different grade levels, came in contact with one set of parents (if the family was intact). Second, students identified as LEP (limited-English proficient) were placed on the same track. This decision was made because the school had only a few English-as-a-second-language teachers—services could not be provided on all tracks. The existence of this de facto linguistic tracking made some Ruff teachers refuse to concede that the school had really done away with tracking. None of the portfolio teachers in this study taught on the LEP track, but two of the examination teachers did.

Who Needs Money?

A third important change also occurred during the mid-1980s. The State Department of Education had made grant funds available to middle schools who were interested in developing "model" programs and becoming "demonstration schools." The funds were available by department. The English Department applied for and won a demonstration grant of approximately $50,000 per year for a five-year period, funds which permitted many of the English faculty to participate in the California Literature Project and the California Writing Project. Soon after the English Department won its grant, the Science Department, the Mathematics Department, and the Physical Education Department applied for demonstration money—and won. During the early 1990s, the school enjoyed almost $200,000 per year in grant funds earmarked for improving curriculum and instruction. Charles Ruff had four demonstration programs operating simultaneously.

Many sites in the district envied Ruff. District-level administrators interested in reserving a slate of substitute teachers for a day, to hold daylong staff-development sessions wherein regular classroom teachers had to have coverage, learned not just to avoid Mondays and Fridays to schedule sessions. They also learned to check the calendar to see whether Ruff had reserved the surplus of substitutes. Ruff had a reputation for releasing its teachers in droves for staff development, a practice which ate up substitute capacity like candy. Ruff was pleasantly surprised when these funds were supplemented in 1993 by the influx of grant money pursuant to Senate Bill 1274, the California restructuring bill discussed in Chapter 3, which brought an additional quarter of a million dollars to the site. This award meant that the school would have upwards of half of a million dollars each year above and beyond its ordinary budget from general funds. Even given the district's cut of these funds, which was substantial, these awards gave the middle school important resources.

The winds of change blew steadily at Charles Ruff Middle School during these years, situated as it was in the middle of a legislated reform movement begun in 1983. The spirit of change was partly responsible for the English Department's request that it be allowed to schedule seventh-grade students into two-period blocks for language arts instruction. This same spirit was also partly responsible for the department's interest in developing an alternative CLAS-like reading test, even before CLAS was formally released, which could provide local data in response to local concerns. So, things *had* changed.

But they had also remained the same.

The Machinery of Grades

The official rules governing how teachers were expected to issue grades, for example, had not changed. Largely a technical matter, the grading system reflected the way in which the school day was broken down. Students attended classes six periods per day of approximately fifty-minutes each; according to the long-standing tradition of the Carnegie unit in secondary education, students could earn one credit per class per grading period, in this case, twelve weeks. The teachers to whom students happened to be assigned held the authority to issue letter grades to the students on their rosters at the end of each grading period. Said differently, each teacher held the power to grant or withhold credit for each period of the school day that she or he "taught," i.e., each period for which the teacher was assigned a roster of students. Teachers who were not assigned students for discrete periods (e.g., counselors, teachers released from instructional duties such as the technology coordinator and the performance-assessment coordinator) held no power to grant or to withhold credit.

Students either passed or failed their classes each grading (or twelve-week) period ("passed" when the teacher-of-record indicated to the office technician, who entered data into the central computer, that a particular student had earned an A, B, C, or D and not an F, which constituted "failure" and loss of credit). The rules governing the accumulation of credits were enforced not by individual teachers, but by site administrators, who held the authority to adjust these rules in accordance with circumstances.

Passing seventh grade meant that students would be placed on the rosters of eighth-grade teachers during their second year at Charles Ruff. The technical rule was that students were required to earn at least sixteen of the eighteen possible credits to pass seventh grade. Passing eighth grade meant that students could participate in the Ruff graduation ceremony if their names were not listed on the "No Activities" list and would be placed on the rosters of ninth-grade teachers at the high school. Students were required to earn thirty-two of the thirty-four possible credits to be promoted. In most cases, these technical rules applied. In some cases, the principal did not apply these rules and "passed" or "promoted" particular students for "social" reasons.

Teachers issued progress reports midway through each grading period. Identical in appearance to the documents which went out as report cards, these reports were handed out by first-period teachers, who were responsible for collecting the parentally signed reports by a given date, and were intended to inform parents of their child's status-to-date as an earner-of-credit. The essential difference between progress reports and actual report cards was this: Progress reports were not subject to the rules governing the granting or withholding of credit. They were simply rehearsals for the real thing.

Though progress reports did not count toward advancement within the institution, they did count toward quality of life within the homes of many students. From the point of view of a large number of students, therefore, Charles Ruff actually issued *six* report cards spaced *six weeks apart*, not three report cards spaced twelve weeks apart. Every other report card counted in school; every report card counted at home. Teachers knew to expect a flurry of activity during the week following the issuance of progress reports. The office staff took more phone calls than usual from parents. Notices to teachers that parents had called would pile up in the teachers' mailboxes, and the counselors would be busy scheduling "all-teacher conferences," formal gatherings of the counselor, the parent(s) or guardian, all of the teachers, and the student. Teachers invariably noted that students who received the greatest number of low grades on their progress reports, however, often were not among those students about whom phone calls were made and conferences were held.

The real report card was issued every twelve weeks. Students with "F's" on these reports were termed "credit-deficient." Credit-deficient students were given the opportunity to make up credits in a program called "Intersession." The following is an excerpt from a document which the school sent home to parents to notify them of this opportunity:

Intersession Registration Form for the June Session (June 12 through June 23)

In order to ensure academic success as well as complete necessary credits for promotion, your child has been recommended to attend Intersession:

___ Based on progress reports

___ Receiving one or more F's on their report card

___ Due to late registration

This program is intended to provide extra time and help to students. Students attending are expected to be on their best behavior and will not be allowed to remain in the program if they are disruptive in class.

The Intersession Program consists of one (10-day) session during regular school hours. Students successfully completing the Intersession course will earn one (1) credit toward promotion. Students must attend all days of the session and pass all classes.

[Charles Ruff] students enrolled in Intersession may ride their regular bus.

The Charles Ruff administration gave teachers a calendar each year with deadlines for turning in documents to report letter grades to the office technicians. Resembling Scantron® answer documents, these bubble sheets contained the names and student identification numbers of each student on that teacher's rosters as well as two sets of bubbles for teachers to fill in with number two pencils: one set containing the letters A, B, C, D, and F; the second set containing numbers 1 through 14, which corresponded to a list of standardized comments teachers might want to issue (e.g., comment #7 was "low test scores"; comment #14 read "Poor attendance is affecting class work"). Parents got the official report card, together with a list of standardized comments, in the mail.

In most cases—certainly, in the cases of those who worked within the traditional disciplines—teachers made decisions about which grade to bubble in on the basis of their own private criteria. An exception to this rule could occur when a student with a designated disability was being mainstreamed with some sort of agreement about grading among the parents, the special education teacher, and the regular classroom teacher. In practice, each teacher kept his or her own grade book as the teacher pleased.

Before the school was awarded its SB 1274 grant, according to interviews with teachers, no one had ever systematically and publicly discussed what those criteria were. Grading practices were individual matters. One might hear a revelation about a grading practice or policy in the lunchroom or the photocopier room or even during a staff-development meeting (a sample of which will be presented shortly), but it would have been a breach of professional etiquette for one teacher to confront another teacher with a challenge to his or her grading practices. In fact, grading practices were usually openly discussed only during "all-teacher conferences" involving a failing student and his or her parents. Even then, however, the intention was never to critique a practice. Rather, each teacher was given the floor to present his or her own grading philosophy and standards.

And to explain why the student on the hot seat was not meeting them.

That this set of rules which governed the credit-granting function of the institution influenced how teachers acted in their classrooms was made clear near the end of the 1994–95 school year, when the site administrator decided to abolish the practice of "retention," i.e., holding credit-deficient students back at their grade level rather than "passing them on" to the next level (what we call "flunking the year"). The principal explained this shift in policy in a memo entitled

"Retention Policy Review and Recommendations," a memo which stirred up a controversy among the teachers. The memo opened with conclusions the principal had drawn following a study he and a small group of colleagues had made of the policy:

1. Charles Ruff Middle School is currently the only middle school in the district that retains seventh- and eighth-grade students. . . .

2. Review of 1994–95 retention lists indicate that many of our retained students do not improve their performance during the retention period and those that do improve initially, often fail when they are eventually accelerated to the appropriate grade level.

3. There is a need to change our students' outlook from "I know you can't keep me here forever," to "Even if I advance to the next grade level, I haven't met the academic standards for a Charles Ruff student."

4. Teachers of retained students often request grade-level advancement due to poor behavior, performance, and apathy on the part of the retained student. Oftentimes spaces are no longer available for such grade-level changes.

5. When teacher or counselor requests have been made to advance retained 7th graders to 9th grade (sometimes after 2 years of retention), [Ruff's] High School has discouraged these requests because the student has not been exposed to eighth-grade curriculum.

The principal went on in this memo to spell out his recommendations for change, as follows:

1. That all course-credit requirements for academic promotion to 8th or 9th grades remain in full effect including eligibility to participate in promotion ceremonies.

2. That the existing informal process of social promotion be officially recognized and that students no longer be retained in either the 7th or 8th grades. Credit-deficient students will advance grade levels under a *credit-deficient social-promotion designation*.

3. That parents/guardians of credit-deficient social-promotion students be notified of their student's status by registered mail. Included in this letter will be information regarding support services including: (a) summer school/intersession (b) parent conferences (c) tutoring (d) teacher team-intervention activities.

This change in policy appeared to undermine the authority which many teachers believed that they had in their classrooms to make students do their work. Here is what a seventh-grade English teacher said to me a week or so after the above memo was circulated:

> I just can't believe what's happening around here with this retention policy. [He shrugs his shoulder and sighs.] I'm lookin' for another job. I'm washin' my hands of this whole place. [He shakes his head in disgust.] I had these kids—most of 'em—workin' really hard, and then *he* has to make this announcement that there's gonna be *social* promotion. Everything came to a stop right then. Just like that. These guys that were payin' attention and doin' some work just because they wanted to go on to eighth grade, well, they just stopped. And they're smilin' at us. And there's nothin' we can do because they know we can't stop 'em from goin' on.
>
> And look at this! [With an ink pen he points to a string of numbers in his grade book sitting open on his desk, which trails off with zeroes.] This girl was doing fine—she got A's first and second trimester. Since they announced the social promotion policy, she just stopped. It's a shame, I tell you. But what are ya' gonna do? My hands are tied. There's nothing I can do. It just boils my hide!

The grading system, which had been in use essentially unmodified since its inception when the school opened its doors, had grown deep roots that intertwined with other school and nonschool practices. To play on the basketball team, students had to prove to their coach that they were maintaining a C average. To attend school dances, students had to stay off the "No Activities" list—that is, keep their grades up. To be deemed "gifted and talented," students needed to show either an extremely high score on a norm-referenced test or one of the following (data taken from a document circulated among parents and students at Charles Ruff):

> Grade-point average of 3.75 over a period of at least two years, beginning in the seventh grade.
>
> [OR]
>
> Staff judgement [sic] on one of the following: 1. Extraordinary ability in the areas of art, music, drama, or leadership; 2. Extremely high potential but low performance due to educational deprivation.

Another example of opportunity for students with good grades was the Discovery Club, which, according to a brochure, was a club "formed by hardworking students for responsible students who are sometimes forgotten in the day to day business of running a school." Here is how the brochure described the "exchange" between the school and the student:

> In exchange for maintaining high grades, attending club meeting
> [*sic*] and performing community service, members are excused
> from school to participate in a variety of prestigious field trips.

Grades accumulated as a ticket to the graduation ceremony from
the eighth grade. Graduation day at Charles Ruff for the 1994–95
school year—actually, there were two graduation days to accommodate the various tracks' schedules—marked the successful completion
of the school's and the students' tasks. The multipurpose room had
been decorated the previous evening. Crepe paper, streamers, and balloons festooned the large room. Red and white crepe paper twisted
into a spiral hung from the edge of the stage; a group of balloons of
various colors hovered at the center of the stage. Two rows of cafeteria
tables ran along one side of the room, each row decorated with twists
of crepe paper and balloons.

Several large posters made of butcher paper were taped to the
walls: "We are the Future—Class of 1999"; "Congratulations Class of
1999"; "Goodbye Ruff . . . Hello High School." Two video monitors on
tall metal stands, their screens facing the empty hall, were set up to
present student-made videos of life at Charles Ruff during the past two
years. The doorway to the multipurpose room was blocked off by the
same tables used at the honor roll luncheon a month earlier. These
tables, stood on end, were also festooned with crepe paper and balloons, and a butcher-paper poster read "Good Luck Class of '99."
Generally, there were signs of leave-taking, signs of a journey. The dec-
orations celebrated a turning point, an accomplishment.

A number of symbols from graduation day showed the depth of
the roots of the grading system. The balloons and the streamers in the
central gathering hall of the institution represented the pride that both
adults and adolescents took in the fact that students had accumulated
at least thirty-two of thirty-four credits. The video monitors represented considerable planning on the part of these adults, who had sup-
plied the equipment, the materials, the training, and the guidance over
two years so that students could see for themselves that they had
"done it." This investment also communicated approval.

The posters with their messages conveying movement and
direction clearly reinforced the advancement goal orientation. Indeed,
the central reason for the graduation ceremony was to communicate to
everyone that a milestone had been reached. The next milestone to be
reached was forecast in several posters that referred to the "Class of
1999." Noticeably absent were symbolic artifacts that might communicate to students that they ought to reflect on what they had actually

learned during their time at Ruff. The emphasis was on the passage of time—and the accumulation of credits.

Ruff students had to pass time at home as well as at school, though they didn't get credits from home, and grades held important consequences for them in both locations. Melvin, for example, a student in one of Martha Goldsmith's classes, told her this during an interview she conducted with him as part of a case study she was doing:

> *Martha:* You seem concerned with getting higher than a C+ . . . How important are grades to you?
>
> *Melvin:* They're very important in my household 'cause without good grades I get in trouble, and I get sent to school like a bum. . . . I can't wear none of my cool clothes or my tennis shoes or nuttin' like that.

In a piece of autobiographical writing intended to describe a terrifying moment, one student composed a long essay from which the following excerpt is taken:

> When the bus pulled up to my house, it was quiet. I prayed a quick prayer that she would be gone. When I walked into the house, so far so good, then I walked into my room and she was asleep. The good thing about that was she was asleep. The bad thing about that was that she would be in a bad mood when she woke up. That was exactly what happened. She read my progress report and was . . . buried six feet deep before she finished reading. "Four F's!" was the first thing that came out of her mouth. I didn't say a word. I stood as far away as I could because I knew she would want to hit or slug me. She yelled, "You are grounded. No TV, radio, and activities for one month. Get out of my room before I do something drastic!" she yelled. I ran out as fast as I could. It wasn't over. In fact, it isn't over till the fat lady sings. The next day she was worse. She made me sit in her room and do homework, and if I didn't do something right, she would get really mad at me. Even till this day she still get mad at me for getting four F's. If I do that again, I don't know what would happen. I would probably be grounded for a whole year without my birthday or Christmas.

The following example illustrates the degree to which students' lives were impacted by the machinery of the grading system at Charles Ruff. In a manner similar to Melvin's aunt, who used grades as an indicator of whether Melvin could wear his tennis shoes to school, Jarod's father used grades as an indicator of whether Jarod could do an activity that he wanted to do. Here is a segment from an interview with Jarod which occurred a few days before the first portfolio scoring session:

Jarod: My portfolio's goin' pretty good, it's just that I'm tryin' to get started with takin' my work a lot more seriously now because I know how much this affects my grade. And now I'm startin' to put a lot more effort into my work and startin' to write a lot more stuff over, and I'm copyin' all of my text logs over because usually I rush through 'em or somethin', but now I'm takin' my time, you know, writin' neat and stuff.

TU: What happened?

Jarod: One thing is I don't want to end up goin' to Intersession [the year-round equivalent of summer school] again. And then if I pass, I get a chance to go see my mom, which who I don't live with, and I get a chance to go see her, and it's just that it'll make me feel good if I get a good grade knowin' that I did good.

TU: When did this dawn on you?

Jarod: Last night when I couldn't get to sleep I started thinkin' about it. And then I started thinkin' that I have to start takin' my work a lot more seriously now in all my classes and stuff. It was just a last minute thing and then I fell asleep.

TU: So something was bothering you.

Jarod: Yeah. I guess 'cause the more she [Jennifer Johnson, Jarod's teacher] started talkin' about how it was my grade, and I just started thinkin' about how she doesn't grade us and then I really have to get all my work done because she told us, you know, if we're missin' stuff, we're gonna get graded down on that. I'm gonna have to start puttin' a little more imagination and neatness into my work.

More was at stake for students than the wearing of certain tennis shoes or the taking of certain trips. Susan, for example, a seventh grader in one of Martha Goldsmith's portfolio classrooms (the same Susan who wrote Mary's letter of recommendation reported in Chapter 2), was deeply distraught when she first learned that her grade would not be determined by her classroom teacher. Here is an excerpt of an interview with Susan from late July 1994:

TU: Tell me how you picture these examination teachers.

Susan: I just see all these people looking at and reading our papers and grading us on *those*, and it—they don't really know what our teacher's like and so they don't . . . *Our* teacher is the one that knows us, so they think differently, so it's like you can't be *really good* for them because they don't *realize*.

This was the first hint in the field record of what became an important theme for a large number of portfolio students early in the project and then faded away later in the year, namely, the positive importance for students of subjectivity in assessment. Susan seemed to suggest, at least early on, that she interpreted letter grades from her teacher as somehow richer, more significant for her than letter grades from an external assessor, perhaps because teacher grades come out of a richer context—a personal context with a shared history. Susan's early view implied that she felt somehow cheated of the satisfaction she had come to expect, i.e., the satisfaction that derived from teacher confirmation of her being "really good."

It is important to note that the machinery of grades remained unchanged for the duration of the portfolio project. Despite changes made in the process through which grades were determined in the portfolio classrooms, and despite the fact that students in the portfolio classrooms were taught explicit criteria with which they would be graded, all of the ceremonies and requirements and uses built upon those five letters remained a part of school life for the portfolio students. Although the original proposal for the portfolio experiment discussed the possibility of exempting the portfolio students from the letter grade machinery and replacing it with discursive reports to parents, the principal at Charles Ruff could not approve that proposition. Here is the language he used one afternoon during a spirited discussion with me of this possibility prior to the school's approval of the project:

> Oh, no, no, no, those kids [the portfolio students] have got to receive letter grades just like every other student on campus. Do you think I'm foolish? In this district? No, it won't happen at this school. Nobody's *ever* going to say that I was the one that tried to do away with letter grades. There's a political reality here that I just can't ignore. It just won't happen, not on my watch, anyway.

Two Spheres of Influence

Analysis of the field record reveals that grades had at least two distinct spheres of influence on students at Ruff. The first sphere, which I've labeled "consequential" to denote the aftereffects of grades, was similar for all students regardless of how their teachers graded and pervaded student lives within the institution and, often, at home. To summarize some of what has gone before, within this sphere grades were important because they were a ticket to pleasurable events like a vacation or a dance or a banquet. Students who earned consistently low grades could be placed on the "No Activities" list, which made them ineligible to participate in events ranging from school dances to athletics.

Until the principal changed the retention policy, those students who were not able to accumulate at least thirty-two credits with a grade of "D–" or better ran the risk of retention at the end of seventh and/or eighth grade; they lost their ticket to "promotion." Many students with low grades were the subject of an "All-Teacher Conference" (an "ATC") involving parents or guardians, a counselor, and all of the student's teachers. Often unpleasant meetings in themselves, such conferences affected students' out-of-school lives to the degree that parents or guardians implemented the sanctions recommended by school personnel (e.g., reduced hours of television viewing, less access to the telephone to call friends, etc.). In giving up their authority to issue grades on the basis of whatever criteria they happened to choose, the portfolio teachers did not remove their students from the effects of this "consequential" sphere.

The rules of the second sphere, which I've labeled the "shaping" sphere to denote the online effects of the presence of grades, were constructed by individual Ruff teachers, not by the administration. It was this sphere that constituted one of the essential differences between the portfolio and traditional teachers. The portfolio-assessment project removed the portfolio teachers' authority to construct the rules that determined grades. As a consequence, the portfolio teachers could not use behavior modification strategies involving grades as tools for shaping classroom behaviors, but the traditional teachers could.

For example, in the following document handed out to all of her students, one traditional English teacher tried to modify student behaviors by using grades as a tool for placing heavy emphasis on the practice of "homework":

> Homework will count as a substantial part of your grade. *I do not accept late homework* except under very special circumstances. If you are absent when homework is due or assigned, see me on the first day of your return so that you can make the work up. *It is your responsibility to make up all work missed during your absence.*

In contrast, another of Ruff's traditional English teachers sometimes flipped a coin as a way to decide whether he would even collect student homework on any given day. This teacher devalued homework by making homework's link to grades dependent upon chance.

The portfolio teachers did not have this option. Homework for students in the portfolio classrooms was spelled out explicitly in the rubric. The following language from the "reading" portion of this rubric, describing an "A" grade, left little doubt about what constituted "homework" and how "homework" would be graded:

Consistency and Challenge

- reading done habitually almost every day, often for long periods of an hour or two
- readings not only entertain, but also challenge and stretch capabilities
- reads widely; experiments with new authors and forms

The concept of "late homework" did not exist, nor was there any opportunity for portfolio teachers to flip a coin and excuse students from the task and the standard. And students had similarly explicit language to help them understand what "homework" would be required to earn a grade of "C":

Consistency and Challenge

- reading done at least once or twice a week, often for brief periods of ten to thirty minutes
- readings mainly for entertainment
- little evidence of concern for experimenting with new authors or forms

The fact that the portfolio teachers could not modify these expectations meant that they could not rely on grades as a tool for shaping student behaviors in whatever direction they chose. Instead, student behavior was shaped by the policy itself, with little or no association with the teacher's institutional authority.

Teachers at Charles Ruff, like teachers elsewhere, had a strong affinity for "points" ("When teachers get their teaching credential," a California Writing Project teacher-consultant once said at a workshop, "they are given an infinite supply of points"). As the following observation, taken verbatim from a tape recording of a teacher who was working with a class of students in the Ruff library, illustrates, points do not have to be linked to any specific grading criterion:

Yesterday—you probably didn't notice this—but I sat there at that computer, and I typed in all of the topics that you'll be writing on, and I *know* that this library has books on those topics. So tomorrow when you come up to me and say "Mr. Solomon, I can't find any books on this topic" I'm gonna say, "You're asking me a question that I've already answered, and that answer is, 'Yes, there is at least one book on that topic in this library.'" So you listen carefully to [the librarian] here because if you ask me that tomorrow, you're going to lose points.

In contrast, the portfolio teachers gave up their supply of points when they agreed to abide by standards that had been written down and published. If anyone had a supply of points, it was the examination committee. The portfolio teachers could not rely on the consequential sphere of the grading system to shape student compliance with whatever the expectation of the moment happened to be. Of course, the portfolio teachers had negotiated those standards among themselves; they could have changed them at any point before the start of the school year (just not during the school year). Had these standards come down from "upstairs," the fundamental nature of the portfolio project as it was played out at Charles Ruff would have been different. Such an external imposition of standards would likely have resulted in a very different history.

Traditional teachers at Charles Ruff found other, perhaps more surprising, shaping uses for grades, uses that were not available to the portfolio teachers. One content-area teacher, for example, told me about a project-based unit he assigns. Students were given a series of projects to do, such as making a board game, designing a poster, etc., that were usually of high interest to them, and grades for this unit were based upon "performance measures"; i.e., students received course credit—and grades—for their board games and their posters instead of for the more usual chapter tests (and end-of-chapter essays).

On a single-sheet handout which summarized the nature of the various projects as well as student responsibilities during the unit, cooperation became confounded with achievement. Under the heading "consequences," the teacher discussed a phenomenon labeled "firing." Students who were "fired" from their groups were given a "stack of worksheets to do," were not allowed to participate with their group, and "can receive a grade no higher than C" (which was in boldface on the sheet).

The question of using traditional end-of-chapter tests as opposed to "performance measures" as a basis for grades was a thorny one for Charles Ruff's content-area teachers. During a staff-development meeting, a second-year history teacher expressed an appreciation for an "activity-based curriculum" that had arrived on site in binders in crates—appreciation because the binders provided a sequence of interesting activities that led to a "culminating activity." This teacher reported that she preferred to give students grades on their performance during the culminating activities as opposed to the end-of-chapter tests.

A more seasoned teacher listening to this discussion volunteered the information that her students always did very poorly on the end-of-chapter tests that came as part of the textbook package. She commented that if she based grades solely on those tests, she would have to give F's to most of her students. The teacher mentioned above in connection with "firing" said, "I don't use 'em much [referring to the end-of-chapter tests]. Just as a kind of grade deflator. See, if I gave grades strictly on their group work and activities, I'd have to give everybody an A—or most kids anyway."

The portfolio teachers did not have these choices. They could not use any particular form of assessment as either a grade "deflator" or "inflator." They could not decide to weigh the products of collaborative groups more heavily than student scores on written tests in their grading, because their grading system involved agreements with colleagues. Just as they could not rely on the power of the consequential sphere to motivate student compliance (e.g., "You'd better listen to the librarian"), they could not select activities and materials in order to predetermine the outcome of their evaluative decision-making process. They did not control this process.

Clearly, teachers' grading decisions in the traditional context were influenced by information beyond that gleaned from assessing classroom work. In the following excerpt, taken from a taped thinkaloud done by one of the portfolio teachers as she looked over her students' portfolios, which had just been graded externally by the examination committee, we see a teacher who is making use of her knowledge of students' families, especially knowledge of parental attitudes. Here, in the language that came spontaneously to this teacher's mind when she first opened Mark Thomas's portfolio with its examination grade, we find a frame of family knowledge that surrounds her entire reflection on this student:

> [Speaking] Next folder: Mark Thomas . . . Shelby's cousin—very different student than Shelby [this teacher had Shelby, Mark's cousin and an excellent student, in class two years earlier].
>
> Mark Thomas . . . in my book here we have C [for research purposes she had written down a grade she would have given Mark if she had been giving him a grade].
>
> [She opens the portfolio and reads the grade from the examination teachers.] Ooooo, hey, D+—well, you know [rising intonation]—*boy, his mother's gonna come unglued* (the teacher starts laughing nervously).
>
> [She spends a few minutes looking at the work which Mark entered in his portfolio, comparing this evidence to the commentary made by the examination teacher. She essentially concurs with those comments, all of which revolve around the theme of unrealized potential ("Mark, obviously you are capable of doing

high quality work," wrote the examination teacher. "Please work on neatness and goal setting"). In the end, however, this teacher's thoughts move toward family life.]

[Speaking] Now he obviously didn't take me up on redoing anything, um . . . most of his criteria is highlighted in the C, D, and especially F range, and this is in reading. Writing is higher-end—B, mostly C's. So, anyway . . . um—*they'll have to live with it, you know*?

[After a rather fine-grained analysis of the written feedback she had given Mark over the term, which had found its way into his portfolio either attached to a piece of work via a sticky note or written on a comment form—an analysis that serves to convince her that she gave Mark ample warning of what lay along the road ahead—she finally closes the portfolio and accepts the inevitable.]

[Speaking] This kid does have real strong potential just based on his verbal skills in class and the way he contributes, but he's pretty lazy about getting stuff out. So D+. But, um, I can see this mom comin' down the pike. But that's OK. We'll go on.

In this example, we see a teacher's envisionment of a future unpleasant parent-teacher conference, a possibility which perhaps ought to have little to do with the grading decision. The following example illustrates that there seemed to be few limits on what sorts of student behaviors teachers might deem relevant to their grading schemes. One afternoon, a staff member at Charles Ruff who was in charge of the computer laboratory was approached by a teacher who was interested in scheduling a day to bring his students into the lab. Here is a transcript of their conversation:

"When can I bring my kids in here?" Teacher A asked the lab supervisor.

"Second week in February?" the lab supervisor answered, referring to a calendar hanging from a filing cabinet.

"Ok, sounds good," Teacher A said. "If I can just remember now."

Teacher A smiled, and the lab supervisor shrugged.

"Well, you know, I just barely remembered to stop by and sign up," Teacher A said. "I keep forgetting, and my kids keep writing me notes. I give them ten extra-credit points if they write me a note to remind me of things, and I've been getting a whole drawer full. Well, at least it helps their grades."

That the shaping power colored relationships between students and teachers is illustrated over and over again in the field record. The following incident is taken from the field record just as it appears in that document, except for name changes:

> Yesterday p.m., [Maria Madsen, a portfolio teacher] told me about an incident when two boys came up to her at lunch and one of them offered her a French fry. She took it, but the other boy laughed and said, "You're only giving her that so you can get an A."
>
> The boy looked at his friend in surprise and said, "Miss Madsen can't give me an A."

As this anecdote revealed, the impulse to shape worked both ways—from teacher to student and from student to teacher. A second incident, this one involving my talking casually to a student whom I had in class during the previous year, further illustrates the depth of the influence which the shaping sphere of grades had for relationships between teachers and students:

> Yesterday as I was crossing the quad at lunch, A. (my student from last year) called me over. He looked at me, squinting in the sun, smiled slyly, and said, "Well, I've decided."
>
> "Decided what?" I asked him.
>
> "That I like this new way of grading us."
>
> "Oh, really?" I said and laughed. "You're kidding me."
>
> "No, I'm not. I do. I like it."
>
> "How come?" I asked.
>
> "Well . . . ," he began and then paused. "It's hard to explain."
>
> "Try."
>
> "Well, I finally realized . . . doing it this way, it's all right for me to like my teacher. I don't have to wait to see what my grade is."
>
> "I never thought of that angle," I said.
>
> A. laughed and said: "And I don't know who the examination teachers are, so I don't know who to hate."

The "consequential" and the "shaping" spheres of influence at Charles Ruff posed interesting problems of interpretation. Once letter grades moved from the privacy of the teacher's grade book to the public realm of the school's computerized database, they became somehow uniform in meaning. In other words, all "A's" were equal, all "B's" were equal, etc. This meant that an "F" given to a student because she or he was "fired" and refused to complete the stack of worksheets, or because the student gambled and lost too many times when the homework coin was flipped, had the same value as an "F" given to a student who couldn't quite wrap his mind around the end-of-chapter tests that his teacher used exclusively. The external consequences of the two different "F's" were potentially identical (loss of vacation, presence on the "No Activities" list, etc.), though some were contingent upon varying parental practices.

However, within the "shaping" sphere, letter grades had foggy contextual meanings determined by individual teachers' wishes. Despite the public assumption that letter grades had meanings stable enough upon which to base decisions about student lives, the actual referential content of those grades was really quite varied and may have had little to do with learning—at least, not with academic learning. It is interesting to note that although grading practices were secret and private affairs, instructional practices were much more visible and public.

From Nancy Atwell to Charles Cooper and Back Again

To fully characterize the Charles Ruff English–language arts curriculum and associated instructional practices with any level of completeness would be a daunting task. Earlier discussions of state and district influences revealed a somewhat chaotic but powerful set of defining factors, and given the broad spectrum of educational philosophies, personalities, intellectual backgrounds, and perspectives on language and literacy represented among the twenty or so teachers in the English Department, one might well conclude that an entirely separate curriculum existed for each individual teacher.

Despite these differences, there were some important similarities in instructional practices at Ruff that can be discerned and explained. Mayher and Boomer (1990) published accounts of historical similarities in English–language arts instruction that cut across geographical and sociocultural divides and appeared in Ruff's practices as well. Mayher's comments about the "long workbook," for example, ring true at Charles Ruff:

> As teachers we have too often not been the questioners. We have believed it was more important to have answers than questions. We have let others determine our curricula, our teaching strategies, and the texts we use. We have resisted change by claiming that "*they* won't let me do it," without recognizing our own role as part of the "they." Or we have incorporated new approaches into the old system, so that teaching the writing process, for example, becomes a kind of long workbook whose only substantial difference from earlier ones is that the blanks to be filled in are longer. (pp. 1–2)

The truth of Mayher's conclusion that "we have let others determine our curricula" has been and will be substantiated by data collected at Charles Ruff. Charles Ruff English teachers historically did what they were told to do by "them," even if it meant simply lengthening the lines that students were asked to fill in. As we have seen, during 1985 and 1986 district personnel worked furiously to keep abreast of stunning changes that the state had made. Ruff's English teachers were not left out of the district's staff-development plan and soon learned how to teach to the new test, as we will see in more detail.

The English Department chairperson at Ruff in 1986 was called upon to develop enough of an understanding of the state's "new" methods such that she could bring the remaining teachers "up to speed" and ensure respectable scores. Evidence of her participation in these efforts was found in that old filing cabinet drawer, in the form of a handout presenting the schedule of the "Third Annual Institute of Issues in English Language Arts" held in early October 1986 at the Los Angeles Airport Marriot Hotel.

Accompanied by the thick binder referred to earlier entitled *Writing Assessment Handbook: Grade 8,* this conference schedule encapsulated the reform philosophy of the times, namely, that assessment *should* drive the curriculum and instruction, which should result in positive changes in classrooms. The opening address given by the manager of the English–language arts unit for the state department was entitled "State Assessment: An Overview of the Status of California Writing Assessment for Grades 8 and 12." Following this presentation, another important figure in the development of the assessment system spoke on "The Relationship of State to District Assessment." In the afternoon two speakers tied the more general threads of the overview and the connections between state and districts to more practical classroom concerns, such as "California Assessment Program and the Teaching of Writing" and "Summary of the Day, Review of the CAP Writing Handbook and Preview of Workshops."

The second day of the conference, according to the handout, was devoted to specific workshops aimed at helping attendees understand the nature of each of the individual writing types that would be assessed. In the "Management Guidelines" section of the handbook that Ruff's English Department chair carried back with her from this conference, there was explicit reference to the intention of the new assessment, that is, to do just what Mayher described: "let others determine our curricula." Here is the language from that document as it was published in September, 1986:

> A management plan can assist district and school site personnel in identifying and organizing key tasks that must be accomplished to prepare for the direct assessment of writing at grade eight. Before the major management tasks can be undertaken,

they must be clearly defined. This requires the early involvement of those affected by or responsible for carrying out identified instructional goals. After determining what needs to be done, district and school administrators can decide how, when, and by whom each task is to be completed. (pp. iv–1)

Proposing that administrators decide "how, when, and by whom each task is to be completed" was hardly innovative (Mayher and Boomer, 1990).

Tucked away inside the flap of the binder's cover was a computer printout of a meeting agenda that was held at Charles Ruff on November 19, 1986. It took just over a month for local wheels to begin turning to get the "early involvement of those affected by or responsible for carrying out identified instructional goals." Here is what that agenda looked like:

AGENDA

DIRECT WRITING ASSESSMENT WORKSHOP

NOVEMBER 19, 1986

CHARLES RUFF LIBRARY

1:30–1:50   Workshop Objective
Background of Writing Program
Overview of D.W.A.T. [Direct Writing
Assessment Test]

1:50–2:00   Writing Process
Rhetorical Stance

MOVE TO ASSIGNED GROUPS

At this point the teachers were divided into groups on the basis of the specific writing type for which their discipline had been assigned responsibility.

Because the state decided to use the lever of assessment to pressure district and site administrators into allocating human resources in such a way that the program would be implemented, writing instruction based upon discrete tasks with artificial audiences, semiformulaic writing processes, and product-focused rubrics gained a strong foothold not just in the Ruff English Department, but across the curriculum at Ruff. Like departments in other secondary schools in the district, the Ruff English Department was enthusiastic about the new writing assessment, according to an interview with one of the writing resource teachers mentioned previously, especially in light of the fact that writing had never before been assessed except through multiple-choice tests of editing skills and knowledge.

Although there was minor resistance to the idea that the writing curriculum ought to be organized around the writing types as articulated by CAP, this resistance was short-lived. By 1987, the English Department had sorted out the writing types by grade level and had made an effort to assign certain types to the appropriate content area as called for in the staff-development literature published by the state. In no time at all, responsibilities had been made clear, and teachers were "teaching to the CAP test" just as the state department wished.

The power items did indeed have power.

But that power was deflected at least a bit by the writing of a young English teacher from the East Coast named Nancy Atwell. Several of the Ruff English teachers realized that Atwell's book took a broad swipe at writing instruction as it was delineated in the CAP manuals. Indeed, in her introduction to the section that explained the birth of the theory of the writing workshop, Atwell even discussed the work of Charles Cooper from UC–San Diego, a principal architect of the CAP writing-domain classification scheme, as representative of the force she was reacting against. Here is how Atwell (1987) described her previous writing program when she had based it on the theoretical perspectives of Charles Cooper and James Moffett—before learning about the work of Donald Graves:

> I had a writing assignment for every week of the school year, my own composition treasure trove. Students role-played, then wrote monologues. Or they talked in small groups, then wrote dialogues. Or they read selections from the anthology, then wrote fictional narratives. Then I wrote all over their drafts and they "revised." On Friday I collected all the compositions. On Saturday I avoided the room where they lay awaiting me. On Sunday I wrote all over them, recorrected too many of the same mistakes, then started pumping myself up for Monday morning's prewriting activity. (p. 6)

Atwell, of course, advocated that students should be free to select—indeed, be responsible for selecting—their own writing topics and make their own plans for getting the writing done. Such a philosophy was perceived to be in conflict with the district's insistence that the teachers prepare students to do well on the CAP writing test. During this period, as the 1980s were melting away (and after the English Department chairperson who had spearheaded the CAP movement on site had become a Ruff vice principal), copies of Atwell's book proliferated at Charles Ruff—well-thumbed copies underlined in ink of many colors—and "teaching to the writing test" grew distasteful to some Ruff English teachers, who had become convinced that students' should have "topic choice" and should show "ownership" of their own "writing process." These teachers had their students keep writing portfolios, usually fat folders stuffed with draft after draft of writings with little organization or format.

Just as the 1990s arrived, however, the English Department got their rude slap in the face: CAP writing scores came back in the single-digit percentile rankings with reference to other schools in the same socioeconomic bracket.

Ruff's principal was shocked. These scores, after all, were not multiple-choice scores, but represented the state's authentic writing assessment. If the new tests were to mean anything, they had to be taken seriously. The principal acted immediately. I was a newcomer to Ruff at the time, but I knew the CAP writing test. The principal found the money he needed to hire a long-term substitute to take my classes and released me from instructional duties. He asked me to design and prepare binders of CAP writing lessons and to lead CAP inservices for the Ruff English teachers.

All of the English teachers began implementing the writing lessons in the Ruff CAP binder: "How to Read a Writing Prompt"; "Features of the Essay of Speculation about Causes and Effects"; "How to Score the Problem Solution Essay"; etc. Posters, upon which the CAP writing types and scoring rubrics had been emblazoned, appeared almost overnight in all of the classrooms, and several of the most vocal advocates of Nancy Atwell's approach found jobs elsewhere, including the department chair who had replaced the earlier chair when she moved from the English building to the administration office.

By 1992, after the CAP writing scores fell into the black hole of the first stanine, the Ruff English Department began to rethink its use of portfolios. Inspired by the workshop philosophy which privileged student ownership, some teachers had been using free-form portfolios. Assessment had consisted of weighing the folders and measuring their thicknesses—the heavier and thicker, the better. After the CAP disaster, portfolios took on a more uniform cast. The teachers began talking about what kinds of work that perhaps ought to go in a portfolio which others—say, other teachers, the vice principal, students' parents— might inspect. There was some concern about the possibility of state-mandated portfolios, which at that time many believed were just around the corner. Making agreements about portfolios could help improve the CAP scores; it could also lay the groundwork for later state assessment mandates.

The department agreed that everyone would keep portfolios; translated, this meant that the vice principal would be able to walk into any classroom, open a filing cabinet, and see manila folders that held identifiable CAP essays. The next year the agreement went deeper: Teachers would direct students to save one CAP-type essay each trimester along with their rough drafts (the CAP essays were to be taught as "multidraft essays"). Although there was no formal plan for anyone to look at these folders, the vice principal (the former department chair who had participated in the original CAP training in 1986) offered to buy dinner for those teachers who actually followed through on the agreement.

I did not hear of such a dinner taking place. No further agreement was reached regarding the use of portfolios until the close of the 1993 school year, when the department voted unanimously to participate in the 1994–95 field trial of the New Standards Project's portfolio system. Although this system did not particularly support instruction in the CAP types, it did provide several instructional components which appealed to some of the English teachers, who had been complaining that they didn't know how to use portfolios and found them simply an extra burden.

The New Standards Project's system provided a student handbook with directions for putting together portfolios, accompanied by samples, materials which meant that the Ruff English teachers would not have to commit the unpardonable sin in education, that is, "reinventing the wheel." In addition, the New Standards Project's system called for just one portfolio which would be put together at the end of the year, a much more attractive option for those who considered portfolios to be just another intrusion. Instead of worrying about portfolios three times per year, all that would be required was an end-of-year portfolio.

That year, too, was to be the year of the Ruff portfolio project funded through SB 1274, about which this report was written. But the Ruff 1274 portfolio project did not involve the entire department, at least not during the first year. The 1274 project would involve just three volunteer English teachers who would implement the system in their classrooms and four volunteer examination teachers who would score the portfolios. Most of the English teachers could go on about their business as usual that year. The rationale for everyone's participation in the New Standards Project's field trial was, in part, that it would provide a common foundation for everyone to enter the portfolio discussion during the following year and beyond.

Although Governor Pete Wilson officially halted the CAP/CLAS assessment system developed by the California State Department of Education in September 1994, the use of the principles and practices put forth by the assessment system was unstoppable at Charles Ruff. The English teachers' earliest efforts to organize a local portfolio-assessment system had made use of the state's model of writing instruction and assessment. Further, district and site administrators had mandated that Ruff teachers in 1986 and then again in 1991 embrace the official writing system. By 1994, many Ruff English teachers had been thoroughly indoctrinated.

Despite the fact that the system no longer held political importance as an assessment method after Wilson's veto, it had proven to be such a strong organizer of instruction that the Ruff teachers—both the portfolio and the traditional teachers—could not let go. Indeed, the state-provided examples of student essays for each of the types at each score point, which had been photocopied and made available in class sets as part of the staff development that had occurred in 1991, continued to be used in lessons. Though these class sets were ragged and worn by the time the 1994–95 school year arrived, teachers still signed them out from the work room and assigned their students to small work groups so that they could collaboratively analyze the sample essays by referring to the appropriate CAP writing rubric.

As we will see later during the analysis of writing instruction in the portfolio classrooms, one of the central challenges that faced the portfolio teachers was figuring out how to break away from the CAP writing model, a challenge at which the portfolio teachers themselves said they failed.

Charles Ruff students of the mid-1980s and early 1990s experienced a writing curriculum shaped by a struggle between the CAP writing-assessment system and Atwell's articulation of the writing workshop. These same students experienced a reading curriculum also shaped by the strong forces discussed in Chapters 3 and 4. In the case of reading, however, as we have seen, the state influence on Ruff's reading curriculum during this period was much more amorphous. Though California's direct writing assessment had been implemented in 1987, with scores reported each year thereafter to the media, the state was not ready with its reading tests until 1992. Nonetheless, the force of the state's English–Language Arts Framework itself had encouraged Ruff's district officials to move in the direction of a literature-based English curriculum long before the reading test had even been designed. In keeping with the vision communicated in the state framework (Glass & Gottsman, 1987), Ruff's English teachers in the mid-1980s were required by district administrators to teach works of "core literature," that is, novels or other collections of literary works that had been assembled by district committees for each grade level K–12.

At Ruff that meant that seventh-grade English teachers would teach Paterson's *Bridge to Terabithia* and Conan Doyle's *Hound of the Baskervilles*; eighth-grade teachers would teach Twain's *Tom Sawyer* and Taylor's *Roll of Thunder, Hear My Cry*. Although these materials showed up in Ruff's classrooms and lesson plans by way of mandate, Ruff 's teachers, according to the memories of English teachers who were on staff in those years, were not opposed to their use. Moreover, the Ruff English teachers voluntarily complied with the state when the state reading test was ready to make its ill-fated entrance onto the reformist stage. In 1991, after the design of the CLAS reading test began to solidify, and after the state began to circulate documents explaining the test's design principles, the Ruff staff designed and implemented its own direct reading assessment patterned after the state model, jumping the gun on the official state implementation.

As we will see in the upcoming chapters, the powerful hold of CAP writing could not be shaken during the 1994–95 portfolio year. Moreover, the design principles of the CLAS reading test, not the notion of core literature as a foundation for democratic citizenship, were very influential in the portfolio classrooms. Although a small group of Ruff English teachers put together their portfolio system, the system emerged quite nicely from forces set in motion several years earlier by the state.

7 Ruff Instruction

The Teachers

In early spring 1994, we observed Ruff's leadership council approve funding for the portfolio experiment. A call went out for teacher volunteers. According to the proposal as funded, the project needed six portfolio teachers across disciplines. It also needed as many as ten examination teachers with credentials appropriate for the evaluation of student work within the respective disciplines. Interested faculty members were advised to write letters of application to the Performance Assessment Committee (PAC), a subcommittee of the leadership group. PAC would interview applicants to make final selections.

The portfolio teachers would design an assessment system complete with rubric and student handbook for their respective disciplines. They would make a clear, practical system, useful to their students, to their colleagues serving as examination teachers, and to themselves. They would endeavor to teach their classes in accordance with this system. Finally, they would report back to the school community with recommendations at the close of the project. The portfolio teachers would be given an additional preparation period, partly in recognition of their design work during the spring, partly in order to safeguard time for planning and reflecting.

The examination teachers would do the hidden work. They would learn to evaluate student portfolios according to the system's rules, each trimester getting more astute, more efficient, better. They would write letters to students commenting on the strengths and challenges they saw for each student through the cracked windows of the portfolios. And they would give the grades.

A key idea driving the project was the notion that the school could build its instructional capacity through this experiment in assessment. A delicate, intricate, yet strong intersubjectivity could emerge that might move the entire school forward. A dominant concern among almost every faculty member at Ruff was student motivation, and there was never a public argument that I heard against the proposal that classroom evaluation practices were related to student motivation. Volunteers for the project promised to examine and report on the impact of precise local criteria and "impartial" grades on student motivation at Ruff.

There was, however, to put it mildly, no stampede to interview for the project.

Three English teachers, a math teacher, a science teacher, and a music teacher volunteered to be portfolio teachers, and that was all. All of these teachers were interviewed; all signed on. Four English teachers volunteered to be examination teachers; though interested in participating, each of these four teachers told me that the prospect of being a portfolio teacher was scary. The portfolio teachers from the other disciplines had no trouble recruiting volunteers from their departments to be examination teachers. In fact, opportunities for staff development afforded by the demonstration and restructuring grants during the past several years had nurtured a number of curious teachers eager to experiment.

Readers have already heard the voices of the portfolio English teachers in previous chapters—Jennifer Johnson, Martha Goldsmith, and Maria Madsen (all pseudonyms). Martha and Maria were both entering their second year of teaching at the time of the portfolio project; Jennifer had been teaching for seventeen years (fourteen at the elementary level). Each was, it should be clear, fairly new to the school, but each of them had worked at Ruff long enough to have learned how Ruff things were done. Jennifer had been a fellow in a California Literature Project and a California Writing Project summer institute. Two years before the project, Martha had student-taught at Ruff—in Jennifer's classrooms. All three disliked the traditional grading system.

The examination teachers from the English Department shall go without pseudonyms. Each trimester this group of four English teachers, three female and one male, gathered to grade portfolios and to write letters to, and read letters from, students. One female examination teacher had taught for five years and was then serving as the English Department chair; she worked in the ESL track and later was asked to be the school's ESL coordinator. A second female had been teaching for approximately fifteen years and had long been a leader at the school. Having done work in a master's program in reading at the University of Arizona, she had been a reading specialist, a resource teacher, and a social studies teacher at several different schools. During the experimental year she was serving as the coordinator for the Ruff School Site Council, a parent-school group with decision-making authority over the school improvement budget.

A third female was a new teacher with a degree in American studies. She was teaching her own schedule of students for the first time; all of her previous experience had come as a long-term substitute.

As a new hire, this teacher worked cross-track—she had a full schedule that was spread across all four tracks. The fourth teacher, a male, was in his second year in the profession. He had earned a degree from a prestigious northern California university and had been thoroughly immersed in CLAS/CAP-like assessment. Credentialed to teach both Japanese and English, he, like the department chair, taught in the ESL track.

Predictably, this contingent of English faculty at Ruff differed in their views on particular instructional issues. They did, however, converge on one important point: They believed that working on the portfolio project would help them to improve their instruction. Further, they believed that the project could begin to create shared agreements about the curriculum across the department. Ruff English teachers exemplified the height of eclecticism. A portfolio system might help smooth Ruff edges.

Comprehension and Conflict

Eclecticism (now, balance?) had always been a Ruff virtue. The following examples of worksheets, one in seventh grade and one in eighth grade, illustrate the prevalence of the "multiple-choice mentality" among some teachers. The first worksheet was used by a seventh-grade English teacher in connection with his teaching of *Bridge to Terabithia*, a core literature title. This novel tells the story of Jess Aarons, a fifth-grade boy, who makes friends with a new student in his class, a girl named Leslie. After sharing magical moments of friendship with Leslie, Jess is ultimately faced with the problem of dealing with Leslie's death in a drowning accident.

According to a conversation I had with the teacher who used the following worksheet, the teacher indeed asked students from time to time to discuss their ideas about friendship, and the role of trust within relationships, as part of their *Bridge* work. He *did* ask students to develop and refine their personal responses to the novel through various graphic, dramatic, and verbal strategies. But as the worksheet below shows, he also provided students with assignments designed to collect proof that they had grasped what Sheridan Blau, during CLAS development work, called the "brute signifiers" of the text. This teacher tested his students on fiction as if they were reading a chemistry textbook:

> *Bridge to Terabithia*/Quiz
> Answer each question with a T or F also [sic] write in your
> bonus spelling word.

1. The name of Jess [*sic*] school was Lark Creek Elementary.
   T or F

2. Miss Bessie was the name of a person. T or F

6. Maybelle lost her cupcakes. T or F

7. Janice Avery wrote the letter. T or F

10. Twinkies were eaten by Jess and Leslie. T or F

20. Who ends up falling in the creek? _____

Bonus Spelling Word: _____

Of course, Lark Creek Elementary was the school, but Miss Bessie was a cow, not a person.

Who ends up falling in the creek?

This question, a carefully phrased item, reveals the tip of an iceberg of core controversy among some of the seventh-grade teachers at Ruff. Every year when students read the ending of *Bridge*, there was always a group of them who, upon completing the chapter in which Leslie's dead body is found in the creek, would shake their heads in confusion. If you asked them to name who had died, they might say, "Someone died?"

Some Ruff teachers thought that these students did not comprehend the plot of the book. How could they have if they did not know Leslie had died? What did they think happened to her? How could they go on to high school if they didn't know that Leslie was dead? What was the point of the novel if Leslie did not die?

Others argued that the reaction was entirely understandable. In fact, their confusion was an indicator of the depth of their identification with Leslie. After all, Leslie's demise threw Jess himself into a state of massive confusion. Even though characters die in cartoons and movies, characters you come to know aren't supposed to die. It isn't fair, and it is not part of common experience. In essence, according to this argument, just as they might have done in real life if a friend were to die, when they learned about Leslie's death, they denied it. Or they may have thought that the author was playing a trick and would bring Leslie back to life later in the book. It wasn't as if these students had misread the novel and thought that Leslie had gone off on a camping trip.

The second worksheet, used by an eighth-grade teacher, illustrates another Ruff attempt to give students explicit instruction in reading comprehension. This example represents a worksheet as assigned to students in connection with Tom Sawyer during the 1994–95 school year:

Study Guide: Unit Five
Reading Assignment
Chapters 13, 14, 15

Directions: Read each paragraph and underline the sentence
that best states the main idea.

   1. Read the paragraph beginning, "As the two boys
      walked along . . ."

      The main idea of this paragraph is:

      (a) Joe Harper and Tom Sawyer share feelings
          of self-pity.
      (b) Joe has been accused of a crime he has not com-
          mitted.
      (c) Joe wants to become a hermit.

   2. Read the paragraph beginning, "The Terror of the
      Seas had brought a side of bacon . . ."

      The main idea of the paragraph is:

      (a) None of the pirates smoke except Huck.
      (b) Joe has stolen a side of bacon.
      (c) The boys behave like pirates as they organize
          themselves.

As David Pearson and others have suggested, exercises such as the
above obscure a cluster of varied mental tasks under the fog of the
term "main idea."

One afternoon during the time when this teacher was teaching
Tom Sawyer, I had occasion to talk briefly with a former student of mine
who happened to be listed on this teacher's roster. I asked him how
things were going in the class. Here is his reply:

Well, you have to have everything in on time. Man, she just
won't accept anything even if it's just a minute late. And you
know what we had to do the other day? We had to copy, like,
five pages of notes from the overhead—notes on Tom Sawyer,
like, when he was born, what his religion was, things like that.
Took all period! My hand ached like crazy after that class!

Clearly, *Tom Sawyer* was being used—to teach punctuality and
responsibility, to teach the concept of main idea, to teach getting the
facts.

The Role of the Reader

Numerous data in the field record suggest that the English teachers
involved in the project differed substantially in their views on reading
instruction from those held by many of their colleagues who were not

involved. The project teachers agreed implicitly from the outset that a primary mission was to teach students to assume the role of a reader of literature as that role was defined by the portfolio-assessment system. These teachers wanted to influence their students' self-perceptions so that the students would come to identify themselves as "readers" as opposed to "nonreaders" and would thereafter *behave* as such.

When they asked them to become readers, these teachers asked students to do more than comprehend texts accurately and gain new vocabulary—though comprehension and vocabulary were given instructional attention and assessment weight on the rubric. Of interest, as we will see, is that the tension between comprehension and reader response was never really resolved and constituted a major frustration for portfolio students. Within the specifications of the portfolio rubric, readers were committed to goal-driven thinking and acting. What did Ruff readers during the 1994–95 school year do? How did they think?

Readers read every day, for one thing, "often for long periods of an hour or more" according to the rubric (see the Appendix). Readers also set goals for themselves, complex goals that took time and required effort to accomplish, important personal goals that promised to sharpen their understanding of life and literature. Readers kept records of their work so that they could periodically analyze themselves. Readers selected texts carefully, not haphazardly, to ensure that the texts presented appropriate intellectual, emotional, linguistic, rhetorical, or cultural challenges and furthered progress toward a goal.

Readers were persistent. Instead of abandoning carefully chosen texts when difficulties arose, readers applied strategies that permitted them to clarify and extend and understand. To acquire strategies and to create original ones, readers attended to instruction and then transferred their insights into the arena of self-selected reading. Readers wrote themselves into the books they read and were, in turn, themselves rewritten by those books Above all, readers "dug deeper."

Digging Deeper

During analysis of the field record, the phrase "dig deeper" became an important coding category. It appeared to be related to what the CLAS reading-test rubric described as probing, challenging, and questioning the text and the author and connecting the text to personal experiences. The phrase first appeared in the field record in an interview with Jennifer Johnson, when her students were putting together their first-trimester portfolio.

Jennifer was afraid that her students' portfolios would be weak, particularly in reading, because her students "[could] respond [orally] to what it is they read in a thoughtful, thorough manner, but their responses orally [were] not often reflected in their text logs that they write." The following excerpt constitutes the first use of the phrase "dig deeper" in the field record:

> *Jennifer:* Oh, [these students are] not anything compared to what we had last year, but they're starting to dig deeper, starting to be more thorough, starting to write more, starting to reflect more and be more self-evaluative. Just starting, though, taking baby steps.

Jennifer had been teaching long enough to know that students vary from year to year—sometimes in dramatic ways—for no good reason. Everybody has a hard year now and then.

The second use of the phrase "digging deeper" appeared two weeks later during an interview with Martha Goldsmith. In the following excerpt, Martha linked reading and writing and incorporated "digging deeper":

> *TU:* What kind of growth have you seen in these kids this trimester?
>
> *Martha:* Well, a lot. Like, Sophie is digging really deep. She's taking a lot of emotional risks with what she's doing, like in her writing she started out writing stories that were, like, horror stories or thriller stories, and now the last story she wrote was on a personal experience, a very very painful one which she had never written about before. I see some kids digging deeper and getting to probably more emotional or reality-based things, personal experiences, things like that. Whereas they started out with R. L. Stine–type books and writing stories that modeled R. L. Stine. I think they're challenging themselves more, probably making things a little bit more personal.

For Jennifer, "digging deeper" denoted "[beginning to be] more thorough, starting to write more, starting to reflect more and be more self-evaluative," especially in students' writings in response to literature. For Martha, this phrase meant that students were "challenging themselves more, probably making things a little bit more personal." Martha saw "digging deeper" as cognition based not in fantasy or illusion but in "reality-based things." These teachers wanted their students to find in fiction not the skills needed to recognize main ideas and the "facts" of a passage, but a deeper understanding of the facts of their lives.

Maria Madsen also used the phrase "dig deeper" during an interview. In the following excerpt, Maria reflected on an alternative instructional possibility that she could have employed during a whole-class reading activity involving a common text:

> *Maria:* I was thinking maybe I should've had them keep a character diary, like, either they're writing to the character or writing from the perspective of the character. So give more—but that only kind of covers plot, and I wanted them to dig deeper. Like, the verbal scale . . .

The "verbal-scale" strategy (Anderson & Rubano, 1991) requires students to make an early judgment about a character with reference to a predetermined trait (e.g., honesty); later in the same piece, students make a second judgment and compare their early and late judgments to determine what change, if any, took place in their thinking. Here, Maria dismissed the idea of a character diary because it tended to direct attention toward the surface. Like Jennifer, who meant "more thorough" and "more self-evaluative" by the phrase "digging deeper," and like Martha who meant more "reality-based" thinking by the phrase, Maria wanted her students to go beyond getting the facts and the main ideas. Digging deeper meant discovering symbol and theme, constructing integrative ideas, uncovering personally transformative meanings. Digging deeper meant looking beyond Leslie's death in the creek toward its significance for their lives as children.

When the question was finally posed to the portfolio teachers, that is, when I finally asked them to explain to me what the phrase "dig deeper" meant to them, neat and tidy definitions would not come easily. In February 1995, we discovered an article that covered all of the ground implied by the "digging deeper" metaphor and provided the theoretical language needed to explain the construct toward which they had been teaching. In this article, Miall and Kuiken (1995) explained the development of a survey instrument potentially useful to researchers interested in examining students' habits of mind with respect to literature. This survey measured several dimensions of literary reading orientation.

One of the dimensions, "insight," defined an important aspect of what the portfolio teachers meant by "digging deeper." Readers interested in gaining insight from text, according to Miall and Kuiken (1995), use the literary text as a guide to the "recognition of previously unrecognized qualities, usually in the reader, but also in the reader's world" (p. 41). The portfolio teachers agreed that this language described "digging deeper," particularly as it related to "reality-based" thinking. Such reading meant reading the text, but it also meant reading the self and reading the world.

It is interesting that Miall and Kuiken (1995) identified a "distinction between a form of absorbing reading that heightens awareness (Insight) and a form of absorbing reading that dulls awareness (Leisure Escape)" (p. 46). This distinction had already been made under the heading "consistency and challenge" on the portfolio scoring rubric, which required students to "select readings that challenge" rather than "readings that entertain." Escaping the world would be an unlikely route to gaining insight into the world.

Miall and Kuiken (1995) identified a second aspect of an orientation to literary reading which the portfolio teachers considered important in "digging deeper": "empathy." Empathy, for these researchers, was defined as "projective identification with fictional characters" (p. 41). The portfolio teachers encouraged their students to "identify with fictional characters" through a variety of whole-class and small-group strategies involving role-playing, writing letters to characters, writing letters as characters, and discussing what characters might have been thinking or feeling in selected situations. Often, such activities led students to an insight, as in the following excerpt taken from an eighth-grade student's "Friday Reflection":

> I think after I finished the *Joy Luck Club* I started thinking about my life and what my mother has taught me. I started asking my mom about her life back in Vietnam when she was my age. It might be a reason I started writing a reflection paper.

Setting Reading Goals

As part of their instructional approach for supporting students through the transition from nonreader or leisure-escape reader to literary reader in the habit of "digging deeper," the portfolio teachers required that their students establish reading goals for themselves early each trimester. The following excerpt was taken from a tape recording of a formal talk that Maria Madsen gave to the examination teachers, prior to the second portfolio scoring, in an effort to clarify for them the role of goal setting in her instruction:

> *Maria:* One of the first things students mention in the TL entry slip is their goals [TL = text logs]. A complex goal, as I explained it to my students, would be: an exploration of a genre such as fairy tales, fantasy, ethnic literature; comparing two or more genres; exploring a theme; searching for strategies to unfold literary works. A simple goal would be

to read for a certain length of time, to read a certain number of books. Students' text-log entries should chronicle their attempt to meet goals.

Although each portfolio teacher approached goal setting in her own way, all three expected students to articulate their goals for reading at the beginning of the trimester, to revisit those goals periodically, and to provide evidence in their portfolios of having worked toward achievement of their goals. Like almost everything about the implementation of the system, goal setting for the first trimester was not as effective as it was for the second and third trimesters. Immediately following the first scoring session, the portfolio teachers recognized the central role that goals played in the assessment, and all three teachers formalized a procedure for setting reading goals at the start of the second trimester.

Depending on the teacher, goals were brainstormed on butcher paper that decorated the walls, or spelled out on 3 × 5 cards in a file box, or written in letter form to the teacher—and each teacher devoted considerable time during the first few weeks of the second trimester to holding goal conferences with students. Sometimes student goals reflected considerable teacher influence. The following example of this influence was taken from an interview with Maria Madsen in February, in which Maria explained what she had come to understand about her students' fascination with horror:

> *Maria:* At first, they think they're just interested in horror stories, but what they're really interested in is, you know, what happens after you die, so then you can guide them toward the *Epic of Gilgamesh* or the Elysian Fields, and kind of get them to look at, you know, 'Why are you interested in horror?' A lot of them say they want to read horror, so I figure I'll just get them to understand why. You know, one kid was talking about he believes—and he's a kid who didn't do anything last trimester—and for him, he wants to know if there are different things that happen for different people, you know? Does morality have anything to do with an afterlife? He's really curious about that.

Challenge

Goal setting was originally listed on the rubric under "self-assessment and reflective analysis," but all of the criteria listed under "consistency and challenge" ultimately became interconnected with goal setting. The notion of "challenge," expressed on the rubric as "readings not only entertain, but also challenge and stretch capabilities," tied back to the CLAS reading test's criteria for test text selection; that is, good texts had to be challenging. Challenge became connected to goals at Ruff because students could not meet the "challenge" criterion if their goals were too easily achieved or too simple. Early in the year the portfolio teachers—and the examination teachers as well—worked hard at figuring out precisely what "challenge" might mean. The following excerpt from an early interview with Jennifer illustrates this point:

> *Jennifer:* Some kids are really challenging themselves—they're selecting more challenging reading materials, which is exciting. They're abandoning R. L. Stine, and they're going on to something like *Treasure Island* or even Michael Crichton.
>
> *TU:* How would you respond to people who say that Michael Crichton isn't all that different from R. L. Stine? I mean, some people might put the two of them in the same category.
>
> *Jennifer:* Oh, I would, too, except that he does use a little bit more meaty vocabulary than R. L. Stine does, and he does allow you to fill in more gaps than R. L. Stine does.
>
> *TU:* So when we think about challenge, we think about vocabulary load and inference load, but we're not really thinking about theme?
>
> *Jennifer:* Well, yes, we are, too, but all of those things need to be considered. We need to look at what kind of a jump a kid makes.

The portfolio teachers carried this discussion of "challenge" into their classrooms. The following segment was taken from an observation made in one of Maria Madsen's classrooms when her students were assembling their second-trimester portfolios. During this event, Maria demonstrated instructional persistence by giving her students a chance to get "unstuck" with respect to the notion of challenge:

> *Maria:* OK. Well, yesterday we got stuck on the challenging part. So let's go back to the challenging part. What kinds of reading challenges you?
>
> *Daniel:* Authors that you might not have read before?
>
> [Maria writes that down on the overhead.]
>
> *Maria* [speaking softly to herself while she writes]: Readings that challenge . . .
>
> [She looks up and sees some male students going on to highlight their practice rubrics, something they will do later in the lesson. She stops them from doing so. Then she calls on Eduardo.]

Eduardo: Books that are for older people?

Maria: How do you know if they're for older people?

Eduardo: Vocabulary?

Maria: And what about the vocabulary?

Eduardo: Harder words?

[A male student calls out: "The material inside the book. You know how some writers put in stuff that only grownups could love!"]

Maria [responding to the call-out, a puzzled look on her face]: What do you mean?

Unidentified male student: I mean stuff like romance and foul language. . . .

Maria: OK. Why don't you hold onto that for a minute—I'll come back to you. Eduardo?

Eduardo [who has clearly been thrown off by the interruption but still responds]: The author?

Maria: What do you mean by that?

Eduardo: Tom Clancy.

Maria: OK. [pauses, looks around the room] You guys had a lot of time to choose books that challenge you. Think about the choices you made. Why did you choose the books you read? Maybelle? Why did you choose Frankenstein?

Maybelle: It had to do with my subject.

Maria: OK. Your subject was stories of the supernatural. You could have read all Stephen King, but you chose Mary Shelley's Frankenstein. Why?

Maybelle: Because that was a challenging book.

Maria: Why was it challenging?

Maybelle: The writing style is a little bit different than what I'm used to.

Maria: What do you mean by that?

Maybelle: She uses words different than I do.

This discussion continued until five more students had explained what made some of the materials they had selected that trimester "challenging" for them. One student, for example, discussed his reading of Steinbeck's *The Pearl* and explained that a dream sequence had caused him to slow down, back up, and reread just to sort out what might be real from what was fantasy. Another student discussed her reading of a novel wherein "this lady doesn't agree with her son's marriage, and so she decides to clam up and not talk about it, and then finally when she does talk about it, she goes overboard, and she loses the relationship with the son"; the challenging part derived from the author's writing about events from several different perspectives.

Martha Goldsmith, the seventh-grade portfolio teacher, knew that something extraordinary was happening when the librarian expressed joyful disbelief about the titles which Martha's students had begun to request. One girl had asked for Faulkner's *The Sound and the Fury*. Shortly after that, Martha asked me to observe her third-period class. The girl was sitting at her desk reading *The Sound and the Fury* with a look of intense concentration on her face. She had a pad of yellow sticky notes at her side on which she was writing comments to fix onto pages in the book. "Jessica's not understanding that book, and she's getting frustrated," Martha whispered as we watched. "But what's wrong with that? Maybe she'll revisit that book when she's twenty, and something will have stuck."

Digging Deeper into Text Logs

An unexpected challenge for students was the recordkeeping requirement built into the portfolio system. Because students had not walked into the portfolio classrooms enculturated to supply evidence of their personal reading to be analyzed both quantitatively and qualitatively by teachers they did not know, the portfolio teachers had to teach them a recordkeeping system to capture their reading behaviors. The system came to be called "text logs."

Mechanically, it was a simple system: Students were directed to read in their self-selected books each evening; during the first five minutes or so of class time each day, they were directed to write a text-log entry which included information about what and when the student read as well as the student's response to the previous evening's reading. At the end of each grading period students gathered together their text logs, self-analyzed their entries according to the grading criteria, and prepared an entry slip to guide the examination teachers to those parts of the text log illustrating accomplishment according to the rubric.

All three portfolio teachers began—and ended—the school year with text logs employed as just described. There was, however, some dissatisfaction with the system which was never fully resolved. Early in the year, after the portfolio teachers understood how difficult it was going to be to motivate students to keep text logs, they talked about changing the text-log system. In early September, Maria explained in an interview that she and Jennifer had been thinking about making a significant modification:

TU: How are they doing with their personal books?

Maria: They're doing pretty well. They seem to like—Jennifer said that her students don't like the text logs. My students *do* like them. But I'm thinking about letting them do those at home and doing journals again because Jennifer and I talked about how the journals are a really good stepping board into a lesson. . . .

Many Ruff English teachers used the practice of writing a journal topic on the overhead to which students responded by writing in their daily journals the moment they entered the classroom and sat down at their desks. Intended as a device to increase writing fluency as well as a means for getting students to think about an issue or topic important in the day's lesson, journal topics were often provocative and stimulated much follow-up discussion. This journal strategy had been particularly appropriate for the study of a work of core literature. Jennifer, in fact, had used the daily journal as a central organizer for her classes for the past few years during which she had emphasized core literature.

Although Martha Goldsmith also had had second thoughts about the text-log system, Martha was more ambivalent about using the journal writing strategy, perhaps because she did not have a long history of teaching core literature. The following excerpt was taken from an interview with Martha just a few days after the interview with Maria, cited above. Martha and Maria had been talking to one another about text logs ever since the topic first came up:

TU: What changes in the system would you suggest?

Martha: We were thinking about doing text logs at home.

TU: What do you think about text logs?

Martha: More what I'm getting from the kids is that they really don't like doing them in class, and I think that they would be OK with doing them at home. For some of them it's hard to remember what they've done, and it would be easier for them to do it at home.

The three portfolio teachers had reported three distinct judgments of the text-log strategy: Jennifer had said that her students didn't like doing them at all, Maria had said that her students did like doing them in class (but she was considering using the journal strategy anyway), and Martha had said that her students didn't like doing them in class but would like doing them at home. Martha found value in the text-log strategy, particularly in the transfer she saw from text logs to "bookshares," classroom events where students "shared" their self-selected books in front of the class. She continued to talk about text logs in the interview:

> *Martha:* I think that text logs are pretty good, and where I see text logs come out the most right now is in their book-shares. The questions that they ask are almost always a lot more challenging and a lot more in-depth—and things that kind of remind me of the text-log question sheet that we gave them at the beginning. So it's just—it's really showing me that they interact with each other about literature.
>
> *TU:* Explain please.
>
> *Martha:* It just seems like what we ask them to focus on in text logs and give them practice on daily—it seems like it's applying itself to other areas. When we do bookshares, the questions that they ask the people who are sharing, they're a lot more in depth, or they're a lot more on a personal experience or a feeling or a deeper interpretation rather than literal questions asking for information.

Martha's analysis of the role of text logs in her classroom culture placed considerable importance on the strategy. When she explained why she was even thinking about modifying such an important strategy, her logic illustrated her concern for her students' and her own comfort. Text logs were awkward:

> *Martha:* Simply because they feel like it's easier for them to be done at home. They just seem like they would like to do them at home. And also when Jennifer and Maria and I were talking, it's like they come in, they do their text logs, and it's like we have this pause, and then we start teaching. Whereas last year when we did the journals, there was a transition all the way through. And they started prewriting, and they started really thinking and sharing opinions with each other when they shared their journals, and it was just a much more smooth thing.

At this point Martha was weighing the organizational effect which the journal writing strategy would have on her instructional composition against the pedagogically powerful effect she had attributed to the text-log strategy. She continued:

> *Martha:* But I've been so *happy* about their personal reading, because almost everybody is into a book. And they've asked if they could take some of the books over the break. And last year things like that didn't happen.

The preceding interview segments with respect to the text-log strategy illustrate a pattern in the field record that was coded "digging deeper into digging deeper," to refer to the intense level of collaborative reflection in which Martha, Maria, and Jennifer had engaged over the course of the year. They talked daily about concrete strategies in light of student behaviors. Under ordinary circumstances, Jennifer Johnson probably would not have discussed changes she planned to make in the text-log system; she would have announced them, if anything. Ruff teachers routinely made those kinds of decisions on their own, often modifying the modifications and then modifying again. But the portfolio teachers' practices were inextricably linked together by the scoring rubric and by the existence of the examination committee. There was no requirement that these three teachers employ identical practices—and, to be sure, they did not—but they were teaching toward agreed-upon objectives using common criteria and were very interested in what their colleagues were doing. They also were often found visiting in the classrooms of the examination teachers during their prep periods.

Jennifer, Maria, and Martha ultimately decided for themselves against asking students to do text logs at home: Students would write their entries in class. The teachers came up with several explicit reasons for their decision, reasons that they could present to students, parents, and other teachers: (1) in-class text logs present a daily reminder that self-selected reading should be done; (2) teachers can monitor self-selected reading behaviors by circulating while students completed text logs; (3) expecting personal responses to self-selected reading during institutional time sends a clear message that such activity is officially valued; (4) putting time between self-selected reading and written responses encourages students to approach their reading with the idea that they need to remember and to reflect.

Since it was clear that text logs were going to be a part of the instructional landscape for the entire year, the portfolio teachers began investing even more effort in teaching students to use them, and the portfolio students began taking their text logs more seriously. During early drop-in observations, I would sometimes count as many as twelve or fourteen students sitting idly during text-log time, either not making an entry or completing the entry quickly. A few months later, idle students were far fewer in number, usually just one or two if any. Further, almost all students used most of the allotted time, and many wanted more time. As students came to realize the importance of the text logs in their portfolios for their grades, the entries became increasingly longer and more legible.

Portfolio students received a heavy dose of direct instruction, modeling, and discussion regarding the keeping of text logs during the first trimester. As Martha indicated above, students got a sheet prepared by Martha, Maria, and Jennifer, with the help of Nancy Atwell (1987), giving text-log prompts. Here are the entire contents of that sheet:

> Questions you might want to ask yourself when responding in your text logs:
>
> How has the character changed?
>
> How am I like or unlike the character?
>
> What would I do if I was this character? Why?
>
> If this character was a real person I could talk to, what comments would I have for him/her?
>
> Would this book be considered a classic? Why? Why not?
>
> Have I ever had an experience like this?
>
> Do the things that happen in this book happen in the real world?
>
> How does this relate to other books I've read?
>
> Would a nonreader choose this book? Why? Why not?
>
> What could people learn about life from reading this?
>
> What have I learned about life from reading this?
>
> What other things has reading this novel made me think about?
>
> How has this text changed my reading habits?
>
> If I could have a conversation with the author, what would I ask or say to him/her?
>
> Do I agree with the author's ideas? Why or why not?
>
> What do I think about the way the author has written his/her book?
>
> What images came into my mind as I was reading the book?
>
> If I were the author, what would I change?
>
> How do I think the author came up with the ideas for the book?

Class time was devoted not just to the writing of text-logs entries, but also to the reading of entries. Students began to share their daily text-log entries in front of the class, much as students in previous years had shared their journal entries. The teachers occasionally scheduled small-group sessions in which students examined one another's text logs in light of the rubric. The following segment was taken from an observation in one of Maria Madsen's classes during the assembling of the first-trimester portfolio and illustrates the level of explicitness with which the portfolio teachers treated text-log instruction:

> [Maria is writing on the overhead. "Count the number of text logs. Write down the average length of time you read."]

Maria: OK. If you've been reading every day, how many text logs should you have?

Students: Thirty to thirty-five?

Maria [writes the number "35" on the board and circles it]: I've seen as many as *fifty*, but that is from people who kept track off-track. How many of you are reading every day? [Lots of hands in the air.] How many of you are reading every day for at least an hour? [Several hands in the air.] So where does that put those readers?

Students: An "A."

Maria: How many of you read every day for less than an hour? [lots of hands] Where does that put you?

Students: "B" [one student calls out "A–"].

Maria: Actually, you may want to be highlighting this as you go along. [She passes out water-based highlighters to students. A few male students take the caps off and sniff the highlighters. Maria ignores their giggles while she continues to pass out highlighters.]

Maria [addressing a female student as she is passing out materials]: Well, either you read for long periods up to an hour or you don't.

Student: But this says that the reading is not only entertaining, but challenging. So it isn't just a matter of reading for an hour.

Maria: So the examination teacher might put you in between.

Martha had begun giving her students instruction and practice in keeping text logs during the first week of school. The following segment was taken from a very early observation in one of her classrooms:

[Students are working on their text logs in Martha's room. Martha has prepared a text-log sheet that includes the grading criteria, and she is having students look at their text logs, decide whether they have evidence for a certain criteria, and answer "yes" or "no" or "yes, strongly" or "yes, weakly." She speaks briefly with three or four students and then stops the class.]

Martha: Can I see a show of hands of people who are totally lost?

[Almost every student in the room raises his or her hand. Martha takes time to re-explain the task.]

Martha: If you see proof or evidence in your text log, then write "yes" next to that criteria.

Elton: Do you do all the grading criteria on one [entry] and then do it on the next one?

[He is pointing to the text-log sheet which consisted of five boxes, one for each day of the week, in which reading notes are to be made.]

Martha: You do it on the whole log, not on one part at a time.

Martha realized that her students needed to know not just how to write a text-log entry, but how to read a text log in its entirety as the examination committee would read one. Above, Elton asked a crucial question with significant implications for his emerging conception of the text-log genre. After Martha explained that evidence for any criterion could come from anywhere on the text-log form, she focused on one particular criterion:

> *Martha* [speaking to the whole group]: Reads widely and deeply—remember, we talked about going widely and how you probably can't do that until you have several entries.

She gave her students a few minutes to examine several entries and then called the group together:

> *Martha:* How many of you did better? [A few students raise their hands.]
>
> *Martha:* How many are lost? [About twenty students raise their hands. Martha laughs.]

Because she had made little progress with her students this time out, Martha tried a different approach:

> *Martha* [goes to the front of the room]: If you were allowed—asked—to design your own criteria, what would they be? What would you like to be graded on? What would you like to be graded on?
>
> *Amanda:* It could show how much you got into the book.
>
> *Another student:* They could see if you're reading books up to your standards and not below.
>
> *Another student:* If you could say what you think needs improvement in the book.
>
> *Martha:* Anything else to add?
>
> *Another student:* Evidence that you are reading every day.
>
> *Martha* [pause]: Anybody else?
>
> [Martha waits, then:]
>
> *Martha:* It's my feeling that if you were to show that you really get into the book, that you read up to your standard, that you think about how to change your book, well, I think that the text logs would show what they need to show. OK, I'm going to give you one goal for your text log. When you do

> your next text log, do not include even one sentence of
> retelling what you read. Give your reactions and responses
> to what you read.

The injunction to "give your reactions and responses to what you read" rather than a simple retelling proved to be a complex factor in what happened with reading in the portfolio classrooms. When the facts of the text were taken away as content for the text-log entry, students sometimes had trouble finding things to say. A pattern emerged in the taped thinkalouds of the examination teachers that was coded "mumbo jumbo." Instances occurred where students talked about their readings, referencing notions in the rubric, but actually said nothing about their reading of the text, of themselves, or of their worlds. Here is a brief example of "mumbo jumbo" from one of Maria's student's text log in response to a work by Edgar Allan Poe:

> I don't really understand what's going on right now. I can
> understand the vocabulary, but I don't really see a moral. It's
> becoming harder as I go deeper into the book. I think that I'm
> starting to understand the book a little more. Although it's
> becoming easier, I still must say it's no doubt the hardest book
> I've ever read.

According to the examination teacher who scored this portfolio, the student's text logs "talked around" the text's words, but never really entered any text with any specificity. Particularly problematic was the lack of any evidence of connection, questioning, resistance, or any of the reading behaviors valued on the CLAS reading rubric. In commentary to the student, the examination teacher wrote that this student was trying to pass off "mumbo jumbo" as insight: "You say that you read a lot of challenging texts in your text logs, but it's all talk. You don't *do* anything with the texts."

Maria Madsen was irate when she read this commentary. In her mind, this student did "a lot." In his entry slip for shared reading, for example, he explained that he was trying to transfer strategies from classroom instruction into his "home book," and in fact he mentioned these attempts at transference in his text logs. Because he did not deal with the texts in any detail, however, the examination teacher did not seem to believe that he had actually read them. "It's an issue of trust," Maria said. "[The examination teacher] doesn't trust him, and I do. I know he read them because I watched him and I talked to him."

The mean report-card grade for portfolio students for the first trimester was roughly a full grade lower than the mean report-card grade for the traditional students (portfolio students averaged a "C" while the traditional students averaged a "B"). Some students were shocked: A male student in one of Martha's classes reported that he had never received below a "B" on any of his elementary report cards (he earned a "D" on his first-trimester portfolio). Generally, this grade deflation was painful. When the portfolio students received back their second-trimester portfolios, which still averaged a "C" grade, there was a period of sagging spirits. In an interview, Maria described her students' reactions when they got back their grades for their second-trimester portfolios:

> *Maria:* I think there were a lot of disappointments. And I was disappointed, because I know some kids worked harder and got lower grades. And that made me angry—and it made me feel . . . It drove me into self-reflection and looking at how I failed them as a teacher more than how the examination teachers failed them. . . . They *were* reading challenging books, and they didn't necessarily get credit for that, you know? They were reading much better books than they were reading the time before, and I don't know what it is that . . . Maybe the entry slips are more important than I realize because those seem to have a lot to do with the grades, but—I'd really like to look back over the portfolios and compare them.

During the third trimester, Maria mentioned again that she saw a need for modifying the text-log system, but this time her concern grew from her sense that the system was not sufficiently expansive to accommodate all of the kinds of reading her students were doing:

> *Maria:* And in their text logs—many of them are saying they need to do more, especially like the kids who are getting into poetry. They're saying, you know, somehow . . . this doesn't work in the text log because I need to do more with the poetry than just write down my feelings or thoughts or compare or contrast. So I said, "Why don't you use the text logs as a place to kind of record what you did, you know, what strategy you used to unfold the text for you? And refer in the text log to what pages or what poems." You know, because I have some kids who are writing the poems down in different ways, and they need to just—they need to have that. They need to keep that evidence.

Transfer

In addition to this self-selected reading program, the portfolio teachers continued to employ works of core literature in their classrooms. During the first trimester, Jennifer and Maria taught *Tom Sawyer* while Martha taught *Bridge to Terabithia*. During subsequent trimesters

Martha and Jennifer taught *The Giver,* but Maria did not (Maria did not agree that *The Giver* was sufficiently challenging for eighth-grade students). To varying degrees the portfolio teachers approached the use of a common text for all students (what was called "shared reading" in the portfolio system) as a means for teaching students how, when, and why to employ a variety of literary reading strategies. The intention was for students to then demonstrate that they had transferred these strategies to their self-selected books.

The following segment was taken from a first-trimester interview with Martha about her use of the book *Bridge to Terabithia.* This portion illustrates Martha's concern with providing her students opportunities to understand why creating images enhances the reading process:

> *Martha:* [We did a] visual imagery activity where I walk them through into *Terabithia,* and they all close their eyes, and when they open their eyes they shared what they saw. And then they drew what they saw on a piece of paper, and they went through—well, actually, first we had this discussion about how you got those images, and the three things they came up with—and, honestly, I didn't do any prompting—but the three things they came up with were their imaginations, personal experiences of being in the mountains before, and, um, the sentences in the book. So we talked about those three things. So we went through the book and they picked out ten lines—or was it five? I think it was five—that allowed them to really visualize, and then they rewrote, reshaped it, rethought it into a poem.

The idea was that students would apply what they had learned about imagery from this lesson to their reading of self-selected books.

Students were required to create a shared-reading entry for their portfolios to provide evidence that they were developing "deep, personalized interpretations" of core texts and that they had experimented with a variety of response types and reading strategies. This requirement forced Jennifer to assign her students more written than oral tasks, as the following excerpt from a midyear interview with Jennifer suggests:

> *Jennifer:* I've done more written things because I would've done more oral things and just quick presentations, but they need to have written things to show in their portfolios. We've done a lot of written responses—like, initial responses, and we've done dialectical journals, double-entry journals—and we've done open mind, image logs, those kinds of things, rather than quickly coming up and

> doing Hot Seat, which I would have done after Chapter 9
> when Jonas [*The Giver*] had just received the instructions on
> how to become a receiver of memories. I would have liked
> to have done that, but I wanted them also to have some-
> thing written. . . .

"Hot Seat" requires students to role-play a character while classmates ask questions. Here, though uncomfortable, Jennifer modified what she would have ordinarily required her students to do in order to accommodate the portfolio system. The kinds of written response tasks she assigned had emerged from her participation in the California Literature Project and from her knowledge of the CLAS reading test.

An emphasis on self-selected reading, goal setting, text logs, transfer of strategies, and "digging deeper" distinguished reading instruction in the portfolio classrooms from other sorts of English classrooms, in which mastery of literary content was a more salient instructional objective. The field record was saturated with data from the portfolio classrooms that showed consistent, systematic instruction aimed squarely at helping students volunteer for the role of a literary reader. Moreover, when the portfolios were graded, the examination teachers weighed heavily students' text logs and searched the evidence for complex goals, transfer of strategies, consistency in reading at home, and insight and empathy. Grades depended on such evidence.

A quantitative analysis of reading-test scores gathered in a pretest/post-test fashion was done in accordance with the SB 1274 proposal funded by Ruff's leadership council to compare the reading achievement of portfolio students with that of nonportfolio students. The scores were taken from Ruff's schoolwide, locally developed CLAS-like reading exam, which the English Department gave twice each year. This testing had been started in 1991 in order to provide the district administration with evidence that the seventh-grade block schedule was working.

According to this analysis, there was a statistically significant difference between the groups with respect to gain scores on the reading test. The mean score of the portfolio students was almost half a point higher on a six-point rubric than was the mean score of a comparable group of nonportfolio students at the end of the year, though there had been no difference at the start of the year (see Underwood, 1995, for full details). Although the pretest/post-test design was not purely experimental and was flawed in important ways that limited opportunities to generalize, the quantitative evidence it provided corroborated conclusions drawn from qualitative data in the field record.

CAP[ped] Writing

The portfolio teachers had made changes in how they taught literary reading throughout the year and implemented a recognizable and systematic approach. A motto capturing the gist of portfolio reading instruction might go something like this: "Understand your life through understanding literature." A metaphor anchoring the nature of instruction in the portfolio classrooms might be a chrysalis, the hard-shelled pupa of a butterfly. Each student was expected to grow in maturity and seriousness over the year, to transform himself or herself for the moment and for the future. The classroom itself was the chrysalis, protecting students from external demands except for those which required students to think for themselves and choose for themselves. Each student wrote his or her own core literature list. Content was, for the most part, the student's choice.

In most of the English classrooms at Ruff, however, particular literary content was chosen by the teacher. Ironically, particular content was often irrelevant to composition instruction. The following observation was made in the library during a lesson in which the librarian was teaching students how to use the electronic card catalog during the writing of a research paper:

> *Librarian* [standing at the front of a group of students who have just been instructed in the use of the electronic card catalogue]: Suppose you were doing a report on, oh, say, salamanders, and you looked in the computer, and there wasn't anything. What would you do? [Selects a student with a raised hand.]
>
> *Student* [after a few seconds pause]: Pick a different topic? [rising intonation]
>
> *Librarian* [laughing heartily]: Oh, no, no, no! You couldn't do that. Your teacher has already assigned you a topic!

A brief interview with a student in the class revealed that students had actually gotten their topics by random selection of a slip of paper from a box.

By the time Martha Goldsmith, Maria Madsen, and Jennifer Johnson started to think about the assessment system that they would implement during the 1994–95 experiment, the CAP writing model had literally become the Ruff writing curriculum. As described earlier, CAP influenced Ruff in two waves: The first wave hit after the English Department chair brought the new system back from a Los Angeles conference. The second wave landed with even more force after Charles Ruff's shockingly low CAP writing scores were reported in 1991.

Maria Madsen taught at Ruff during the 1993–94 school year, more than two years after the second wave, but she had nonetheless become thoroughly imbued with CAP. According to a reflective interview held near the end of the portfolio project in 1995, Maria had been grateful for the system when she first arrived at Ruff. "They never taught me how to teach writing in my teacher-preparation program," she said. "All I knew how to teach was literature—and I didn't even know how to teach that very well. And then when I came here, you guys had these writing types with lessons all worked out in a binder. I mean, it made it easy to plan your day, and I knew that I would be OK if one of the administrators came poking around. I knew—at least I thought that if they came in and saw me teaching autobiographical incident, they could see that I was a team player. I was doing what they expected me to do. Nobody seemed to care if it was really helping the students become good writers or not."

Maria brought CAP with her when she started the 1994–95 school year as a portfolio teacher. The following observation, done early in the year, shows her application of the technology. Maria had asked her students to read an essay classified as an "autobiographical incident" in accordance with the state's definition of that type. For students to receive high scores on these essays, official scorers determined whether there was the recounting of an incident (an event which takes place in a few minutes, a few hours, or at most, a day—anything longer was defined as an autobiographical "phase"); whether this incident was narrated in a context that neither overshadowed nor left vague the incident itself; whether the student writer had communicated the significance of the incident for himself or herself either explicitly or implicitly; and whether the whole essay was written in a sincere and engaging "voice."

During several lessons prior to this observation, Maria had given her students direct instruction in the features of an "AI," including the injunction that the "AI" essay is about an incident and not, heaven forbid, a "phase." At the following point in the lesson, Maria had just asked her class to report their answers to four questions she had given them on a handout. Her students had been organized into groups of four and had been given ten minutes to develop answers. Here, she had just called the class together and asked each group to report back to the whole group:

Maria: What did you think the incident was?

[No responses.]

> *Maria* [waits five seconds by the clock and then repeats]: What did you think the incident was?

> *Student* [after five more actual seconds, raises a hand and is given the floor by Maria]: How to make a figure eight.

> *Maria* [nods]: OK. [Scans the class for more hands, waits, sees no more hands, then directs her question to a specific student.] What did you think the incident was, Joseph? How to make a figure eight? [Joseph looks down at his desk. Maria waits two seconds.] Does anyone have a different point of view?

> [Maria waits ten seconds, looks over the group of students. Several hands begin to go up tentatively. Some quiet talking, including a few giggles, occur.]

> *Maria:* Can we have some quiet hands please?

> [There is more murmuring while Maria waits. The vocalizing subsides, and students begin to put their hands down.]

> *Maria* [apparently deciding to abandon the first question]: Who has the answer to the second question? [This question is about the significance of the essay.] How about your group, Kathy?

> *Kathy* [shrugs]: I dunno.

> *Maria:* Who took notes?

> *Kathy:* Juan.

> [Maria does not speak again for fifteen seconds. She makes her way between the clusters of desks over to the vicinity of Juan's group. There is a shuffling of papers and some mumbling while Maria waits for Juan, whom she has spoken to very quietly, to respond.]

> *Maria* [after ten more seconds]: Juan, are you having trouble reading your handwriting?

> [She waits eight seconds.]

> *Alvin* [a member of Kathy and Juan's group, says in a somewhat resigned tone]: I don't think there was any significance.

> *Juan* [smiling]: Yeah, and if it wasn't significant, why would the guy write it?

Maria commented during interviews that she felt something was wrong with her writing instruction, though she couldn't put her finger on the precise nature of the problem, and that she had sought out readings and discussions with colleagues to help her clarify her thoughts about it. This observation had been made early in the project, at a time when Maria had told me that she was not yet comfortable with my presence in her classroom. Although her instruction in the above instance was probably uncharacteristic, the presence of CAP was clear.

Though Maria was troubled by her writing instruction, many English teachers showed little, if any, dissatisfaction with CAP as the hub of the Ruff writing curriculum. In an interview in September 1994, just days before Governor Pete Wilson vetoed the CAP/CLAS legislation, Jennifer said that teachers at Ruff should continue to be guided by CAP during the upcoming year, the portfolio-project year. The following excerpt began with my asking Jennifer to think back to the period three years earlier when Ruff's CAP writing scores had bottomed out, CAP writing scores across the state had been low, and Ruff's principal had called for binders and inservices to return the English teachers to "CAP-compatible" instruction. I asked Jennifer whether she thought this emphasis on teaching the CAP writing types had been positive for Ruff's teachers:

> *Jennifer:* Yeah, our teachers are talking more about writing *types*
> rather than free-for-all writing workshop. They're looking
> more at *form* rather than writing fluency. They're expecting
> more out of students . . . is what *I* see. They've *really*
> bumped up their expectations in writing here.

"Free-for-all writing workshop" and "looking . . . at . . . writing fluency," for Jennifer, characterized the kind of writing instruction that had been carried out in several English classrooms at Ruff just after the publication of Atwell's (1987) *In the Middle.* Jennifer argued that although students from more homogeneous populations with smaller classes, like those in Atwell's eastern area, could select their own topics and plan their own writing and do well, the Charles Cooper perspective on guided writing procedures, as embodied in the CAP model, seemed more appropriate for West Coast teachers with their crowded and diverse classrooms. When it came to writing instruction, one size did not fit all.

The portfolio teachers began their 1994–95 year fully expecting to teach autobiographical incidents, firsthand biographies, essays of speculation, and all the rest of the CAP menu, just as they had done the previous year ("Probably because [the principal] had been patrolling D complex pre-CAP testing to make sure I was preparing students for the test," wrote one of the portfolio teachers in the margin of an early draft of this chapter). In fact, the CAP model had been built into the portfolio student handbook (entitled "Building a First Trimester English–Language Arts Portfolio: A Handbook for Charles Ruff Students"), the document that students received the first day of classes in the portfolio classrooms. The following quote comes from the third page of that document and illustrates the degree to which portfolio writing instruction was framed according to CAP tasks:

WHAT GOES INSIDE YOUR FIRST TRIMESTER ENGLISH–LANGUAGE ARTS PORTFOLIO?

What pieces of work will you include in your first trimester portfolio for your first trimester grade report? Your regular English teacher will give you instruction in and practice with writing formal essays which will be due every three weeks.

The CAP system appeared neat and tidy on the surface, but there were tensions and paradoxes in its design which showed up at Ruff and were embodied in the above quote. Ironically, although the state's CAP writing test required students to write an essay in one class period, Ruff English teachers had found that students needed at least three weeks to complete one CAP essay from start to finish. And even though the state test required students to write their essays in isolation, the state handbook paradoxically recommended social composition practices, so the Ruff teachers employed such practices as student-led writing conferences, formal response groups, and author's chair during this three-week instructional period. Although Jennifer had expressed the view that CAP had improved writing instruction at the school by muting "free-for-all writing workshop," she did not want the portfolio teachers locked into teaching particular CAP types on a schedule. So the portfolio handbook did not specify types. It used code instead: "writing formal essays."

The degree to which a particular instructional theory has become embedded in a school culture can be determined, in my view, by the forthrightness with which the practice is discussed by teachers with parents. Here is a quote that provides evidence of CAP's deep penetration into the school culture, taken from a presentation given by Maria Madsen near the start of the school year to her students' parents during a "Back-to-School Night":

> *Maria* [standing in front of a roomful of parents who showed up at Ruff on a warm summer evening to learn about their child's school]: First of all, your [children] will have writing assignments every three weeks in this class, and we're starting out with autobiographical incidents. That's a story about an important event in their life, something that they learned from, something that was important to them. And as you can see [referring to a note written on the chalk board giving a due date], the rough draft is due tomorrow.

As we have seen, observations and interviews early in the year confirmed that the three portfolio teachers taught at least one of the CAP essay types during the first trimester in a manner reminiscent of the *Writing Assessment Handbook: Grade 8*. In Maria's classes, students were assigned a CAP task, that is, the creation of a particular text type with certain specified features, and taught to define the type through abstract language. They were taught to identify features in model essays (e.g., the figure-eight essay). They were given an explanation of the task with student-written examples, they drafted, they responded to peer essays by keying on the features, they revised in light of feedback, and they turned in final copies on a predetermined date. Students did not, however, get grades on their writing—unless they determined them themselves—until their portfolios came back from the examination session. Even then, their grades reflected a collection of work, not an individual essay.

Martha Goldsmith, however, did not begin teaching that year with quite the same brand of CAP instruction that characterized Maria's instruction. Martha had decided to begin her year by assigning her students the task of writing a story. Never as firmly rooted in the CAP instructional model as her two portfolio colleagues ("Maybe because testing didn't occur until eighth grade," wrote Maria Madsen in response to an early draft of this chapter), Martha's practices in the early months of the year were ambiguous, partaking of both an Atwellian workshop and a Cooperish "guided tour." There was something about "story" which made it hard to assess using CAP technology. The state assessment system had abandoned "story" as a discrete type; it no longer used prompts designed to evoke a "story" from students. For one thing, students couldn't seem to write stories that were any good during a single class period, and scoring the long, meandering texts that they did write had been problematic (Weiss, personal communication).

There *was* an official scoring rubric for story in existence in the filing cabinet that housed the official state handbook, however. The type had been *acknowledged* as an official part of the curriculum at Charles Ruff. But because the type was no longer tested, Martha was not bound so tightly by the state rubric. And as Maria had pointed out, because Martha taught a nontested grade level, Martha was probably less carefully monitored by the administration. This freedom, perhaps, permitted her to move more in the direction of the Atwellian workshop than had her colleagues been permitted. The following observation from early in the year illustrates how Martha negotiated this greater freedom with her students in her classroom:

[Martha is standing in front of her class of about thirty seventh graders, in the center of the "U" formed by student desks, discussing with them the fact that they will choose their own topics to write about. She tells them that she knows how "intimidating" this can be.]

Martha: There is a whole world of things to take from. How does a writer choose? How do you choose what to write on? The best way we can find out is to ask you. You are the masters. Personally, how do you select your topics?

[Martha scans the room and waits until eight people have their hands in the air. Then she calls on them and listens carefully to them, making notes on a scratch pad, while they explain to her some topics they might want to write about and why.]

[After these students have shared their ideas about where they find topics, Sophie, who turns out to be perhaps the best writer in the class, raises her hand again for clarification. Martha calls on her.]

Sophie: Can we, like, write a letter?

Martha: Only if you are done, like, with the story you are working on.

Martha had opened the class period by asking students to pay attention: "Ladies and gentlemen, eyes and ears up here. Have out your pens and paper. Put away your reading books. I'm going to pass out some folders." She spent the next few minutes giving students manila folders, multicolored dividers, whatever they would need to put together their work-in-progress folders. When she finished distributing materials, she called students' attention to the "rules for writing workshop" at the front of the room. She had to lift the overhead screen so that students could read the "rules" she had posted on butcher paper.

Andrew, a student who was sitting just to my left, began whispering. Martha walked over to stand beside Andrew's desk, all the while talking about the rules for writer's workshop. The first rule was "Everyone writes"—"No reading, no talking unless you are in a conference," she explained. She told her students to save everything in their work folder. Then she announced that they would be writing a story and that "the story is due on the 26th." Martha mentioned that there would be conferencing and asked, "What do you predict, what do you guess you'll do in your conferences?"

Sheila: You go over your paper. Somebody corrects it. You go over your paper and talk about your mistakes.

Martha: Any other ideas?

Sophie: You talk about your paper and give each other ideas.

Martha: Any other ideas?

Fred: You tell them how to make the paper better, how to improve it.

Martha: Any other ideas? [Long pause.] Marcus?

Marcus: [No response.]

Martha [after waiting a few seconds]: So let's see. Let's just review what you've said. . . . Make improvements, make the paper better, get ideas, talk about mistakes. . . . You have things to do today if you conference—share ideas, correct mistakes, improve the paper.

Martha had collected their ideas in her notebook while they talked and then fed them back to the students. The lesson continued:

[Martha goes over the rules governing conferences. There are designated conference areas in the classroom, in opposite corners and at the table in the center; the rest of the room is a silent area.]

Martha: You writers won't hear more than a whisper. There will be no talking in this work area. Oh, if you're desperate for help, like [whispers] "How do you spell this word? What's a better way to say this?" then you can whisper.

[She goes on to talk about never erasing, saving this record of thinking.]

Martha: You guys don't use pencils in here so you can't erase. Keep that thought there so that you know where you've come from. You can cross it out later—don't use Wite-Out.

Martha ended this period by taking a "status-of-the-class" just as Atwell described, asking students to report the topic for their story. She got topics like a boy who is killing his parents, a riot where everyone is going to be fighting, a horror story about a black widow, a houseful of people and there's a murder, a whole bunch of scary stories—an abundance of silly topics which students on the East Coast would never choose to write about—then:

Karen: I'm going to write about a doll house. They'll be scary stories. See, these little people live in the doll house, they're really alive, and it's in this attic, and there's a door, a real shiny door, and if you stay there for thirty minutes you become a doll.

Jim [the guy sitting behind Andrew; he raises his hand, and Martha calls on him]: I want to ask her—Did you make that up?

Karen: Yes.

Martha: I'm glad you asked that question, Jim. We're going to talk about that in just a little bit.

Pedro: Can I write about O.J. Simpson?

[The class bursts out laughing. Pedro tells the plot of what has happened to O.J.—football star, murders wife, etc. After the class settles down, Martha goes back to Jim's question.]

Martha: Karen, where did you get that idea?

Karen: I was watching a movie, a film on TV. Then I fell asleep and missed the end, so I made up an ending.

[Martha asks the girl who will write about the black widow where she got her idea, and she says the movie *Arachnophobia.* Martha says, "Another movie." She asks Susan where she got her idea. Susan replies, "There is a book called *Scary Stories That Glow in the Dark,* plus when I was in fourth grade, me and my friend wrote a book of scary stories and dedicated them to my cats."]

[While this discussion is going on, Martha again walks over near Andrew, who has begun to talk to a neighbor, as she takes notes on her yellow sticky pad.]

Elsie [referring to the black widow]: I really didn't get it from a movie. I saw a black widow in my backyard.

Laurie: I'm going to write a mystery, and I got that from the movie *Clue.*

Martha [moves to the center of the room, holds up the note pad]: If I was stuck, I could get a topic [reading from the yellow sticky] from films, the dollhouse; the news, Pedro's O.J. thing; a book I read when I was younger, like *Scary Stories;* brainstorming; overhearing conversations; real-life experiences, Elsie's spider. . . .

This excerpt reveals CAP's less-than-monolithic influence on writing instruction in the portfolio classrooms. CAP had determined the genre, Martha had determined the due date, but the students were determining their plots. Though Martha assigned story and taught students to apply CAP-compatible criteria (detailed setting, dialogue, well-developed characters, pacing, etc.), she did not give her students guided questions to lead them through the analysis of model essays and to structure peer responses. In contrast, Maria and Jennifer, at least initially, followed closely the template established by the CAP assessment system.

The examination teachers were just as heavily under the influence of CAP as anyone else when they assessed essays students submitted in their portfolios. The following segment was taken from a taped thinkaloud made by one of the examination teachers as she scored a portfolio during the first-trimester scoring session, and reveals a thorough grounding in CAP methodology:

> *Examination Teacher:* OK—as I open up she has a cover letter— it goes on, basically restating what she's already stated in the entry slip, telling her step-by-step procedure. Um . . . "Autobiographical Incident" is called "My Two Flower Senders in the Seventh Grade." [She reads from the student's essay.]
>
> "It was May 27th, my last day of school at [***] before I moved to [***]. The sun was out, and the wind was blowing lightly. As I made my way through the crowd, the bell rang. At that moment everyone ran to their class. I made my extremely slow walk to the office. I opened the door. It made a loud squeak. I asked the lady for my grades. She went and got them and then handed me them. I made my way to Language Arts, first period. As I opened the door the class was decorated. The decorated class had purple white streamers with balloons, cake, ice cream, presents, and loud music playing in the background. As the class was finishing decorations, I went to the front and yelled 'Thank you for giving me this party.'" [She stops reading from the student's essay.]
>
> Um . . . she seemed very preoccupied with description, focusing mainly on writing details both about the places that are in the autobiographical incident and the people, um . . . a little attempt at dialogue, generally one-line responses bouncing back and forth from two speakers. . . . This doesn't seem to be about one incident. She's talking about a lot of things that occurred in one day at school.

Her selection of weaknesses illustrates a solid understanding of AI per the CAP model. "She seemed . . . focus[ed] mainly on writing details both about the places that are in the autobiographical incident and the people" echoed the substance of the state rubric, which explained that weak autobiographical incident essays sometimes dwell too much on the context at the expense of the incident. "This doesn't seem to be about one incident" and "She's talking about a lot of things that occurred in one day at school" echoed the official definition of incident. Later in the thinkaloud the teacher commented that "I don't find much resolution; there's no significance in this piece at all," providing evidence that the examination teacher thoroughly understood the significance of "significance" in the state rubric. Note that *the portfolio rubric made no mention of these state criteria.*

The following excerpt came from a taped thinkaloud made by Jennifer Johnson as she looked through her students' portfolios after they had been scored for the first time by the examination teachers. This excerpt illustrates a foundational tension between the CAP rubrics, which applied to individual essays as products, and the portfolio rubric, which applied to collections of work products and to processes as well. Jennifer used the acronym "FHB," which stands for "firsthand biographical sketch," as she thought about a problem she saw with the grade one of her students had gotten. Jennifer would have given this student a "B," but two examination teachers issued a "C minus":

> *Jennifer:* I'm rereading her entry slips about what she wanted the examination teachers to notice about her best essay, um . . . Mostly she says that her cover letter talks about the process she went through and the changes she went through. She also wanted the examination teachers to consider that [reading from the student's entry slip]—
>
> "Even though it's not the best, I worked very hard, and I put a lot of effort into my FHB. I'd also like them to look at my first draft and my final draft so they can see the changes that I have done and how much I have tried to improve on it. Number one I don't think it has stretched my abilities as much as they have been challenged, but I think that picking this topic helped me show how much I could think about my cousin, and it showed me that I could write a lot of things in one incident." [Stops reading.]
>
> And, um . . . OK . . . [pages turning] OK. Let me go back. I forget this paper. It's been a long time. . . .

In the end, Jennifer concurred that the portfolio was accurately scored "C minus" according to the portfolio scoring rubric, primarily because the student had not demonstrated "B" level work in writing in the areas of consistency and challenge, control of processes, and self-assessment and reflection. However, Jennifer was unsettled because the essay itself looked much better than a "C" when viewed through the CAP FHB lens. The student *had* demonstrated skill with the defining feature of the FHB: the state scoring guide said that firsthand biographies should bring the subject to life on the page. This student had accomplished this task competently.

During a discussion among the examination teachers near the beginning of the second scoring session in February, the issue of the lack of fit between the CAP rubrics and the portfolio rubric was raised again. Discounting the fact that the CAP rubrics did not take into account the student's capacity to self-assess, the student's control of processes, and the consistency and challenge of the student's work, whereas the portfolio rubric was largely concerned with those issues, there was still a glaring discrepancy. Here is what one examination teacher, the department chair, had to say in this February conversation:

> *Examination Teacher:* If we were scoring these AI's [autobiographical incidents] and FHB's based on CLAS [CAP] rubrics, when you're looking for things like significant and interesting opening, I mean, these are basic showing writing, um—they would be very low from what I've seen so far. But there's nothing that reflects any of that on our rubric. So . . . what I find myself looking for more is that I'm looking at sentences, sentence structures, paragraphs, you know—that they *can* . . . that they can *write* . . . with paragraphs and sentences and ideas . . . and I'm not reading what it is they're saying . . . as much as the way they're saying it. There has been one story that I read that when I was done my reaction was more to what was said, but I'm looking more at how they're saying it.

This examination teacher had noticed that CAP scoring required the rater to consider how clearly the writer's essay painted a portrait of the subject of a firsthand biographical sketch, how compellingly the writer's autobiographical incident communicated the significance of a discrete event, and so on—the form of the essay specified the content, and the scorer's job was to see how well the content fit the official forms. In contrast, neither form nor content were specified by the portfolio rubric, and the examination teachers had to invent ways to look at each writer's unique effectiveness (or lack thereof). They were thrown back to pre-CAP days when "writing was writing was writing." The rub was this: Students were being taught to write CAP types, perhaps being penalized for becoming skillful at writing good one-draft essays because they weren't experimenting with revision (see Jennifer's concern with the FHB essay discussed above).

Maria had struggled during the first trimester to teach her students to "experiment with drafts," to "select topics that challenged them," and to "become aware of their writing processes"—all prized criteria on the portfolio scoring rubric. The problem for Maria was that she couldn't figure out how to assign CAP tasks in a lockstep fashion in accordance with the kind of instruction that was sanctioned at Ruff, while simultaneously requiring students to set their own goals and make their own plans. This situation forced Maria to fall back on the traditional grading system as a threat:

TU: How have you handled giving assignments and setting deadlines without being able to refer to giving a grade?

Maria: Well, it's been—I think it's been more confusing for them than it has for me. But I give an assignment—well, for the writing, I give them a sheet of the criteria and the requirements, you know, what they should include, you know, the cover letter, the final draft, the rough draft, um, the prewriting, and anything else that goes along with what they're to include. So that's listed, and what they're going to be graded on is listed—or what the features of that paper are. And then—so they have that, and then the deadline's on there. And then . . . I just tell them that's when it's due, and . . . for my first period class it's been a real problem because, like I said, I got five in on Monday. And then more came on, um, yesterday. But then they'd ask me, "Well, what happens if it comes in late? Do we get a lower grade?" And I tell them, "No, but it's going to be reflected in your letter of recommendation." Well, that's still pretty abstract for them. And, um, for the first paper, I just kept reminding them that it was due, you know, that they needed to get it done.

It should have been clear to all of us that the tension between an assignment-driven, lockstep writing curriculum and an intentional-learning–based writing curriculum would create instructional problems. But it wasn't clear to any of us. Moreover, the problem had roots not just in CAP, but in the entire academic enculturation process which the students had experienced since the elementary grades. The interview continued:

TU: What do you think would happen if you didn't have due dates?

Maria: Well . . . I think that the students who have a tendency to get behind anyway would probably just put everything off. And I think that they would get kind of lost. I guess, for me a due date is a way of calling my attention to the fact that this kid's not doing his work. I don't know—I go back and forth on that. I was going to ask the kids when we came back if they thought due dates were important or effective or if they thought they needed 'em. And you know, I talked about why I had due dates, which was to keep them . . . um . . . because we had so much work to do that I didn't want them falling behind and then becoming overwhelmed and that's why I, you know, set these dates. But I don't know. I'd like to ask them what they thought, because they're usually pretty honest with me.

TU: There is a non-negotiable due date, which is when the portfolios are going to be graded. Any other due date should be negotiable. What disadvantages do you see in giving these students a due date?

Maria: Um . . . Some of them need more time, I think. But they *have* more time, I mean, they can revise at any time.

TU: So why should they turn them in on time?

Maria: So that they've got *something*, you know. It forces them to get something done. And for some of them, that's all they'll *do*, you know? Does that make sense? Without that, I don't know if they'd do it. I guess I should see, you know? But it's been a frustration for me.

TU: Have you thought about just making it a requirement that everybody writes? You know, they all have to write. It's just that some will take longer than others. Then where your recommendation is going to come in is just whether they work or not.

Maria: That would be a lot more comfortable for me, because I don't like feeling that—I know when I, um, last year I didn't worry about due dates and deadlines. If they got it in to me, they got it in. I never really took off credit for late assignments. But then—I felt this year that it was part of my responsibility to get them moving.

TU: What in the pilot made you think that?

Maria: Well, because in the handbook it says an essay is due every three weeks.

TU: You think that we should change that for second trimester?

Maria: What I would like to see is a certain number of papers required to be submitted in the portfolio, and I'd like to see that the kid could approach those papers in different ways—more freedom about the way they approach papers.

Week after week, the gap between instruction aimed at encouraging intentional writers and instruction aimed at creating competent form crafters, as Lucas (1988) called them, grew wider for Maria. In an interview in November, Maria wanted to talk about her writing instruction so that she could design a way to free herself from the CAP model. As illustrated by the following section excerpted from this November interview, Maria had developed serious reservations about Ruff's CAP approach:

Maria: I mean, when they come [to me after seventh grade], they go, *"More autobiographical incidents???"* They're ready to barf autobiographical incidents, and they say, "Well, I've exhausted my ideas." And so you're—in some ways, you're asking them to dig deeper, but really what you're asking them to do is tune out, I guess. I don't know. So then comes the question . . . How do I get them to set writing goals . . . because that's part of what they're supposed to do. And . . . where should that come in?

In October 1995, after reading a draft of this section of the report, Maria telephoned me to explain what had happened historically that resulted in her being thoroughly "CAPtized." She reminded me again that she and Jennifer were more enmeshed in CAP-compatible instruction than Martha was because she and Jennifer taught eighth-grade English, the grade level which the state, in its infinite wisdom, had selected as the target grade for assessment. Seventh-grade students, whom Martha taught, did not take the CAP test.

Further, during her first year as a Charles Ruff teacher, the principal had told her he wasn't convinced that she would be capable of teaching CAP (recall that the Ruff staff had received their CAP staff-development blitz before Maria arrived). In fact, the principal told her that he was considering moving her from an eighth-grade to a seventh-grade teaching assignment because of CAP. Before he made his decision, however, he gave her the opportunity to teach a writing lesson while he observed. Maria made sure she understood how the CAP machine worked.

Maria also reminded me during this phone call that when the portfolio year started for the portfolio teachers, the state assessment system had not yet been vetoed. She and everyone else in the English Department had assumed that students would be assessed by the state using CAP rubrics and prompts. What else were they supposed to have assumed? Maria, who did not have tenure at Ruff, was under even more pressure to teach CAP than was Jennifer, who did have tenure.

Maria's early concerns about writing instruction foreshadowed later instructional problems that unfolded over the course of the year. "How do teachers get students to set writing goals, and where do those goals fit in the classroom?" Maria wanted to know. What kinds of goals should teachers expect students to set? What should they look like? Jennifer also began to complain about a lack of fit between the portfolio system and CAP-compatible instruction. Midway through the second trimester she told me that she had given her students more opportunities to plan their own writing projects, but that many students wanted her to stay at the helm and lead them through the writing of short stories:

> *TU:* So they're all writing stories?
>
> *Jennifer:* Yes. Most kids are writing short stories. Some are writing—they wanted to write another autobiographical incident, so that was fine.

TU: How are you handling instruction?

Jennifer: For those that are not doing short story, I'm meeting with them pretty much individually. And for the rest of them it's whole-class, with mini-lessons, with, um, dialogue instruction, and instruction on characterization, and instruction on show-not-tell writing.

A few moments later in this interview, Jennifer made it unmistakably clear that she was dissatisfied with the instructional arrangement described above:

Jennifer: I've been floundering all trimester because the way I've been teaching this writing assignment, this story, doesn't fit with the portfolios. It doesn't *fit.* . . . So I'm feeling *real* frustrated. Because—what would have been better is if I could have had writing workshop, but *that* isn't what I wanted to do exactly. . . .

Jennifer could not forget the alleged failure of Atwell's writing workshop in the late 1980s at Ruff. The approach had been tried, and it had failed as judged by the California writing-assessment system, an "authentic assessment" system that had been designed by teachers, for teachers, to replace standardized, multiple-choice tests of editing. CAP had been seen as a powerful tool for reform of writing instruction by colleagues involved with the California Writing Project, an organization to which Jennifer felt allegiance. To turn to a "free-for-all writing workshop" would have been to turn backwards in Jennifer's mind. But Jennifer could see that something was wrong.

Maria had discovered that she needed to turn away from instruction as outlined in the CAP handbook, though she, too, wasn't sure that she ought to turn in the direction of Atwell. Here is an excerpt from one of many interviews with Maria over the middle portion of the year, wherein she explored her approach to writing instruction in ways that might threaten less tenacious teachers:

Maria: I just . . . I'm kind of stuck because I have this very safe way of introducing writing that could leave little room for error. You know, I had a real specific way of introducing a writing task which would be for a very specific task which was either one of the [CAP] writing domains or a history report or something like that. And I could teach to that. It was, um . . . I knew what I expected from the writing, I had these set criteria to achieve, and all that, and so now—I see that asking kids to do that kind of writing, well, it's counterproductive in so many ways for the grading rubric we're using, because. . . . They would do some drafting before— no, we did it two ways. They would do a draft first before I showed them a student example and we took it apart, and then I did the student example first, and then they wrote based on that. And so what you're really asking the kid to do—what I was asking the kid to do is not to use the draft as a means of discovery, but to use it as a kind of dress rehearsal for the final, and then maybe to add a few things to it to tighten it up. So . . . I think that my teaching really limited student achievement, and I see that now.

The idea of using drafts as a tool for discovery was explicitly stated in the portfolio rubric, and the examination teachers looked carefully at students' self-analysis of their processes as well as at early and late drafts to find evidence that students were, in fact, shaping ideas through multiple drafts. Some of the examination teachers visited students in the portfolio classrooms following the examination process to give them general feedback, and they told the students that the examination committee needed to see more evidence of true revision. The following excerpt was taken from a tape recording of one such presentation and indicates generally what the examination teachers were seeing midyear in the student portfolios:

> *Examination Teacher* [speaking to a large group of portfolio students who had been gathered together to hear her feedback]: For your writing the main thing that I would work on for the future is to work on showing us when you're doing your revisions. I believe that many of you did revisions, and you talked about the revisions in your entry slips, but we could not see them. What I would see in many papers, even though you mentioned revisions, I would see your first draft and your final drafts looked almost identical except that your final draft was neater, maybe in ink, and had the spelling corrected. I didn't see those revisions you talked so much about in your entry slips, which would have really helped your papers. I didn't see that you experimented with the lead. I didn't see that you experimented with writing dialogue—not all of you, but many of you.

As the year moved toward its close, the portfolio teachers continued to investigate their writing instruction, none of them satisfied with what they had done during the experimental year, each of them probing and exploring for ways to improve their writing classrooms. Freed somewhat by circumstance from the state's influence, Martha Goldsmith, perhaps, had enjoyed a broader opportunity to explore her writing instructional practices than had Maria and Jennifer. She had greatly relaxed the use of genre assignments, lockstep activities, and due dates in her classroom by the end of the year, preferring to "keep the work open" as long as necessary, to use a phrase from Simmons

(1992). Here is an observation made in Martha's room in March 1995, wherein Martha modeled for students what it was like for her as a writer to get a project going:

> *Martha* [seated on a stool in front of her class, a few pieces of notebook paper in her hands]: I was thinking a lot about what I said about setting goals and writing with you, but I never did it, and so I started doing it this weekend. And what I realized was that while I was writing I was revising a lot. How many of you stop and make changes?
>
> *Denny:* Usually, like, when I'm writing I will stop and, like, leave room. I don't know how to say this. If there is something wrong with it, you can change it right at that moment instead of waiting until the very end.
>
> *Martha* [nodding with understanding, acknowledging a hand raised]: Charma, what about you?
>
> *Charma:* Well, you can come up with a better idea while you're writing and you just get it down while you are going along.
>
> *Martha:* Some other people had their hands up?
>
> *Sally:* Well, sometimes you get really into your writing, and you just get better ideas while you're working.
>
> *Martha* [nodding in confirmation again]: So I heard several things. One is something isn't right. Another is don't like the idea. How do you know when something is wrong? See, I'm trying to figure out what it is that for you causes you to know there is something wrong with it.
>
> *Denny:* If you're able to have other ideas about it, you know you're not satisfied.
>
> *Martha* [acknowledging a raised hand]: Tina?
>
> *Tina:* When you read other people's drafts, you get more ideas from reading them, so it makes you want to revise.
>
> *Martha:* So are you reading other people's drafts while you're working on your own stories?
>
> *Tina:* Yeah.
>
> *Martha:* And you're comparing?
>
> *Sally:* Yeah, and you just want to make it better.
>
> *Martha:* So Denny is saying when he can think of other things, he knows it's not the best. But how do you know?
>
> *Sophie:* I was gonna say, like, it's a psychic thing. If it's interesting or not, then you know.
>
> *Martha:* I've been thinking a lot about it because when I wrote this poem this weekend, I got this, like, five lines of a poem, and I got all of these brainstorms, and I crossed out these

> five lines, and I wrote four more lines. And then after two
> hours I had about four pages, and I went through, and I
> found that I had some friends with five stanzas and some
> with three, and I thought, "Oh, my God, if my friends read
> this poem, those people who only got three stanzas are
> going to be upset." So I went back and wrote in stanzas for
> them, and I was changing things constantly, and I really
> didn't know why. So I wanted to ask you guys why you
> make changes, and now I'm going to think about what
> you've said.

A quantitative analysis of prompted essays written in a pretest/
post-test fashion was done in accordance with the SB 1274 proposal
funded by Ruff's leadership council to compare the writing achievement
of portfolio students with that of nonportfolio students. According to
this analysis, there was no statistically significant difference between the
groups with respect to gain scores. That this analysis showed no difference was unsurprising in light of the instructional patterns in the portfolio classrooms that I saw emerging in the field record.

The portfolio teachers were changing how they taught writing
throughout the year, but they never implemented a recognizable and
systematic approach, as they had clearly done in their reading instruction. No mottos capturing the gist of portfolio writing instruction, no
metaphors anchoring the nature of instruction in all three portfolio
classrooms can be provided—unless mottos like "If only I had known
then what I know now" or metaphors like "stormy weather" convey
writing instruction in the classrooms of these three portfolio teachers.

From what I could see, ironically, there was much more predictability and consistency in the writing instruction provided in the
nonportfolio classrooms, governed as they were by the powerful CAP
plan. According to informal interviews, nonportfolio students were
almost universally taught to write CAP types all year long, with an
occasional excursion in the direction of rewriting a fairy tale from a
modern perspective or some other favored assignment. The writing
prompts used as pretest and post-test measures were CAP-type
prompts designed to evoke autobiographical incident essays. What
explanation could there have been if there *had* been a difference
between the groups? For much of the year, Ruff students received
essentially the same type of writing instruction—and almost all students, portfolio and nonportfolio alike, were taught to write autobiographical incidents according to the state handbook.

What was surprising to me was that the portfolio students did
not differ from the nonportfolio students on Allen's (1991) postwrite
procedure, a measure of metacognitive awareness of writing process.

Because the portfolio students had had many experiences with self-assessment and reflective analysis, I expected them to do better at discussing their approach to the writing task as well as their assessment of their product. In contrast, from what I could gather from occasional opportunities to view student work samples from the traditional classrooms, from open discussions among the teachers during various professional meetings, and from "eavesdropping," as Schatzman and Strauss (1973) used the term, the traditional students were not getting consistent experiences in metacognitive reporting.

The portfolio students did not score significantly higher in writing than a comparison group of nonportfolio students, but the portfolio teachers still believed that their students profited from their experiences with the portfolio system. It had not been a disaster. In fact, each of the three portfolio teachers believed that if she had understood the conflict between CAP-driven and portfolio-driven instruction earlier in the school year, the portfolio students would have had more opportunities to develop their own learning intentions as writers and would have shown significantly greater achievement than would CAP-taught students even on an on-demand measurement of written product. Of course, this is speculation.

An important lesson from this portion of the exploration, in my view, centers around the role of goal setting in learning, especially in the arena of writing instruction, particularly when dealing with adolescents. Martha underscored this point in an individual interview conducted in July 1995, during her first month of instruction in a new school year with new students—and no officially organized, funded, and sanctioned portfolio system:

> *Martha:* And I was going to add, too, what's *extremely* important is goal setting, and I'm afraid now that some of them are setting goals that I have a feeling are going to be really hard for them, and they're going to want to change them and not stick with them, and I really just have to go, "OK, OK," and let it happen, and just squeeze my hand, and not be afraid to let them fail if they need to, because my instant reaction was, "Oh, God, I should have started with stories like I did last year." But that's not right any more. They can think for themselves about what they want to do. And the younger they start doing that, I think the more powerful they will become. I didn't start with really really letting them go on their own until third trimester last year, and I think if I start that now, yes, it may be scarier, but by the end it's going to pay off a lot more.

At a later point in the same interview, Martha spoke more specifically about the translation of her lessons from the last trimester of the portfolio year to the first trimester of the new year. Her description of her approach to writing instruction suggests that she, indeed, was convinced that the portfolio system resulted in greater achievement despite the lack of quantitative support for the hypothesis:

> *Martha:* Writing is becoming more of an apprenticeship model—now that I'm beginning to understand it a little more . . . but I think the way that I want to start things out is just getting kids to write, period. That fluency, cohesion, correction model, I guess. But just get them to *write* and get them to feel comfortable and *confident* and know that they have some sort of voice and that they view writing with some sort of purpose—they have a *purpose* for writing. So it starts with goals, like reading starts with goals, too. And then what I really want them to do is just write, and then when they get going, I like to work—sometimes I give them general revision strategies, but most of what I like to do is do the one-on-one conferencing, because then I really get into their mind and know what they want to do, and I can give them steps—whether it's just sitting down and talking with them about ideas about where they want to go or. . . . It's almost like taking steps on a map—or they just need techniques for getting out more detail or whatever they need to do. I really like to do it personally one-on-one rather than address it in a large group. But sometimes I'll have *kids* come up and get feedback from the entire class.

Scoring High

In a separate interview with Maria Madsen, as she started the new year after the portfolio project was over, similar points were made regarding the centrality of goal setting in writing instruction. Ironically, as the following segment illustrates, Maria saw her attempts to use what she had learned from her experience as a portfolio teacher being thwarted by a district mandate to assign exercises from *Scoring High,* a commercially prepared series of workbooks designed to increase student scores on standardized multiple-choice tests. CAP/CLAS was gone, but the district's standardized test system had remained. Moreover, reading scores on this instrument had continued their persistent downward slide. The district administration had purchased enough copies of *Scoring High* to supply all of the secondary schools with the materials. The administration had also mandated to the principals that they see to it that every teacher used *Scoring High* in their classrooms. There was no option. When I spoke with Maria, she seemed almost as dejected as her students:

> *Maria:* Having them set challenging goals, you know, that's the way I started off this year, and I feel like I'm starting off—at least as a reading teacher—knowing what I'm doing, and I'm still trying to discover that as a writing teacher. I'm trying to get them to set goals, but um. . . . When they went into the library, another teacher came in and said, "Wow, these kids are really focused." And they were looking for books that they wanted to read. And I told them, "Just go look at the books. Just look at 'em, you know. Look up books—find your interests, but just look around, and see what you see," and—the kids are all reading now. And so that got off to a good start, and then all of a sudden I'm told I have to do the CAT-5 stuff, so everything's just come to a dead halt, and I'm going to have to rebuild that momentum again, and so . . . I'm just thinking about [an assistant superintendent's] conversation with Martha last night [the Ruff Open House was held the previous evening]. He didn't speak to me, but he said to Martha, "You know, can't you find a way to combine these two?" And she said, "They just don't mix." And . . . trying to do CAT-5 and then trying to get the kids back to their personal goals—I tried to do it the first day, you know? "Here's CAT-5. OK, you're done. Now let's talk about your goals and the books you're reading." And there's no momentum, you know. . . . They're just kind'a—this just drains all the enthusiasm out of 'em. And . . . you know, I don't think the CAT-5 necessarily has to be such an awful thing. I *don't*. . . . I think the awful thing is trying to teach to it. I don't think that was the original intention of that test at all.

To be sure, the publishers of CAT-5 did not intend that the test be "taught to," if we can take them at their word. Indeed, standardized tests such as these are intended to be "curriculum free" (Mitchell, 1992). As we saw in the chapter about the state's reform activities, however, the CAP test *was* intended to be "taught to." Was the state's ambition to professionalize teachers by making them the authors of the tests that counted a step in the right direction? Or was the state handbook simply a disguised version of *Scoring High*? Perhaps, as Maria said about CAT-5, the awful thing about any test truly *is* trying to teach to it.

8 Ruff Students and Their Portfolios

Pressure, Stress, Transformation

The portfolio teachers often spoke of the 1994–95 school year as a period of transformation. Jennifer Johnson commented at least three times during interviews several months apart that she felt as if she were student teaching again. Maria Madsen talked about sweeping changes she made, ranging from seating arrangements to writing projects. Martha Goldsmith described her "metamorphosis" and wished that she had had "this kind of training" during her teacher-preparation work.

Many students in the portfolio classrooms were transformed as well—in one way or another. Life had changed for them, but they had had very little to say about that change. Students reported feeling excruciating pressure just before report cards came out. Just before report cards, they had to organize and package their portfolios for export to the examination committee, the committee which exerted lower-intensity pressures on them throughout each grading period. I asked Elsie, a seventh grader, and two of her peers during an end-of-year interview how they would feel if they found out that they would have to do portfolios in eighth grade and got a telling response:

> *TU:* What would people say if I went into your classroom and said, "OK, guys, next year you're going to do the same thing." What would happen?
>
> [All three students gasp, sigh, and groan.]
>
> *Elsie:* Oh, no, really, they wouldn't like it. It puts a lot of pressure on 'em—all of them—and they *hate* having pressure. I don't think that they liked having to do portfolios. Everyone that *I* know just moaned and groaned about portfolios. They didn't like 'em. We always used to wish we were in [another teacher's] class because everybody said, "Oh, it's so easy, because all you have to do is just read."

Pressure went by another name in the field record: stress. Sophie submitted the following poem as part of her second trimester portfolio:

> [From Sophie's Free Choice entry slip:]
>
> A lot almost all my poems come from my feelings and thoughts. I selected this topic because during portfolio time I get stressed out. I knew I would have a lot of feelings about this topic so I

wrote on it. It challenged me by stress could be a lot of different feelings and I wanted to thoroughly describe them.

> Stress
> Stress . . .
> you begin to read things
> over
> and over
> again.
> you can't think
> straight.
> Confusion . . .
> fills your head like
> thick fog.
> Constantly
> blinking
> that
> thick fog
> has also
> filled your
> eyes.
> Tired . . .
> you try to figure out the
> time.
> When you do
> you realize that you have
> only
> 2 hours
> to finish.
> The trembling
> of your hands
> that are
> wanting
> to pull all your hair out.
> you
> clinch
> your teeth
> and try to
> regain concentration.
> You can't . . .
> pushing
> everything
> off your desk.
> you are breathing
> heavily
> now as the
> Anger . . .
> builds up inside,
> you begin to grunt,

holding on to your pen
you squeeze it with
all
your strength
while it
Relieves
Some
of your
anger.
Throwing
yourself to your bed,
you grab a
pillow,
bury
your head in it.
The
salty tears
slowly run down your
sagging cheeks
you don't cry because you're
sad,
Confused,
Tired, or
Angry, but because you
feel
helpless,
like a
wounded animal
all alone,
No one
to
Help
you.

Stress . . .

One of the deepest changes students were called upon to make involved the symbolic capital of the institution: grades. As we have seen, grades had two spheres of influence at Charles Ruff, a shaping and a consequential sphere. The rules of the shaping sphere were altered by the portfolio experiment, often in ways that complicated life for some students. Recall the two boys who approached Maria at lunch one afternoon, and one of them offered her a French fry. She took it, but the other boy laughed and said, "You're only giving her that so you can get an A." The first boy looked at his friend in surprise and said, "Miss Madsen can't give me an A." Perhaps this transfer of the credit-granting function of the institution from the classroom teacher to a distant external committee lay at the root of Sophie's feeling of helplessness, like "a wounded animal."

Although the portfolio teachers had agreed not to give any of their students any grades at all, the absolute value of grades had not changed—grades were still the center of gravity. The consequential sphere of influence remained the same. Grades still meant graduation, allowance, dances, cool shoes, television, telephone, basketball games, self-worth. During the early weeks, more than a few portfolio students complained in interviews that their English teacher was not putting letter grades on their work, and they had no way to index their worth. The following excerpt from an August interview involving Amy, Amanda, and Jimmy illustrates this theme. Amy was a talented reader whose parents had emigrated from Vietnam; Amanda and Jimmy were in Jennifer's class with Amy:

> [I ask the students how they feel about not getting letter grades on their work.]
>
> *Amy:* I'm . . . kind of disappointed. I like how my teacher gives me . . . their opinion. You know, like that, I can improve my papers. But I would kind'a like it if, um, the teacher would give you a grade so you would kind'a know how you are in writing and reading.
>
> *Jimmy:* I like seein' my grade that's on my paper.
>
> *Amanda:* I miss having . . . I mean, I never know *where* I'm at in my grade. I don't know how good I did on this paper. All you get is these little notes saying . . . 'Da da da da da . . .' et cetera. I'm like . . . Oookaaay, but, uh, where is my grade? How do I know what I'm supposed to show my parents? My parents got real disappointed when they saw my papers and my papers didn't have grades on 'em. My parents like me to get grades on my papers.
>
> *Amy:* My parents don't really care about grades. They care about, um . . . what I'm learning and if I'm learning what I need to be learning and I understand it, um . . . It's fine with them. Grades isn't a big thing. As long as you understand what you're doing and know what it's about, that's fine.
>
> *Jimmy:* My mom gets really mad if I get poor grades.

Amy and Amanda reacted quite differently to Jennifer's substitution of verbal for normative feedback. Though Amy missed the reinforcement grades provided, she appreciated the content of the feedback and saw that it could help her improve her work. She also reported that her parents harbored little concern about grades; they cared about whether Amy was learning "what I need to be learning." But Amanda viewed Jennifer's commentary as "little notes"—"'Da da da da da . . .' et cetera"—and reported that her parents were "real disappointed" to learn that Amanda would not get grades. Similarly, Jimmy's mother responded emotionally to letter grades. It is possible that parental views influence student perspectives on grades, but Amy's need for grades shows that other factors beyond parents are operating as well.

Why Me?

The field record was saturated with evidence that many portfolio students were painfully aware that they were being treated to a more challenging English classroom than were students in the traditional classrooms. To make matters worse, their teachers were not giving them grades for their effort. The following observation from one of Martha Goldsmith's classes illustrates this point:

> It is late in January, and I am observing in [Martha's] third period. Martha is called over by a male who is supposed to be freewriting on the portfolio process.
>
> "How come we have to do more work than anybody else?" he asks in an angry tone. Martha told me earlier that this boy is the one she is looking at for her case study—he wants to know why, in all of the other classes, all you have to do is do the work and the teacher adds up the points. In here you have to save everything and be able to explain it and do entry slips and all of this extra work. He says that it is unfair. She is having him write down all of his thoughts, and she will respond to his writing.

In addition to what many students saw as an unfair work load, the portfolio students were also aware that the usual connection between grades and behavior did not apply. Jennifer Johnson, for example, felt a bit helpless when her student Saul earned A's on his report card despite his "noncommittal" behavior and his acting like a "smart aleck" in class. Kendra, one of Maria's students, believed that the system was unjust because it failed to put a premium on classroom life. Consider what Kendra had to say in this regard in April, after almost a year of participation in the portfolio system:

> [I ask students whether they want to keep the system. They do, but they want the portfolio to be just a part of the grade.]
>
> *Kendra:* Somebody could be there for, like, maybe one or two weeks every month or somethin', and then they turn in a good portfolio, and they get a A, but they're not really doin' it, the in-class work. And, like, somebody could yell across the room and act all rowdy and everything, and then *they* turn in a good portfolio, and they get a A.
>
> *TU:* Has that happened?
>
> *Kendra:* Yes.

TU: Tell me about that. You don't have to name names.

[Laughter]

Kendra: Like, they get a A or a B.

TU: So it is possible to really mess up in class and still get a
good grade.

Kendra: Yeah, and it's because the examination teachers don't
see you work.

The phrase "the examination teachers don't see you work" or
some variant came from the mouths of students virtually every time I
raised the issue of whether grades should be given by the classroom
teacher or by the examination teachers. Of interest is that even though
the most confident and competent students seemed to thrive on the
disconnection between their grade and their classroom teacher and did
not want the portfolio system changed, almost all of the remaining students that I interviewed near the end of the year suggested that their
grade should derive partly from the classroom teacher and partly from
the examination committee, in a sort of checks-and-balances system.
They saw that the examination teachers cared about the quality of the
work, which many students perceived to be missing from the traditional approach. But the classroom teacher cared about student attitudes and behavior, which many students perceived to be missing
from the portfolio approach.

Examination Teachers as the Audience for Student Work

Despite their existence at a distance, the examination teachers did have
a constant presence in the portfolio classrooms that affected both
teachers and students. During observations of instructional episodes
throughout the year, I recorded examples of the portfolio teachers'
integration of the examination committee into their lessons as an audience for the students' work. For example, all three portfolio teachers
routinely asked students to read their text logs from the point of view
of the examination teachers and to ask themselves whether they, if they
were the examination teachers, would understand and value the
entries. When students handed in work to their teachers, it was almost
as if the students did so as a rehearsal for the real audience, i.e., the
examination teachers.

This situation required students to read the grading criteria for
themselves, not simply to accept the classroom teacher's interpretation
as gospel. It further placed students in the position of having to judge

the feedback they got from their regular classroom teacher and from their peers in relation to the criteria—"all alone, no one to help you" according to Sophie's poem. Just as the distance of the examination teachers unsettled many students, it unsettled the portfolio teachers as well, as illustrated by the following excerpt from a midyear interview with Maria:

> *Maria:* One thing I think that you get out of the examination teachers, you know, is fresh eyes looking at their work, and going through it, and giving unbiased feedback. Sometimes students might think that what I am saying to them as their teacher is just my opinion. But now there are two audiences, and—am I working for my teacher as the audience? Or am I working for the examination teachers? And does my teacher really know what the examination teachers are going to want and how they're going to view my work? Sometimes I feel that that is there.

In this quote, Maria expressed a part of the core of the difference in student-classroom teacher relationships which the public criteria made. Traditionally, students may "think that what [their teacher is] saying to them as their teacher is just [the teacher's] opinion," but the students have no recourse. Traditionally, what the teacher says usually goes. In this case, there was space on the floor for students to ask, "Does my teacher really know what the examination teachers are going to want?" Essentially, the portfolio teachers had to defend their judgments of student work with specifics. Students had to engage simultaneously in the same process. This position, to say the least, was at times unsettling.

We have seen that many students claimed to need grades "so you would kind'a know how you are in writing and reading" or so they could "know *where* I'm at in my grade." Indeed, grades had been ubiquitous in the elementary schools that fed Ruff (recall the Ruff principal's vigorous rejection of the proposal to do away with grades completely for the portfolio students—"Not on my watch," he said). Daily doses of grades had helped these students index themselves within any number of social matrices for several years. Beyond this enculturation, credits and deficiencies and Intersessions, the credit-granting mechanisms of the institution, suddenly made grades a matter of unusual importance. As the year progressed, however, students stopped complaining so much. Whether this absence of complaint revealed resignation or agreement with the portfolio system became a big question for me.

Our Survey Says . . .

Near the end of the school year, I administered a survey to a random sample of 102 portfolio students to gather some quantitative data as a way to describe their perspective on their experiences with portfolios, including their views about how they received their grade in English class. The following table presents this survey as it was administered to students:

Table 1. Survey Given to Portfolio Students to Measure Their Views at the Conclusion of the Project

Directions: Read each of the following statements. Using a scale of 1 to 5, indicate how much you agree with the statement (1 = I don't agree at all; 2 = I agree a little; 3 = I agree somewhat; 4 = I agree quite a bit; 5 = I agree completely). Thanks for your help!

Mean	Standard Deviation	Item
3.4	1.4	1. I worked harder in my English class this year than I would have worked if we had not done portfolios.
3.1	1.3	2. Doing entry slips for my portfolios has helped me understand more about my own learning in my English class.
3.0	1.2	3. Doing text logs this year has helped me improve as a reader.
3.8	1.0	4. After working with the portfolio rubric for the whole year, I believe I understand it well.
3.7	1.2	5. I learned some things that helped me from the comments which my examination teacher(s) wrote to me.
2.3	1.4	6. Using the portfolio system, I got better grades than I expected to get.
2.9	1.4	7. I did not understand portfolios first trimester.
3.1	1.1	8. Most of my peers learned more than usual this year because they participated in the portfolio project.
3.3	1.4	9. I did not understand the portfolio rubric first trimester.
3.2	1.4	10. I am glad that I had this opportunity to participate in the portfolio project this year.
2.3	1.4	11. I liked the fact that my grade was determined by the examination teachers instead of by my English teacher.
2.0	1.2	12. The portfolio system really had no effect on me.

Items 6 and 11 on the survey asked specifically about grades. Unfortunately, item 6 provides ambiguous information. Most students did not agree that they got higher grades than they expected using the portfolio system (item 6); this item, however, tells us nothing about whether they got *lower* grades than they expected. I should also have asked them about lower grades but did not. It is reasonable to assume, however, that many students did get lower-than-expected grades, given the general downward pull on mean grades by the portfolio system. The data from report-card grades for nonportfolio students bear this out: Nonportfolio students on the average got one letter grade higher (B) than portfolio students on their report cards (C).

Further, the typical student in the portfolio classrooms did not agree that she or he liked having grades determined by the examination committee; 62 percent of the students surveyed circled either "1" or "2," indicating that they disagreed completely or only agreed a little with the statement "I liked the fact that my grade was determined by the examination teachers instead of by my English teacher." Disagreement with item 11 suggests that students would have preferred to have had their grades issued by the regular classroom teacher. There was a mild correlation between responses to items 6 and 11: Students who claimed that their grades were not higher than they expected tended not to like the way grades were derived (the Pearson r for item 6 and item 11 was 0.47). This finding suggests that those students who expected to receive higher grades than they earned would also have preferred the regular classroom teacher to issue grades. (It is interesting to note that the mean and standard deviations of distribution for items 6 and 11 are identical.)

The typical student did not agree that the portfolio system was weak and uninfluential (item 12). Perhaps as a consequence of the fact that the examination committee made it harder, not easier, for students to advance in the institution, students appeared to have been inclined to exert greater effort in their English class. Item 1, for example, indicates that students tended to perceive themselves as having worked harder with the portfolio system than they would have worked otherwise. The extent to which this perception of effort reflects actual effort was impossible to determine with any real confidence, but in interviews the portfolio teachers reported their perceptions that more students than they expected worked harder than they expected, especially after the first portfolio scoring session.

These observations support the notion that the examination committee played a pivotal, if complex, role in the assessment system. Remember that this committee evaluated *portfolios*, which are by definition collections of work over time, as opposed to curriculum-embedded examinations or on-demand tasks, which occur quickly and go away. This organization of power meant that the influence of the external committee seeped into every nook and cranny of the entire grading period (Elbow's dystopia). Just as students in the non-portfolio classrooms were always subject to the shaping influence of the teacher's grading practices, students in the portfolio classrooms could never escape the shaping influence of this external, distant body. The difference was that the portfolio teachers had tried to make the wielding of power visible, clear, and impartial by way of the rubric, and students did indeed come to understand the content of the rubric (see item 4). It would have been interesting to have collected data with respect to students' claims of understanding of grading criteria in the nonportfolio classrooms.

Although students reported dissatisfaction with the existence of the examination committee, they nonetheless—and perhaps surprisingly—reported moderate agreement with the claim that they were glad to have had the opportunity to participate in the system (see item 10), though only 47 percent responded with "4" or "5" to this item, while 34 percent responded with "1" or "2." The examination committee issued lower grades than students in nonportfolio classes were getting, but according to item 5, students tended to agree with the statement that they "learned some things that helped [them] from the comments which [their] examination teacher(s) wrote to [them]." Regarding item 5, 60 percent responded with either a "4" or "5," while only 15 percent responded with a "1" or "2." Further, according to item 3, students were inclined to believe that doing text logs helped them to improve as readers (81 percent responded with either "3," "4," or "5" to item 3).

In summary, then, it appeared that roughly four out of five portfolio students believed that they had learned from examination-teacher commentary and from the text-log system. The dialogic subsystems seemed to promote learning for most students. Nonetheless, one out of three students were somewhat less than glad about having participated in the project. These findings lend credence to the conclusion that Ruff students were not always enthusiastic about what they reported to be good for them as learners. The examination committee and the text-log subsystem required more effort and more responsibility than students perceived they would have been expected to exert in nonportfolio classrooms. And judgment was harsher than it would have been if the classes had been nonportfolio classes.

Taken together, the foregoing observations support two broad inferences. First, middle school students in settings like Charles Ruff are inclined to exert greater effort when their daily classroom work leaves the classroom for evaluation by an external committee who has the power to determine advancement in the institution and consequences at home, particularly if the rules are clear. Many of these same students would prefer not to face an external examination committee; instead, they would prefer that their regular classroom teacher issue their grades. Second, these students are inclined to agree that they learn from the examination committee and from the increased work demands, especially from the dialogic subsystems within the portfolio system that include written commentary from the examination committee. One might argue that portfolio systems which provide students with simple evaluative feedback (e.g., letter grades or numerical scores) *in the absence of substantive commentary* syphon power from classrooms and students while returning few of the learning benefits.

Parents

There is abundant evidence in the field record that students—and some parents—who were involved in the portfolio project gradually came to revise their achievement goal orientations. Just as Amanda and Jimmy and their parents were unsettled by ungraded daily work, many others demonstrated early on a kind of dependence on evaluative, normative feedback. Further, even when that feedback came from the examination committee, many were more concerned with the grade than with the commentary.

After the first grading period, Maria told me about a meeting she had attended the previous evening which involved several parents of students in portfolio classrooms. One parent, Mrs. Good, was upset: "My son is really discouraged," she had said, "because he got two C's [he was actually in two portfolio classrooms, a music and an English portfolio classroom]. He doesn't know what's going on here and neither do I." Student Good was accustomed to getting at least "B's."

Another parent at the meeting, Mrs. Harp, the mother of Dana from one of Maria's classes, responded: "I didn't understand either until I watched Dana work," she had said. "She would be working on an assignment, and I'd ask her, 'Well, what does your teacher want?' And she would say, 'It doesn't matter what my teacher wants. *This* is what I have to do.' I've never seen her work on assignments like that before, and I don't remember ever going through this when I went to school. I mean, for me it was always 'What does this teacher want?' If I could figure that out, I'd be fine. Dana has to figure out what the *assignment* is."

Caring More (or Less) about the Grade

Richard, an eighth-grade student who was angry when his first-trimester portfolio earned a "B" instead of an "A," changed his views by the end of the year. Here is what he had to say in his end-of-the-year text-log entry slip:

> *Richard:* From what I've talked about you can see how this portfolio project has helped me understand literature. I've also found out a lot of things about myself as reader this trimester, and what I'm interested in. I learned that when I'm challenged I'll think of ways to understand things. After the first trimester I thought this portfolio project was a bad idea, because I didn't get the grade I wanted. I cared more about my grade than what I was learning which I won't be doing any more. This portfolio to me has been successful in challenging myself to the fullest.

"Car[ing] more about the grade than what [was being learned]" by no means disappeared from the portfolio classrooms. Certainly, no one could look at the field record and fail to see the enormous influence which letter grades had on these students. But by the same token, Richard was not the only student claiming to have refocused himself.

Together with this revaluing of grades, some students learned during the year to set real learning goals for themselves. Clarissa, a student in one of Maria's classrooms, told of her transformation in her "Autobiography of Me as a Reader and Writer" written for her third-trimester portfolio. She opened her autobiography with a broad look at her change as a student and as a writer, a change that paralleled Maria's own transformation in her writing instruction:

> In the first trimester, we were given something to write about when we did the First-Hand Biography, and Autobiographical Incident. I think that by that, it limited my creativity and freedom of what I could write about. But as I grew as a writer, learning strategies to help me write. Or learning about plans and goal setting. It showed me about all the possibilities and changes

there are during writing. Like comparing the work that I did in the beginning of the year, to my poems. My poems seem to be more me and more meaningful, where the essays seem like writing from "the past."

In varying degrees, each of the portfolio teachers was nudged to, in her own words, "let go" or "give them permission to fail" or "back off" by certain of the criteria in the portfolio rubric, particularly those that required students to set their own goals, to experiment, and to discover their own meanings through drafting. Not surprisingly, each of the portfolio teachers made important changes in writing instructional practices when the second trimester began, changes which carried through to the third trimester and were noticed by students. They taught their students how to set writing goals, to experiment, and to use drafts as windows on new ideas. Clarissa again captured the change in her autobiography:

> In the second trimester, I learned about experimenting. In the diary I made, I used experimenting as a way to achieve criteria. But in this [the third] trimester, though, I used experimenting as a way to help me write. Not to experiment just to experiment. I used experimentation as an answer to when I got stuck in writing poetry. As a result by learning about experimentation helped me to achieve my writing, not criteria.
>
> These challenges stretched me as a writer because it allowed me to find a solution *through* writing. Or expressing an idea *through* writing. When I wrote my poems I think that I have persisted greatly. Like in writing "A World of a Garden." I think that I have written 3 different versions of that poem. Trying to use the right words, the right form. I think what pushed me into doing these was when I letted someone read it, and they didn't get the meaning. I know that I knew what it meant, but the reader didn't. That was important.

Clarissa summed up her changes in a sweeping paragraph that encompassed the changes made by the portfolio teachers:

> In the beginning of the year I wasn't really aware with my steps when I wrote. I remember doing a 1st draft-revision-final draft. But now my steps in writing has changed—Goals - Plans - prewrite - draft - revise - final draft. It is more longer. But I think it is better. That way I can make it exactly how I want it. The biggest change in my steps are planning and prewrite.

Just as "[good writing instruction] helps students discover how to navigate through the earliest stages of task representation, rather than taking the helm only when the vessel is safely underway" (Lucas, 1988a, p. 7), good teacher development involves helping teachers map for themselves "the earliest stages of task representation," in this case the task being writing instruction. Ironically, the CAP writing machinery, with the best of intentions, might have guaranteed that students would not achieve their potential as authors because it put teachers in the position of "taking the helm [of their own teaching] only when the vessel [was] safely underway."

Another illustration from a classmate of Clarissa's, Amy, whom we met before in a discussion of grades, shows the kind of thinking about writing engendered in the portfolio classrooms in part because students finally were given the helm before "the vessel [was] safely underway." In this case, Amy decided to work on a writing issue which would have been impossible for her even to conceptualize if she had been in a completely CAP-driven system. The following segment was excerpted from her third-trimester "Autobiography of Me as a Reader and Writer":

> *Amy:* My first experiment was on genre. I wanted to see if
> changing the genre would make the topic more significant.
> First I wrote the topic in a story form, then in a poem, then
> a speech. I felt the speech only told and the poem only
> described. The story was showing, telling, and describing.
> So I continued to work with the story. My second experi-
> ment was on leads. The purpose is to see which type of
> lead would be most effective and be eye-catching, and set
> up a problem so the reader would read on.

Despite grade deflation in the portfolio classrooms (some might argue perhaps because of it), we saw students "digging deeper" just as we saw their teachers digging deeper. The phrase began to appear not just in the language of the portfolio teachers, but also in the language of their students. The following was taken from an "Autobiography of Me as a Reader and Writer" prepared by Jane, a student in one of Jennifer Johnson's classes:

> This trimester I have challenged myself by trying to be more
> thoughtful, thorough, and truthful. What pushed me there was
> an annoying comment on some of my papers saying "Dig
> deeper, Jane." I tried writing more too. I didn't want that com-
> ment on my paper.

During an interview with Simon, one of Martha students, fol-lowing the first portfolio scoring, the phrase appeared again. This time, Martha had written it in some commentary she had composed for the student (on her own initiative, Martha wrote commentary for her stu-dents each of the three trimesters to complement the commentary pre-pared by the examination teachers). Simon was not a model student. In fact, he had said earlier in this interview that he had never really been interested in any of his work in elementary school, except for math. Here is the relevant portion of this interview:

> *TU:* And you said that you're reading more than you used to.
>
> *Simon:* Yeah.
>
> *TU:* Let's look at these comments: "I applaud you for becoming aware of one of the challenges you face while reading. It's often difficult to point out challenges." Um . . . what's the challenge that you pointed out?
>
> *Simon:* Um . . . I think it was about the hard words, or . . .
>
> *TU:* OK. She says, "Dig deeper." What does that mean?
>
> *Simon:* Uh, that I should start thinking more and digging deeper into my stories and reading.
>
> *TU:* How do you go about digging deeper?
>
> *Simon:* I'll try to, like, um, review the, uh, try to, like, uh, picture the book that I'm reading. I'll try to make a picture out of what's going on. And in my story I'll try to do the same thing. So I can write more or read more.

Supporting students in making the transition from reading for "leisure escape"—or from not reading at all—to reading for "insight" was not easy, though it was perhaps the single most hoped for change in students. Such a change often brought with it a new willingness to research allusions, to investigate language features and patterns, to explore technical aspects of genre and structure. More important, though, it brought with it a seriousness of purpose, a resolve, a willingness to tolerate uncertainty that lent an unusual maturity to those students who had made the transition.

Between Two Worlds

Certainly, not all did, and many struggled. In the following segment from a text-log entry, Betty, an eighth-grade student, chronicled her effort to move from leisure escape to insight as she tried, with only partial success, to make the transition from an R. L. Stine novel entitled *The Dead Girlfriend* to a serious adolescent novel about a girl born in Mexico:

> I am sorry that I am reading a new book [my teacher] gave it to me to Read and I'm going to Read it. Lupita is A little girl. She comes from Mexico and she wants to find a job that she will have enough money to help her mother with. So she crosses over the boarder. I am going to read both books.

Betty wrestled with a difficult issue. On the one hand, she knew that there was value in reading about Lupita; Betty herself had come to California from Mexico and had the background experience to respond quite personally to the novel her teacher recommended. But Betty would not give up her right to read escapist horror: "I am going to read both books." This right showed up in her writings as well. The following excerpt from her story "The Dreaded Party," during which a teenage Hispanic girl is forced to join a Satanic gang in a midnight ritual in a cemetery, was a real hit among her peer audience in her English classroom:

> When I opened my eyes, I couldn't breath. It was so creepy, So evel. Their were signs of the devel, candles, and blood everywhere. It was so gross. I couldn't beleve what I was seeing. I was sitting on a chair. It was different, like a weird person's chair. Mark told me to go into the bathroom and change into the dress that he had. It looked like an expencive dress, It was really pritty.

Betty faced a conflict. Her peers valued her ability to write scary stories, and she got ideas from R. L. Stine. Her teacher, however, wanted Betty to grow beyond creepy and evil midnight cemetery scenes. Betty never completely made the transition from an escapist reader to a serious reader of complex literature. But she took steps in that direction—baby steps, as Jennifer referred to them. And, as we will see in an upcoming discussion of Sophie's growth as a reader, reading for escape and reading for insight are not always mutually exclusive. Betty's decision to "read both books" could be interpreted as evidence that Betty had learned to read for various purposes.

Students who had learned to understand "digging deeper" were on the way to becoming what Martha Goldsmith called "brand new learners":

> I think I have learned a variety of things. Besides ways to improve my textlogs and new vocabulary, I have learned if I set a goal and work hard at it I will be very pleased. I was pleased with my interpretation of *Child of the Owl* because it had sort of an affect on me and made me think more about who I am and who I'm supposed to be. Those were the kind of books I wanted to read, "thought provoking," and by making that one decision of reading that book, I think it will help me with later choices.

This excerpt from a text-log entry slip illustrated important learning. First, the student came to know the satisfaction of goal-driven engagement. Second, she entered a book and left it profoundly changed as a human being. Third, she understood that the experience was pivotal, and she predicted a long-range impact.

There were, of course, portfolio students who did not take even baby steps toward assuming the role of a reader who reads for empathy and insight. The following excerpt from an eighth-grade student's entry slip for third-trimester text logs illustrates just how mechanical the reading process, as it was defined at Ruff, could be for such students:

> These are my text logs personally I think that they are pretty good because I filled them in pretty good and put the date and the time that I read in each one because that shows on the grading criteria. Also last time they took points off of my portfolio for not writing that. I think on each log I put all of the information that I read because that is also on the criteria for the portfolio.

Clearly, this student's goal was to earn credit for the class. What kinds of goals did other students actually set for themselves? Myers (J. Myers, 1992) classification scheme for the kinds of "literacy clubs" students join applied almost perfectly. One type Myers termed the "achievement club" (p. 308); like the student who wrote the following in a text-log entry slip, students who joined the "achievement club" sought to align their literate behaviors with sanctioned behaviors, in form if not in substance. The goals expressed in this excerpt are not all that different from goals implied by the student cited above:

> When I started this trimester, my goals for reading were to keep up on my text logs, build my work around the criteria sheet, and increase my vocabulary. I feel that I have met all three of these goals. This trimester, I read something every day. Most of the time I read my book, but in between the books I read other things like magazines and newspapers. I have written text logs every day, whether I read a book or not, and I have made a list of the vocabulary that I have been introduced to while reading. All of my work has been built around the criteria sheet, and I have used the criteria sheet to make revisions to my work.

Myers called a second type of club the "academic club," made up of students concerned not just with earning credit, but also with learning as much as possible, students like the one represented by the following excerpt taken from a third-trimester text-log entry slip:

> This trimester I did not have a goal set quickly. I was interested in Asian American literature, which I had already explored in the second trimester. Ms. [Madsen] was helpful and threw a book on my desk. It was *The Hobbit* by J.R.R. Tolkien, a fantasy. I didn't like fantasy and had little interest in it. I never exactly

knew what a fantasy was. Since I knew little about it, I just thought it would be a good topic to explore.

That became my goal, to explore fantasy and know more of its criteria. Also to read fantasy by different authors and of different genres.

To meet my goals I read five times a week from 30 to 45 minutes. For each time I read I wrote in my text logs in a variety of responses. This trimester in exploring fantasy I read the listed: *The Hobbit,* J.R.R. Tolkien, Novel; *Baucis and Philomon,* Edith Hamilton, Short Story; *The Zoo,* Edward Hoch, Short Story; *Rip Van Winkle,* Washington Irving, Short Story; *I Cremated James McGee,* Robert Service, Poem; *The Trout,* Sean O'Faolain, Short Story; [several additional short stories are listed].

The opportunity to set personal learning goals within a rigorous context of personal responsibility, as shaped by the examination teachers, seemed to motivate some students to incredible exertion of effort in the name of learning. Sophie, one of Martha's students, expressed her view of goal setting in an end-of-year interview, as follows:

> *Sophie:* With the portfolios, you made your own way. You didn't just do, like, what was done and nothing more. You set your own rules. You set your goals and it was just, like, out in the open. Like, usually, in my other classes you do, like, what was told when it was due and nothing more. And then—but here, you're writing your own entry slips, you're doing your own stories, and you're reading your own books, and you set your own limits. And so you have, like, your *own* criteria.

Sophie realized that once a student accepts responsibility for his or her own learning rather than turning that responsibility over to the teacher, that student can no longer be satisfied with doing "what was told when it was due and nothing more." Students also reported that goal setting helped them learn by anchoring their efforts in what they perceived to be important areas in which they should work. Molly expressed this sentiment this way:

> *Molly:* I thought it helped for me because when I wrote 'em down [goals], whenever you're working on, like, a writing piece or a quickwrite, I'd always, like, look back at my goals and see what they were and try to achieve them through my assignments that we were given. But on a couple of 'em—especially at the beginning—I couldn't really think, like, what to write, like, what goals to set for yourself. But then I kind of based 'em upon first and second trimester, you know, what I did, and how I could do better third.

Myers's third type of club, the "personal literacy club" made up of students who were unwilling to embed their literacy activities in either an academic or achievement context, was also represented at Ruff. Such students were rare, but when they showed up, the portfolio teachers had a hard time engaging them in goal setting. One quite capable student in one of Maria's classes, for example, actually read every day in her room at home, or so her mother reported to Maria, though much of what she read seemed geared toward "leisure escape."

Nonetheless, despite the fact that she could have earned a "C" or perhaps a "B" by simply keeping track of what she read in her text logs, this student refused to comply with the requirement that she chronicle her effort. Never overtly defiant, never unpleasant, she sat quietly at her desk day after day while her peers completed their text-log entries; every trimester, when the time came for her to prepare her text logs for submission to the examination teachers, she claimed to have lost them.

Not all students responded by setting goals and accepting challenges; not all students joined a literacy club of any sort. One eighth-grade male, Eric, presented Maria with as great a challenge as she presented to him. For Eric's second-trimester letter of reference from his teacher, Maria wrote: "As a reader Eric has been struggling with the novel *All in the Family* for the last two trimesters. I believe he has shown some persistence in continuing to read this novel even though it's taking him a long time to complete." Eric's own entry slip for his second trimester text logs read, using his own spelling system, as follows: "I realate to my novel by see a telling in a thoughtful writing. As you look at the one that says Goals. You will see what I had in mind and will see that I set them up good." The following excerpt is from the field record and illustrates the kind of text logs Eric submitted in his portfolio that trimester:

> Text log #1 (Feb. 13, 1995)—The word "goals" is written in the lefthand box where date, title, etc. should be recorded. The word "goals" is circled. Under it is a sketch of a face with eyes wide open wearing glasses. [Eric] has written "I have a good way to start off and, get a good grade. I have to start reading more."
> The next day, Feb. 14, [Eric] indicates that he read from 7:00 to 8:00. His entry reads "I wonder about how the book is going to end. As I look back and reread I see that is going to take a while before I can understand then I am finish."
> The next several entries are dated in mid-February: "I see Jackie in a city. In the book he gose to see his dad a Politician. But I can't see how he can be a movie star's husband to a governer." Next entry: "One question I would like to ask is that will

it get any harder to understand the plot is mind bogoling." Next entry: "I like Jackie because of his bravy in dealing with a problem."

The text log is silent for two weeks. Then on March 2, 3, 6, 7, and 15 there are a few scribbles. On the 21st: "Today I just didn't get a grip on the book."

That's the last entry in the text log.

In an interview, Maria commented about Eric: "His brother is a straight A student, and his mom just beats him up—and he beats himself up—because he's not his brother. I talked with him about trying something else, but he wouldn't. He carried that book around with him for the longest time."

There were several students like Eric in the portfolio classrooms at Charles Ruff, some with much more serious problems than Eric faced. Nonetheless, the portfolio teachers saw some transformations after students got back their first-trimester portfolios with commentary from the examination teachers urging them to seek challenges. Jennifer Johnson spoke about one such student, Lilly, in an interview. Lilly received a lower grade than she expected, primarily because she had not "set complex goals," nor had she particularly "challenged" herself:

> *Jennifer:* Lilly was a little . . . I think she knows. I think she *knows.* She didn't have . . . J.T. was more upset than Lilly. And Lamar was at first upset. Lamar received a C—or earned a C—and feels that he should've, well, just feels that he tried harder, but in actuality he didn't. But then he came up to me afterwards and said, "I don't know what kinds of books to read to challenge myself." So he's making the first step. I recommended to him *Old Man and the Sea,* and I recommended to him *Mutiny on the Bounty* that he might go and try out over the vacation, because those are the only two that came to mind right then, but . . . kids are making overtures.

The Problem with Text Logs

It was clear quite early on that many students had genuine trouble understanding just what the portfolio teachers wanted them to do. Following the second scoring, students were interviewed from each of the three portfolio teachers' classrooms in an effort to understand what they perceived to be the most difficult aspect of the portfolio system to grasp. Many students named "text logs." The following segment of an interview with several of Maria's students illustrates two problems. The first was coded the "gettin' up and gettin' ready" text-log problem, a problem mentioned only by students in Maria's classrooms. The second was coded "Catch 22." Recall that Dana was the student whose mother had expressed appreciation for the portfolio system during an evening meeting when Mrs. Good had attacked Maria Madsen about her son's "C" grades:

> *TU:* What about text logs?
>
> *Dana* [groans]: Ooohh!
>
> [Laughter]
>
> *TU:* Text logs. What do you think?
>
> *Dana:* Just because you read a book? You might understand it, but you don't always like writing it down.
>
> *Kendra:* It's like, when we had—we don't want to spend every morning writing down what we read. And, plus, it's like we don't have time to read in class, like, and so we read before we go to sleep, and then we have to worry about *gettin' up and gettin' ready* [emphasis added] and everything [Dana begins laughing] and we might forget about what we read last night. It's not, like, "You should'a read this *book* last night!" and then we come to school and talk about it or somethin'.
>
> *Dana:* It's not even that—you just don't like writing about it sometimes, because they tell you not to, like, tell what happened, but then they don't understand what's going on.
>
> *Kendra:* Yeah!
>
> *Dana:* They'll say, "I don't know if you read this book," but then they'll say, "Don't summarize."
>
> *Kendra:* Yeah, they'll say, "Don't tell us what happened," and then they don't know what's going on, and then you write, "Oh, this was so exciting!" and you can't tell 'em what was exciting 'cause they don't want to know 'cause it's a summary!
>
> *TU:* So you're kind of caught in a bad spot.

For Kendra and Dana, two capable and engaged students, text logs became just one more thing to worry about in an already hectic existence made even more nettlesome because "they"—the voice of the institution ventriloquated through the examination teachers—set up a seemingly absurd hurdle. First, the examination teachers established the rule "don't say what happened." Next, those same teachers read the entries, and "they [didn't] know what's going on"—they saw "mumbo jumbo." Finally, they made the judgment that they "[didn't] know if [the student] read the book."

And so they gave low grades.

Even Maria had been baffled by the low grades that came back after the second scoring, grades lowered substantially because the examination teachers generally had highlighted the rubric in the lower score-point categories for reading. Recall Maria's words: "They [her students] were reading much better books than they were reading the time before, and I don't know what it is that . . ."

Students in Jennifer's classrooms, however, saw this text-log problem in a different light. To be sure, these students identified text logs as one of the most difficult aspects of the portfolio system, not because of "gettin' up and gettin' ready," not because of "Catch 22," but simply because text logs were "too hard." Text logs demanded not just that students read every day, but that they "dig deep" into challenging books. Text logs forced them to think about serious issues when they had other things to think about that didn't come out of books, when they wanted to relax and be entertained.

Jennifer's students did not find the "Catch-22." In basic agreement with the values of the rubric, Jennifer's students thought that simple summarizing *was* worth little as evidence of a reader's performance, because summarizing involved giving somebody else's ideas (i.e., the author's ideas), not one's own. Besides, students *could* write good text-log entries *without summarizing*; it was possible, even desirable, to provide sufficient details for the examination teachers to get a good idea of a text's content without devoting space to long summaries. Consider the following segment from one of these interviews (we had been talking about the value of feedback from the examination teachers):

> *TU:* Can you give me an example of some feedback that you paid attention to?
>
> *Lillian:* Text logs.
>
> *J.T.:* Yeah.
>
> *Lillian:* It helped there because when you got feedback on a text-log entry, then you could improve on your next one.
>
> *J.T.:* Mostly, on text logs, they told you, like, you can, like, do different things for your writing. Like, not to always write just a summary. Don't write what you read, just write your thoughts.
>
> *TU:* What's wrong with just writing a summary?
>
> *Ben:* It doesn't show anything about *you* as a reader because . . . you're just writing what the writer wrote.

TU: Well, what would you say to people who argue that it's important for teachers to know whether you know what the author wrote?

J.T.: That ain't right. Through your text logs, even *without* writin' a summary, they should know that you already knew, because you show it right in your text logs.

This difference in the perceptions of students who worked with different teachers who used the same assessment strategy called for further exploration. On the surface, it appeared that Maria and Jennifer had implemented identical procedures: Students were given the same set of criteria, the same text-log forms, the same directive to read at home at night and fill in text logs during the first five minutes of class, the same opportunity to discuss text logs with classmates, the same time line and examination committee. Furthermore, the portfolio teachers worked closely together and discussed virtually every instructional and assessment issue of which they became conscious, including issues related to text logs. Yet Maria's students believed that the text-log system was logically flawed, while Jennifer's students believed it served them well (it was just too hard). Why? Why were very capable students in Maria's classes caught in a Catch-22 while similar students in Jennifer's classes bought the ideology of the portfolio rubric? The answer lay in the complex folds of classroom cultures—and in the history of small, nearly invisible instructional decisions.

Observations revealed that text logs had gradually evolved in the separate instructional cultures as different genre or discourse structures. In Maria's classrooms, text logs were viewed as chronicles of events, historical documents to be submitted to the examination committee in raw form. Students were asked, in essence, to become participant-observers in their own growth as readers, to keep a response diary. Like ethnographers, they developed their own field records and analyzed and coded the data for the examination committee. Maria sometimes collected text logs and prepared written feedback for her students, but this feedback was directed largely at helping students reshape their roles as readers, not at helping students revise particular text-log entries. Maria's feedback was geared toward helping students make better text-log entries somewhere down the line; if they improved as readers, naturally their text logs, as historical documents, would reflect that growth.

In Jennifer's classrooms, however, text logs were viewed not as historical chronicles, but as compositions. Text logs could be revised. Students often shared entries with classmates by going up to the stool at the front of the room and reading aloud what they had written that day, much as in earlier days when they had shared journal entries. Later, students could revise their entries using feedback from peers. Jennifer also gave students written feedback on their text logs, some of it geared toward helping them reshape their roles as readers, but much of it geared toward supporting revision of specific entries in the document. For example, Jennifer would place sticky notes next to a particular entry with a comment like "Why? You need to say more!" or "Dig deeper!" Students could then revise those entries prior to submitting the portfolio.

The distinction between Maria and Jennifer's implementation of the text-log strategy was not nearly as neat and tidy as it appears. Students revised text logs in Maria's room to some degree, though not routinely, and students in Jennifer's room understood that text logs needed to provide a factual historical record. However, as a matter of emphasis, the distinction was real. During the first scoring session, the examination teachers were surprised to note that some students actually commented on their text-log revision process; the examination teachers had been expecting a historical chronicle, not compositions. The examiners needed to know whether the dates and times recorded on text logs could be taken at face value—or whether students could revise that information as well as their responses. Of course, students were not free to alter the facts of their reading behaviors—just their responses.

By the second and third scorings, the examination committee and the portfolio teachers had explicitly agreed that dates and times were to reflect historical accuracy regarding what pages were read in what book on what date. Of interest is that nobody even asked about the rules governing *when a particular response to those pages had been written*. This decision, we now know in hindsight, was left to the individual teacher. What mattered to the examination teachers, in the end, was that students were reading daily and that their responses were varied, complex, and thoughtful.

This finding is reported here because I believe it represents an important example of how consequences for students depend not just on the technical nature of a particular portfolio-assessment strategy, but on how a particular strategy actually enters the classroom culture and becomes part of that culture's discourse. After all, capturing a response on the fly early in the reading of a novel is very different from revising that response several weeks later after the novel has been read. In this instance, one might have expected uniform implementation because the portfolio system had been locally developed and implemented, not imposed from afar. The text-log assessment strategy had been the focus of critical attention for several weeks early in the project. But the rules governing participation across teachers differed—and created differential consequences for students.

The encouragement of text-log entry revision in Jennifer's rooms minimized for students the problem of selecting telling details or of writing brief gist statements; students could take their time to make sure that the examiner audience had enough evidence of comprehension to warrant belief that the student actually read the text. The down side, perhaps, was that students need not necessarily learn to hone their responses during online reading. They could wait, collect the responses of others, and reflect on early responses in light of later information. Such social and reflective work might have been expected to yield deeper, clearer, fuller products. But clearly its emphasis was not on process.

Maria's encouragement of text-log entries as chronicles not subject to revision made the summary restriction a big problem indeed. Summary work could not be done after the novel had been read. It had to be done online during moments when readers may not have fully understood what was happening in the book. Telling details had to be included in entries at points where incomplete knowledge of a character or event made such details difficult to spot. The up side, perhaps, was that students had to learn to respond online while reading—what they thought during the moment of negotiation with a text was appropriate content for text-log entries. Of course, such entries tended to be viewed as mumbo jumbo much more often than were entries which had been carefully revised.

After reading a draft of this manuscript, long after she could have done something about her practice with the portfolio students, Maria told me that the preceding discussion of the difference in text-log approaches needed further exploration. While she did not question the veracity of the description nor the logic of the analysis, Maria did believe that the two approaches, chronicle versus composition, were oppositional. She wanted to know which of the two approaches was better. I could not answer her question.

Shortly after this question was raised, however, one of the examination teachers, the assistant department chair who had been involved for at least two years in a teacher-research group, began a teacher-research project involving text logs. She wanted to look critically and carefully at text logs in her own classrooms during the subsequent year, the period during which all of the English teachers agreed to implement a text-log system for all students. Despite a full year's serious and sustained examination of the text-log strategy, Ruff teachers were left with more questions than answers.

Displacement Effects

We knew for a fact, however, that text logs required students to write, as did all of the other important portfolio-assessment strategies used in the system (e.g., autobiographies, goal-setting contracts, entry slips, letters of recommendation, etc.), and we have already seen in Jennifer's practice that the portfolio system led to a reduction of oral activities and an increase in writing activities. Martha, too, commented that her use of talk in her classrooms was affected by the portfolio system. During the previous year, Martha had become a strong advocate of "bookshares" as defined earlier, because she saw that bookshares encouraged students to read carefully and refine their interpretations of works presented publicly, and because bookshares provided a forum through which students could hear about books that they might want to read.

Martha cut back on her use of this whole-class discussion strategy during the portfolio year. She also reported feeling pressured to do more writing activities. Her *students* reported that they, however, did *not* suffer from a lack of opportunity to discuss their views orally. In the following excerpt, Jackson and Sophie contrast their perceptions of the kinds of talk about books that went on in their classroom with the kinds of talk that went on in one of the traditional classrooms which they had had the opportunity to visit and observe:

> *Jackson:* Like, um, with *The Giver,* we would get into discussions after reading, like, a chapter or something, and our discussions—we'd get into theories, and a discussion could last both periods, and still we could say more [Martha taught students in a two-period block].
>
> *Sophie:* And they were, like, reading Sherlock Holmes and stuff, and their questions were, like, "What happened in this and this?" It was nothing, like—*we* were into theories like Jackson said, but they were just, like, proving that they read it, you know, and saying who was mentioned and that sort of thing.

Jackson and Sophie agreed that these group discussions wherein students became involved in theory building were important for their growth as readers. For one thing, these experiences helped them understand the significance of persistence, an understanding that was transferred to their writings about their self-selected readings. But the portfolio students were expected not just to show deep understanding of self-selected books. They were also expected to demonstrate that they had constructed a "deep, personal interpretation" of *shared* literature. Class discussions helped them construct their own interpretations.

The following excerpt was taken from a thinkaloud done by an examination teacher during the second trimester scoring and illustrates the point that writings in response to self-selected readings, though important, would not earn students an "A" by themselves. Students had to understand the content of core literature. (Note: The words of the examination teacher are in italics; when the examination teacher is reading from student work documents, the words are not italicized):

> *Examination Teacher: Um, the next entry is a double-entry journal on chapter eleven of "Tom Sawyer." The first comment is,* "'I didn't do it, friends,' he sobbed. 'Upon my word and honor I never done it.'" *Her response is,* "My reason for this quote is that Muff Potter is trying to prove his innocence and wants everyone to know he is incest"—*which, I'm sure she means innocent. Um . . . then her next quote is,* "'Is that your knife?' And it was thrust before him by the sheriff." "The sheriff, I think, is trying to see if the knife is his, and then accuse him of the crime and then put Muff Potter in jail for the crime." *And her final quote is,* "'Everything was swimming before Tom.'" "The way the author put this is to tell you that all the memories came to Tom and he remembered every little detail from the scene." *So not only is she showing exposure to shared reading, but I think that she's showing some understanding. Um . . . I think in some respects that this is merely superficial understanding. I think she gets some hints of definite understanding of shared reading. I don't really think that she's interpreting at all. Um . . . There's no real personalization here.*

This student was able to comment on the textual significance of the lines she selected from the novel, but she did not discuss larger themes or personal connections—what might be thought of as contextual significance. Though students were expected to understand the content of core literature, they were also to "dig deeper"; these experiences would create habits of mind that would transfer to their personal readings. The following example, excerpted from a midyear observation in one of Jennifer's classrooms, shows Jennifer's concern that students should understand the basic intentions and uses of particular strategies so that they could apply the strategies learned through core book experiences to self-selected reading. It also illustrates that in the portfolio classrooms, students were truly expected to derive their own interpretations. In this segment, Jennifer discussed a misunderstanding regarding the "open-mind" strategy with her student, Amy:

> *Amy* [working alone at her desk during a "catch-up" session in third period; has raised her hand for help and Jennifer approaches]: I'm not quite sure if I did this right.
>
> *Jennifer:* What do you mean?
>
> [Jennifer kneels down near Amy's desk. Amy is showing her a sheet of binder paper with the outline of a head on it. Inside the head are sentences—complete sentences with capital letters and periods.]
>
> *Amy:* Well, I wasn't sure if I was supposed to put what the author says the character is thinking, or my own interpretation of what the character is thinking.
>
> *Jennifer:* You mean, you weren't sure, and you didn't ask? Amy!
>
> [Jennifer gets an alarmed look on her face, more concerned now about Amy's not having gotten clarification than she is with Amy's not having understood the open mind.]
>
> *Amy:* Well, the sub . . . he never really . . .
>
> *Jennifer* [groans]: Oh. Well, anyway, you should put *your* interpretation of the character thoughts. Why do you think I'm asking you to do it that way?
>
> *Amy:* Because if I just put what the author says, I'm not really doing any thinking for myself?
>
> *Jennifer:* Exactly. Exactly.

Substitutes could not really "substitute" in the portfolio classrooms. Because the substitute could not speak the instructional language that had evolved between the students and teacher, he could not communicate. Further, Jennifer's concern about Amy's not having asked a question pointed to a value scheme within the classroom culture of which the substitute could not be aware. In this instance, the larger value rested with the student's willingness to risk asking a question; the secondary value rested with the student's understanding of the particular strategy. Even further down the chain was the value of understanding particular content. Within the network of values defining the "good" reader in the portfolio classrooms, reader-students were always to be in charge of thinking.

Without a doubt, this endeavor to structure a literary reading classroom around goal setting, self-selection of challenging materials, closely monitored and analyzed recordkeeping, ample large- and small-group discussion opportunities with a shared text, direct instruction in literary reading strategies with the expectation of transference, and one-on-one coaching to help prepare for an external audit presented challenges to both teachers and students. But when the year was over, even though many students had found the experience painful, virtually everyone who was involved in the portfolio project—students, portfolio teachers, examination teachers, and interested colleagues who looked in from time to time—was convinced that important growth had been accomplished by an unusually large number of students in the portfolio classrooms.

From the Mouths of Children

Near the end of that year, portfolio students were interviewed to explore their thoughts about why they scored higher on a local direct reading test than the traditional students. Elsie, a student from Martha's first period, expressed her belief that the portfolio students scored higher because their instruction required that they approach and respond to texts as "thinkers":

> *Elsie:* Like I said earlier, one of the advantages of doing a portfolio is that you become a better *thinker*. Like, when you read, you were supposed to just write down your thoughts and your questions and what you *thought* about the book, and that's what I meant by critical thinking. It really put a good advantage to you because, um, lots of other kids would just read—their teachers tell them to read and then maybe they'll just write a little report about what they read, but other than that—

Susan, another of Martha's first-period students, interrupted Elsie at this point to mention the intersection between instruction and assessment in self-selected reading within this particular portfolio system, namely, text logs. In the following section, Susan and Elsie refer to a short story entitled "Joan and the Ants," a narrative in the locally adopted anthology which was used as the test passage for the end-of-seventh-grade local direct reading assessment:

> *Susan:* —us, we had to do, like, text logs and things, and so it's, like, we *have* to think about our reading. And, um, that's pretty much what we had to do. It's, like, was it "Joan and the Ants" [the title of the story on the reading post-test]?
>
> *TU:* Yeah.

Susan: "Joan and the Ants"—because we, um, we had to read, and then it's, like, really easy for us to write down notes because we had to do text logs, and I guess for other people it's like, um . . . maybe they don't do text logs or . . .

Susan and Elsie both suggested that writing about their reading had been important in helping them develop their ability to "think" about texts. "Text logs" were not the same as, in Elsie's words, "writing little reports." But simply engaging in writing was not the key, at least not according to Elsie. She added the following thought to round out her and Susan's explanation of the difference between the groups on the reading measure:

Elsie: Maybe they summarize. See, we're supposed to write our thoughts and our reactions. We're not supposed to summarize and tell what happened in the book. I mean, if we summarized and told what happened in the book, we probably wouldn't have got the scores we got on our "Joan and the Ants" because of all we probably would have done is said, "Oh, Joan found the ant hill" or something like that.

Students from Jennifer Johnson's classes were also asked to explain this difference in scores on the reading measure. J.T. claimed that the explanation lay in the portfolio classroom's requirement that students "understand what [their] work is" and "analyze":

J.T.: I think you grow more because it's more based on understanding what your work is. I'm not saying you can't understand it if you're in a regular classroom. It's just that in this class it's based mostly on understanding and if they can analyze, you know, well, it helps you work more and then you learn more.

Elsie and Susan pointed to portfolio students' having had more opportunity to "think" about their readings; J.T. extended their explanation by connecting analysis to "help[ing] you work more and then you learn more." Piggybacking on J.T.'s remarks, Lillian pointed to the ongoing, recursive nature of portfolio-based instruction as an important factor in stimulating "work at a higher level":

Lillian: And I was going to say, you work in both classes, the traditional type but also in the portfolio type, but I think portfolio makes you work at a higher level, because it makes you analyze your thoughts and all your work, because in the traditional, you do your work and, I mean, that's it. You don't have to go back and look over it. And it helps you—portfolio classes help you improve your work by you looking back at it, but in traditional, you know, you do an assignment and it's the same the next time you do it. But when you go back and you look over it, you improve the next time you do it in the portfolio classes.

Sophie took exception to the notion that the portfolio system was responsible for the difference in scores:

> *Sophie* [responding to the role of portfolios in explaining the difference in the reading test scores]: I don't think it had anything to do with portfolios, because when we were doing portfolios we were getting entry slips ready and things like that, and we were putting our work in there, but when you say the direct assessment test, that, I think, has to do with the teacher and how the teacher taught.

Here, Sophie had keyed on the mechanical aspects of the portfolio system, the actual "doing [of] portfolios" at the end of the term when selection, reflection, and inspection was occurring, when folders were being stuffed for the examination committee—the physical aspect of a culturally significant set of agreements. This aspect of the portfolio system, in and of itself, could not explain the difference. I asked Sophie a follow-up question:

> *TU:* Do you think how the teacher taught was influenced by whether or not the teacher used portfolios?

> *Sophie:* Yeah, probably, because they weren't really grading us, they were preparing us for the portfolios and the public criteria.

This question, of course, led the discussion to precisely the same points made by Elsie, Susan, J.T., and Lillian, students from other portfolio classes. Later, Jackson, a boy who had read the voices of the institution which told him to read *The Hobbit* as "pressure," explained why the portfolio system had had an influence on his teacher:

> *Jackson:* Because she wanted us to get—she wanted to prepare us to the point where we could get a good grade because if she hadn't prepared us, students in the class wouldn't be getting A's or B's. You know, if they were just prepared like [names a traditional teacher], we would have been getting lower grades. If we would have been taught by [names the traditional teacher again] if were doing portfolios, we would be getting lower grades because we wouldn't be totally understanding it, I don't think.

After Jackson finished making his point about the teacher's need to make sure that her students learn what they need to learn in order to meet the standards, Molly raised the discussion to the level of institutional morality:

> *Molly:* Why don't we all do portfolios? Because, like, they're
> gonna be kind'a behind next year, and I think that's, like,
> kind'a wrong unless they go to, again, a traditional English
> classroom.

I explained to Molly that the portfolio project was experimental, that it could have been considered wrong to have tried it in the first place since nobody knew what kind of influence it was going to have on students such as herself. If the project were to have any lasting importance, I told her, the parts of it that had made a difference for her and for other students would have to be identified. Sophie responded:

> *Sophie:* Probably the public criteria made a difference. I don't
> think the traditional classrooms have the criteria, and since
> we did our work based on those criteria, I think that it
> made us grow a lot more than the traditional classes would
> because they didn't have that criteria. I mean, you have,
> like, a goal and you want to meet that goal, and I don't
> think their goals were as high as ours were.

Sophie's analysis of the consequences of public criteria echoed debates going on in the conference rooms of policymakers across the country. It provided evidence from the mouth of a seventh-grade learner that mind is transferred through social processes, that schooling is a primary social arena for such transference, and that professional agreements regarding criteria for learning can have a powerful influence on students. Of course, the nature of the criteria—their values—makes all the difference; indeed, a difference in values with respect to the "good" reader lay behind Governor Wilson's veto of CLAS legislation. As we have seen, even without explicit rubrics, schools and districts still have implicit learning criteria, and those in power positions have the edge in imposing their favored criteria.

Near the close of the school year, a traditional teacher who had not taught her students any specific criteria nonetheless asked her students to put together an end-of-year portfolio. One of these students approached Molly for help. Here is Molly's account of what happened:

> *Molly:* My friend asked me for help because she knew that I
> was in portfolios, and I tried to help her, but it was difficult
> because they just don't understand the criteria. They were,

like, completely confused, like, "What does this mean?"
And I tell them and they still don't understand.

Sophie offered an explanation for their confusion that illustrated the importance of providing multiple opportunities for students to translate and internalize complex criteria for learning:

> *Sophie:* Because they never had that criteria where they had to work with them because, like, when we first started school, it took us a while, and we finally got it. I mean, you can't just *teach* someone these things in, like, a week. It takes time to teach someone something like that. And so it was really confusing for them because they had never had it, and they had never seen it.

Sophie's explanation applies equally well to teachers. As the field stumbles through this dawn of the era of portfolios, it will be increasingly more important that we all realize that this work is confusing, especially for those of us who "ha[ve] never had it, and . . . ha[ve] never seen it."

9 Conclusions and Implications

Putting on the Brakes

The story of assessment-based school reform in California started in 1983 with the passage of legislation; for all practical purposes the story ended in 1994 with the state governor's veto of supporting legislation. As Chrispeel (1997) discovered, however, putting the brakes on California's reform movement has not been easy. Echoes of changes in classrooms and schools made during the era of CAP/CLAS reverberate in schools like Ruff to this day despite vigorous legislative activity to eliminate such vestiges (e.g., California's Assembly Bill 1086—phonics legislation—passed in 1997). To reform the schools, the state relied heavily on its assessment system—"power items," as Superintendent Honig referred to mandated test questions—as hortatory devices (McDonnell, 1994). To return the schools to their pre-reform days, the state is now relying on raw power—the power to fund, to credential, to certify. Whether the method involves test scores or credentialing criteria, however, one thing is clear: The state of California appears now to have adopted intimidation as its primary tool for managing its schools.

It is less clear, however, whether the state has ever given sufficient consideration in its plans to the role of the district, at least not to the district involved in this study. To be sure, Ruff district officials spent money on and devoted energy toward fulfilling the state's objectives. We have seen the district's warehouse personnel working double shifts to make sure that core literature books were available on site. We have seen the district office basement turned into offices for a squadron of resource teachers whose sole function was to support the implementation of the state's vision.

But the state did nothing to change the district's standardized test system, the real yardstick to which district officials had become committed—nothing, that is, except talk. In conferences like the "Beyond the Bubble" conference in 1989, state leaders argued against the "multiple-choice mentality," argued that the old standardized multiple-choice system reinforced a lower-order curriculum dedicated to rote memorization, argued that the right-answer perspective meant the trivialization of knowledge, and argued "WYTIWYG" ("What-you-test-is-what-you-get").

Within the Ruff district, however, the standardized test system went on like clockwork in parallel with the state's short-lived "authentic" assessment system. Despite all of the new legislation, nothing changed the heart, the engine, the core of the curriculum of low literacy: The right-answer, multiple-choice perspective was protected in standardized test systems across California. In the Ruff district this test system had become integral to the daily professional lives of the district's officials and, through them, the daily professional lives of everyone in the district. If Ruff's principal was even partly right in his description of the intense pressure created by these tests on district officials, the impetus to drive instruction, wherever possible, toward alignment with values embedded in the standardized test must have been overwhelming.

What Might Have Been

What might have happened if the state had legislated the abolition of multiple-choice, standardized tests while it simultaneously replaced them with an open-ended, constructed-response test system like CAP/CLAS? Undoubtedly, the structure of power in the district that had been assembled over the years deriving from the standardized test system would have remained. The tactic of intimidation, the strategy of you-scratch-my-back-I'll-scratch-yours would likely have remained. Instead of a commercially prepared standardized test system as the tool of intimidation, however, the state's tests would probably have been used. Such abolitionist legislation might have done away with standardized tests, but it would not have done away with the underlying relationships among the people operating the institutions.

Even if CAP/CLAS had won, however, as we have seen, there was still the matter of a foundational contradiction in the design of the CLAS reading test and the state instructional framework. Undoubtedly, this contradiction would have become apparent over time, and either core literature or CLAS would have had to change. Moreover, as we have also seen, the design of the state writing test resulted in important constraints on writing instruction. Arguably better than constraints imposed by standardized tests of editing, the CAP constraints nonetheless would likely have become the focus of reform in the next century. Instead of chanting "beyond the bubble," the next wave of reformers might have chanted "fight the formula!"

Comparisons, Contrasts

It is interesting to note that the portfolio assessment system implemented during the 1994–95 school year looked, on the surface, much
different from both the state system and the district system. Both the
state and the district systems relied on "snapshots" of performance to
make evaluations, bubbles or not; the portfolio system relied on data
collected over time. Both the state and district systems prescribed content and task dimensions for students and teachers; the portfolio system required student self-selection of content and self-development of
task dimensions. Both the state and district systems intruded into the
classroom and brought with them external packages of materials and
ideas for collecting data; the portfolio system relied on ordinary classroom work as it actually was done for purposes of learning.

But in important ways the portfolio system was not all that different from the state and district systems. In all three cases students
were expected to conform to values spelled out in the assessment system. In all three cases teachers were expected to fashion instruction in
alignment with those values. In all three cases the assessment system
had been born of political agreements which located power outside the
classroom. In short, regardless of the form of assessment and the shape
of the values inherent in it, all three assessment systems were socially
and politically situated and demanded compliance.

The traditional, autonomous classroom-evaluation system was
really the different creature. In this system values were not spelled out;
they were fluid and idiosyncratic, and they could change on a
moment's notice. In this system teachers did not fashion instruction to
align with assessment values; instead, teachers could shape instruction
as they wished and then look at values. In this system there were no
specific agreements among the adults in charge beyond the mandate
that everyone would use the credit-granting machinery of the institution. Power was located within the classroom. Because values in these
classrooms could and did change to fit new situations, they were perhaps more amenable than the portfolio values to change in response to
exhortation from external others who occupied positions of power—
hence, *Tom Sawyer* could become the site of a multiple-choice worksheet, and Leslie had to die in the creek.

Assessment as Political, Not Scientific, Activity

If this study does nothing else, it provides compelling empirical support for an important theoretical notion developed in the recent literature on educational assessment and evaluation (McDonnell, 1994):

Educational assessment and evaluation is *not* a rational and principled search for truth—at least not as it was practiced in California between 1983 and 1995. At every level of organization, as we have seen, assessment in California during this period operated in accordance with political agreements among those with power—the classroom teacher, the principal, the superintendent, and so on. What the assessment measured—the "truth" in all of this—depended on a vote or a signature. Yet nothing in a percentile rank, a normal curve equivalent, or a grade suggested such "truth."

Looked at in this light, the whole era seems absurd and bizarre, rife with inconsistencies and anomalies. On the one hand, Superintendent Honig repeatedly expressed the view that test validity is a social construct and a site for power to make itself manifest. The unabashed California view was that what tests measure ought to represent what those in power consider useful and important. On the other hand, the results of tests were reported as estimates of some universally "true" score, and decisions about lives were made on the basis of such scores as if the "truth" had been seen.

Psychometricians and statisticians can turn cognitive cartwheels trying to establish an assessment's reliability as an instrument for discovering the truth. But reliability is irrelevant in light of the real question: Whose version of the truth? Whose construction of the construct undergoing assessment? As Honig (1987) understood all too well, assessment and evaluation in California were ideological enforcement tools designed to evoke compliance. Any other psychometric concern was simply a veil of scientific respectability. Honig could use these tools to enforce acceptance of his version of truth. What he didn't understand, however, was that his version of truth was a deeply contested version, even within his own camp, even among those who thought they were with him.

Just as power is layered in concentric circles bounded by political agreements, the assessment tools examined in this book were layered and tailored to their specific uses within particular circles. Of interest is that within each circle, participants cared about their own tests, but they cared little about tests owned by the next higher or lower circle. The state, for example, cared about CAP/CLAS while the system existed, but not about standardized tests. The district cared about standardized tests, was irritated by CAP/CLAS, and ignored classroom evaluation practices. The classroom teachers cared about CAP/CLAS to the degree that it promoted their version of the truth, but the portfolio teachers were profoundly concerned about the results from the portfolio assessment—and they cared little about the district's standardized tests. Instructional conflicts arose because each circle had its own values and goals; when these values and goals coincided, things were fine. When they didn't, problems arose. Particularly important is that political agreements rarely crossed the boundaries of the circles—the norm was for agreements to be reached among members of the same circle.

All of the tools, however, from each circle of power, were significant factors in the lives of the students who worked and learned at Charles Ruff Middle School. The tools were significant because they gave control to more powerful individuals who defined and imposed literacy values on students. Ruff students, presumably the most important players in the game, had no opportunity to participate in truth making. The following table depicts important aspects of relationships among individuals involved in Ruff education as those relationships were linked to assessment tools:

Table 2. Assessment Power Tools

	Nonportfolio Classroom Evaluation	Portfolio Classroom	District Test	State CAP/CLAS
Control	individual teachers	teacher collective	district officials	state officials
Subjects	students	students, teachers	teachers, principals	district officials, principals
Consequences for Subjects	graduation, quality of life	graduation, quality of life, reputation	recrimination, employment opportunities, resources	recrimination, employment opportunities, real estate values

This table shows that individuals who occupied the sites of control of a particular assessment practice held power in the form of consequences over the subjects of each practice—real, tangible power over important personal aspects of life. In most instances, the subjects had little control and virtually no reciprocal power over the owner of the assessment practice. Individual teachers in the nonportfolio classrooms, for example, could determine whether students advanced in the institution and whether they were given privileges at home. Students, however, had no control over what would be assessed; they had no power to alter circumstances for the teacher. Principals, who were under the thumbs of district officials, could determine whether a particular teacher was given a preferred or a disliked teaching assignment (recall Maria's loose grip on eighth grade). Particular teachers, however, had no structural power over the principal (although, as we have seen, it sometimes took carpet to make the principal's power understood).

There were important differences in the relationship between the controller and the subjects of classroom evaluation systems with respect to portfolio versus nonportfolio classrooms. Although the portfolio students were subject to the same consequences as nonportfolio students, the portfolio students had a bit more control over their assessment than the nonportfolio students had, in that the portfolio students selected work for evaluation and explained their own views of its worth. Moreover, the portfolio students were given greater control over their work processes and products simply because the assessment system itself built that control into its ideology.

Of importance is that the portfolio students did have some measure of power over their teachers. The portfolio teachers felt as though they themselves were undergoing assessment during portfolio scoring sessions; their reputations and professional self-worth were on the line, especially important elements because these teachers had agreed in public that the values of the assessment were their values. Also of interest is that principals and district officials probably felt that their reputations and professional self-worth were on the line with respect to the district's standardized tests—perhaps even the state tests. However, neither the principal nor the district leadership had taken an active role in specifying the values of the standardized testing system.

However, each assessment tool both reflected and shaped the values of its owner. Individual teachers, for example, used an autonomous tool, the traditional grading system, and could mold it in whatever fashion they liked. The teacher collective that owned the portfolio system reached agreement with respect to its values and located them on the rubric. Although not every teacher agreed with every value, there was enough agreement to bring coherence to the group. District officials may or may not have defined their own values for themselves as the portfolio teachers had done. But the standardized multiple-choice tests that they had used for many years had been chosen by these leaders and so embodied their values just as vigorously as the portfolio rubric embodied the teacher collective's values. The state clearly had gone to great lengths to establish its own values in the form of framework documents. Despite the mismatch between the state's approach to core literature and the CLAS reading test, the perception was that the test reflected the state's values.

Curiously, traditional classroom evaluation practices had remained largely untouched through all of these efforts at assessment-driven reform. Ruff district officials as well as principals had long permitted each teacher to develop his or her own individual grading standards. District administrators had always spelled out general curricular directions in alignment with the standardized test system, whatever textbooks had been adopted, and state frameworks. But teachers had discretion to emphasize topics and to implement instructional practices as desired—if they could manage to keep their standardized test scores up.

The schoolwide credit-granting machinery—one credit per class period, use of letter grades, etc.—held for every teacher regardless of content area, but teachers could decide to grade whatever they wished according to whatever weighted scale they devised. As Crooks (1988) pointed out in a summary of research on classroom evaluation practices, this laissez faire attitude toward classroom evaluation is common, despite the power classroom evaluation practices hold over students:

> Classroom evaluation affects students in many different ways. For instance, it guides their judgment of what is important to learn, affects their motivation and self-perceptions of competence, structures their approaches to and timing of personal study . . . , consolidates learning, and affects the development of enduring learning strategies and skills. [Yet] . . . classroom evaluation currently appears to receive less thought than most other aspects of education. Its power to affect students is not widely perceived or discussed. A more professional approach to evaluation would demand regular and thoughtful analysis by teachers of their personal evaluation practices, greater use of peer review procedures, and considerable attention to the establishment of expectations and criteria within and among educational institutions. (p. 467)

It would be a mistake, in my view, to assume that teachers interested in using portfolios in their classrooms are also automatically interested in "greater use of peer review procedures" to ensure effective evaluation practices, or in "the establishment of expectations within and among educational institutions" to create coherence in terms of grading criteria. In fact, according to data collected by Murphy (personal communication) in connection with the first-year field trial of the New Standards Project, teachers often completely disassociate student portfolios from grading schemes, though some teachers rely on portfolios to form a small portion of classroom data taken into account when report-card grades are issued.

When Jennifer Johnson first began to explain the Ruff portfolio-assessment system to colleagues from other schools with whom she was involved in a teacher-research group, she found that they were surprised, skeptical, even shocked that Ruff English teachers would use student portfolios as the basis for an entire student report-card grade. After all, how could students choose pieces of work that were *truly* meaningful to them if they had to simultaneously choose pieces of work that would meet external evaluation standards? How could students *own* a portfolio put together according to the specifications of more powerful others? How could portfolios maintain their status as counterhegemonic, emancipatory instructional tools if they were embedded within the controlling, credit-granting function of the institution?

Evidence collected in this study indicates that Crooks (1988) was probably right that (1) classroom evaluation practices affect students powerfully, and (2) classroom evaluation practices are not widely discussed nor analyzed. This conclusion could be broadened to include assessment practices from the other circles as well; that is, those practices also have powerful effects and are also analyzed little if at all. Data from this study strongly suggest that classroom evaluation practices associated with the portfolio-assessment system at Ruff did, indeed, influence student motivations, self-perceptions, and learning strategies in important ways. Findings also suggest that schools could improve their motivational climate if teachers were encouraged to bring their evaluation practices into the light of collaborative dialogue. Quantitative analysis of an achievement-motivation survey that was administered to both traditional and portfolio students (see Underwood, 1995) revealed a significant difference between the groups, with portfolio students registering approximately two points higher than traditional students on a scale assessing the degree to which students put forth effort in order to learn.

Achievement Motivation and Ruff Portfolios

Why was there a difference between the groups on the learning-orientation scale? A part of the explanation probably derives from the nature of the evaluation system itself as it was implemented in the portfolio classrooms. On the one hand, in the traditional classrooms, teachers occasionally taught students to apply one or more of the state direct-writing rubrics to particular student compositions, but grades did not reflect those rubrics. We have seen that grades were issued for idiosyncratic reasons. On the other hand, portfolio students were explicitly taught, and they discussed, how grades for their work products would be determined; they were taught to apply the same holistic, external standards to qualities of their work products that would be applied by the examination committee.

For example, as writers, they were taught that the examination committee would evaluate compositions on the basis of how well organized they were; whether they were composed for a variety of purposes with careful attention, in the final copy, to conventions of usage, spelling, etc. As readers, they were taught how to demonstrate transfer of strategies from whole-group, direct instruction to work products from self-selected readings. They were taught how to demonstrate their having constructed rich and complex meanings through transactions with texts. This work occupied center stage in the portfolio classrooms for both teachers and students.

Students were also taught how grades for their work *processes* would be determined. In this evaluation scheme, how students went about their work, how they planned and revised their plans, and what they learned from monitoring their processes counted just as much as products counted. They were taught that their grade depended partly upon their capacity to set their own learning goals, to make plans for the accomplishment of those goals, to monitor and self-assess their work processes and products, and to articulate what they learned from their effort. Borrowing a page from the portfolio system developed in Pittsburgh in connection with Arts PROPEL (Wolf, 1987), this portfolio system weighed reflective analysis quite heavily, and it was possible for students to create less than stellar products while still earning passing grades—so long as they could demonstrate their seriousness and intention to learn.

This portfolio-evaluation system privileged academic behaviors that demonstrated a learning orientation (complex goals, reflective analysis, etc.). Ironically, the power to privilege these behaviors came from *the attachment of letter grades to these behaviors*. In other words, an institutional mechanism, which encouraged an advancement orientation, appeared to lay at the foundation of the portfolio-evaluation system, which encouraged a learning orientation. Because students were taught that advancement in the Ruff portfolio system depended on developing a learning goal orientation, the portfolio system succeeded in stimulating a learning goal orientation.

Of importance is that quantitative evidence discussed elsewhere (Underwood, 1995) suggests not *just* that the portfolio students adopted a more intense learning orientation, but also that they actually *learned* more, at least about reading as reading was defined by the local open-ended test patterned after CLAS. Although some portfolio advocates have maintained that the phrase "portfolio assessment" is an oxymoron, evidence from this study of the linkage between letter grades and portfolios at Ruff suggests that the application of external standards coupled with judgments of consequence tapped two arguably healthy motivational orientations: the urge to improve one's status *and* the urge to learn.

As educational psychologists and anthropologists of education alike have pointed out (e.g., Midgley, 1993; Ogbu, 1992), students' achievement goal orientations are influenced by broad sociocultural and historical forces located both inside and outside the school. Changes in isolated classroom practices are likely not powerful enough to interfere with such deep forces as, say, family views on the value of schooling or student perceptions of the connection between school and employment (e.g., MacLeod, 1987). Although some theorists maintain that changes in whole-school culture may make a difference (e.g., Anderman & Maehr, 1994), the power of the school is probably not equal to the broad-based influence of the society of which the school is but a part.

Indeed, students at Ruff claimed on the achievement-motivation survey that often they exerted effort because they believed that such effort would contribute to advancing their status socially and economically over the long run, an orientation that likely grows from the very roots of American society (Collins, 1979). Certainly, the explanation for the intense advancement orientation measured by the motivation survey, a much stronger orientation at Ruff than either the learning or approval orientations, derived not from any experimental intervention done at Charles Ruff. Charles Ruff's administration implemented no special schoolwide plans during the 1994–95 school year to boost the advancement goal orientation. Moreover, the advancement-orientation scale registered equally strong scores in both portfolio and traditional classrooms, indicating that the classroom assessment system in place in these different classrooms had no impact on the students' advancement orientation.

Theorists disagree about the use of methods like letter grades and honor rolls, designed to encourage students to adopt an advancement orientation, as strategies for stimulating exertion of effort to learn in school. For one thing, such strategies may work for middle-class students, but not for students from other socioeconomic backgrounds. For example, in his ethnography of working-class Italian-American teenagers on the East Coast, MacLeod (1987) theorized that many poor youths learn from their life experiences to reject connections between the "achievement ideology" found in schools and later socioeconomic success. Rejecting the message that good grades and high school diplomas translate into better lives, MacLeod's children of poverty instead read their futures in the lives of adults inhabiting their social landscape who had earned passing marks in school but had never gained their economic footing. "Aspirations" among these children became "leveled" over time as they came to understand that regardless of how hard one worked in school, life in the project seemed not to change. Honor rolls and good student banquets held no allure.

On the other hand, Hayamizu and Weiner (1991) approached the issue of advancement from a different perspective. These theorists argued that "advancement" is just one of three distinguishable goal "tendencies," none of which is in itself either good or bad, and that other theorists must look more carefully at their assumptions before they make value judgments regarding the efficacy and morality of stimulating an advancement orientation:

> We think the meaning of the performance goal as defined by Dweck and Leggett (1988) [who argued that this goal orientation is maladaptive intellectually, morally, and personally] is somewhat different from ours. . . . We do not assume that the learning goal tendency is socially desirable, whereas the performance goal tendencies to gain approval and to advance in school are socially undesirable. (p. 227)

Earlier, theorists like Dweck and Leggett had implied, in varying degrees, that learning and advancement/approval orientations are mutually exclusive. The suggestion was that schools ought to develop practices to encourage learning orientations while simultaneously eliminating practices that encourage advancement/approval orientations (see Covington, 1992, p. 259; also, Midgley, 1993). In alignment with findings showing decreases in intrinsic motivation when extrinsic incentives are introduced (Deci, 1975), this perspective would suggest that by eliminating practices such as honor rolls, which stimulate advancement/approval orientations, schools might boost intrinsic motivation to learn. However, Hayamizu and Weiner (1991) surveyed college students and found that learning and performance goal orientations can co-occur; students often exert effort for many reasons, including the desire to learn and the desire to improve one's status in life. Framing the issue in an "either/or" format distorts the options open to schools.

Clearly, this debate will not be settled here. Grades and academic rituals are political issues. But in my view, MacLeod's (1987) convincing analysis of leveled aspirations speaks to a need for schools to recognize that children of poverty may *not* respond to practices that are aimed at stimulating the advancement goal orientation—the kinds of practices on which Ruff and many other schools with large populations of poor children typically rely. For these children, the connection between what Covington (1992) termed "the star-spangled scramble for grades" (p. 259) and employment may not exist. The consequences for subjects of the classroom assessment system—advancement in the institution, privileges at home, a good job in the future—simply do not seem real. For these children, an assessment system aimed at stimulating a learning goal orientation wherein self-satisfaction and personal interest drive exertion of effort is probably a better option. As we have seen here, such a system can exist within the traditional institutional-advancement mechanisms.

Making Assessment Ethical and Useful

When the portfolio project ended in June 1995, the English Department decided that it would embrace the portfolio rubric across all of its classrooms and that each teacher would implement the kind of instruction implied by the system to the degree that she or he could make it fit, particularly in the area of reading instruction. In short, the teachers decided that they would support students in making the transformation from either a nonreader or an escapist reader to a serious student of thought-provoking literature; that they would help students set complex goals for themselves as readers and learn to self-assess both their processes and products; that they would invite students to act as if they were serious and literate human beings who know how to make and interpret texts deeply and personally. Moreover, they agreed to take a hard look at their writing curriculum with a view toward its revision. Of importance is that this decision was made on the basis of both quantitative and qualitative data gathered on site over the course of the 1994–95 school year. This decision was not made by individuals at a distance from the school, nor did it have the effect of marginalizing anyone.

But district administrators did not know what had happened during the portfolio project. Unlike the reading program in the History Department, which caused the principal to send image-building documents to the district office, the portfolio project had received little attention from the decision makers. What seemed even more puzzling from the perspective of the portfolio teachers, as they expressed their sentiments in end-of-project interviews, district administrators did not appear to want to know. The portfolio-project teachers had entered into the experiment during the 1994–95 school year with passionate intensity, hoping to make school better for their students. Consider what Maria Madsen wrote in her application letter for one of the portfolio-project positions:

> Through close examination of student work, I have come to realize that our present system of assessment is crippling student growth and achievement. Grades have been put upon students as inescapable laws, and the formulas for fulfilling these requirements are unclear to both students and teachers. In the meantime students scramble to please their teachers, the bestowers of grades, busily completing projects and composing essays in order to pass courses. Our classrooms have become wastelands for students who are fulfilling purposes that belong not to them but to their teachers.

Like Maria, Martha also addressed the issue of students' needs in her letter of application:

> Most of the students I have seen are not aware of themselves as learners because they are dependent on teachers. Traditional methods of schooling and assessment produce a dependence on teachers by students. Students are conditioned to believe that we have all the right answers and therefore, own the right to judge. I think they begin to regard our answers as more important than their questions. Students forget their questions and begin to look for answers we already agree with. The wisdom is in the question, not in the answer. True learners welcome the questions that come from questions rather than answers. I see the [portfolio project] allowing students to become independent learners by making standards known and then allowing the teacher to act as a coach and fellow learner, rather than a judge.

Guba and Lincoln (1989) argued that evaluation ought to start and end with the "claims, concerns, and issues" of stakeholders—that the claims and issues raised by individuals within each circle ought to be taken seriously. If district administrators had observed this principle, they would have first articulated their own claims and issues with respect to their own effectiveness in promoting student learning. They would have spelled out what they had been doing, how they had been doing those things, and where they perceived those actions to be effective or ineffective. Assessment practices would then have been directed toward gathering and analyzing data to illuminate their claims and issues in order to help them improve.

These administrators could have observed and interviewed teachers and students at each of the schools under their supervision in order to learn what the claims, concerns, and issues were for those individuals. Such an approach would have given the administrators the opportunity to really understand the schools from the point of view of those who lived and worked in them. Administrators would have learned, if they had applied Guba and Lincoln's hermeneutic circle, about the reality of the Charles Ruff school, including teachers' concerns that "the formulas for fulfilling these requirements [i.e., grades] [were] unclear to both students and teachers" and that "most of the students [Martha had] seen [were] not aware of themselves as learners because they [were] dependent on teachers." The administrators could then have explored these concerns to determine how widespread they were among teachers and students; they could have gathered data to analyze in an effort to understand their dynamics. They could then have played their findings back to the site in an effort to help it improve.

Instead of channeling its resources into handbooks and conferences and tools of intimidation, the state could have made its own claims about its activities. How, for example, were state officials promoting student learning? Was there evidence of effective and ineffective practices? And what claims did legislators make with respect to their contributions? Assessment practices could have been implemented to discover whether actions were accomplishing what they were supposed to accomplish. Lines of communication across the circles would have had to have opened; considerable data would have had to have been collected and analyzed; changes could have been proposed on the basis of knowledge of realities rather than on inferences based upon psychometric instruments.

Guba and Lincoln (1989) offered a series of arguments in favor of grounding evaluation processes in the lives of stakeholders:

> These five arguments seem to us to be compelling reasons for insisting upon the use of stakeholder claims, concerns, and issues as focal organizers for evaluation: the fact that stakeholders are placed at risk by an evaluation and, thus in the interest of fairness, deserve to have input into the process; the fact that evaluation exposes stakeholders to exploitation, disempowerment, and disenfranchisement so that they, in the interest of self-defense, are entitled to some control of the process; the fact that

stakeholders represent a virtually untapped market for the use
of evaluation findings that are responsive to self-defined needs
and interests; the fact that the inclusion of stakeholder inputs
greatly broadens the scope and meaningfulness of an inquiry
and contributes immeasurably to the dialectic so necessary if
evaluation is to have a positive outcome; and the fact that all
parties can be mutually educated to more informed and sophisticated personal constructions as well as enhanced appreciation
of the constructions of others. (p. 57)

These arguments are embedded in four standards of quality of a
particular act of assessment, as articulated by Guba and Lincoln (1989):
ontological, educative, catalytic, and tactical authenticity (pp. 248–250).
"Ontological authenticity" is achieved if the evaluation has "improved,
matured, expanded, and elaborated" the understanding stakeholders
have of their own circumstances. "Educative authenticity" is achieved
when individuals' "understanding of and appreciation for the constructions of others outside their stakeholding group are enhanced."
"Catalytic authenticity" is achieved when "action is stimulated and
facilitated" among stakeholders by the evaluation. And "tactical
authenticity" is achieved when "participants [are] fully empowered to
act at the consummation of the negotiation process."

It is probably true that district administrators in the Ruff district
would like to improve the understandings of teachers and principals, to
enhance understandings among various groups of stakeholders in the
school community, to stimulate action, and to empower teachers and
principals to do what must be done to help students learn. It is also
probably true that the Ruff standardized test system is not an adequate
method to achieve those ends. What is unclear is the extent to which the
patterns of control and influence operating in the Ruff district, which
created this inadequacy, also operate in other districts. If this pattern
is widespread, then one could argue that a root internal cause of
California's problems with schools derives from the fact that the organizing concerns of evaluation feeding into decision-making processes
do not represent the concerns of those who actually work in classrooms
and on campuses, but rather the concerns of those who make important
decisions from long distance without firsthand knowledge.

Assessment systems have two cycles of influence on curriculum
and instruction: Data from their application describe the past while
principles from their design prescribe the future. Though many at all
levels in the Ruff district professed a belief that the district's norm-
referenced assessment system as well as the state's assessment system
ought to provide teachers with information useful in strengthening

day to day instruction, I encountered no evidence in the field record to support the claim that teachers acting on their own behalf actually did look at test scores as the impetus for specific instructional behaviors. Therefore, description of past student performance (cycle one) seemed less than useful.

But the curriculum that teachers implemented in their classrooms was heavily influenced by the design of tests (cycle two). What happened at Ruff regarding writing instruction after CAP is evidence of that claim. Ironically, curriculum and instruction had been shaped in important ways by test design as preparation for future testing. When those future test scores came back to the site, however, they would be used as tools of intimidation, not as data to inform decision making.

Although the portfolio assessment system was flawed, the system provided teachers not only with a curricular frame. It also provided teachers with a rich source of data that were factored into their day to day instructional decision making. The following segment from a thinkaloud taped by Jennifer Johnson, as she looked through a set of scored portfolios, provides a simple but powerful example of this:

> *Jennifer:* "What a story!" [the examination teacher] says. [Jennifer is reading from the written commentary prepared by the examination teacher for the student.] "But I don't see any drafts. I realize it's a long story." Yep. These guys just don't get revision. Hopefully, that's something I can work on next trimester.

A number of assessment theorists have argued that designers of assessment systems ought to show evidence that data from an assessment actually result in positive changes in instruction. Fredrickson and Collins (1989), for example, referred to the need to demonstrate "systemic validity," a notion which takes into account instructional changes brought about by the use of the test. Lucas (1988a) called for a shift from an accountability model to an ecological model of assessment. The accountability model puts a premium on getting good scores in a cost-effective manner without regard for "what that effort does to the teacher, the learner, or the curriculum" (Lucas, 1988a, p. 1). To ensure that assessment systems do not damage what they seek to measure, Lucas suggested "a radical shift [in the] worldview in which learning is done in the service of evaluation to one in which evaluation is done in the service of learning; from teaching to the test to testing for teaching" (p. 2). In an article exploring both reliability and validity in assessment, Moss (1994) advocated Darling-Hammond and Snyder's term "professional model of accountability," wherein assessment involves "seek[ing] evidence that teachers are engaging in collaborative inquiry to make knowledge-based decisions that respond to individual student needs" (p. 8).

Discussions among teachers about what students are really up to, what students are really learning, are evidence of a useful link between instruction and assessment. The portfolio project at Charles Ruff seemed to engage the English teachers who participated in it—including the examination teachers and the portfolio teachers themselves—more deeply and seriously in a thoroughgoing examination of their practices and their students than any of the teachers had ever experienced in connection with any other assessment system. As Maria suggested in an interview near the end of the project year, the portfolio-assessment system provided data that helped her understand herself (ontological authenticity) and the views of other stakeholders (educative authenticity), and data that stimulated (catalytic authenticity) and empowered her (tactical authenticity) to act:

> *Maria:* I've had to look so closely at my assumptions as a
> teacher. What do I really want my kids to do? Who am I
> really as a teacher? What am I asking of people? And every-
> thing comes screaming back at me when portfolios come
> back, and sometimes that's a little bit hard because you
> have to really look carefully at yourself, and I think it's still
> possible to, you know, sugarcoat it because you can look as
> much as you want, and you can stop looking when it hurts
> too much. But it's really forcing me to examine myself, and
> I'm really thinking about which parts of this are important
> to me. And I think . . . for me, having this happen my sec-
> ond year as a teacher was ideal, because I think it's going to
> shape who I am as a teacher for the rest of my life.

In the end, if we are to provide access to mind to the young people least likely to find an easy path, we must be wide awake. This study illustrates that assessment is indeed a value-laden enterprise which has at least as much to do with defining what is learned as it has to do with measuring it. The power to define rests with those who choose assessment practices, a political act fraught with danger. As a society we must learn to make this choice wisely. How? Perhaps we need to learn to assess ourselves before we shift our focus to the assessment of others.

Epilogue:
Three Years Later . . .

TU: It's been three full school years since the portfolio project. You're starting the fourth school year now.

Jennifer: Yeah . . . yeah. [sighs] Seems like much longer, though.

TU: Tell me about that. Why?

Jennifer: Because it's *hard work*. It's very hard work when you do not have the kind of support and time you had when we were doing the pilot project. [Looks at Sylvia] Would you agree with that?

Sylvia [a project-year examination teacher]: Yes.

Jennifer: It's *really* hard work. That's the biggest [reason] . . .

Sylvia [nodding head in agreement]: Um hm . . .

Jennifer: Probably [a reason it seems much longer is] because we have this *body* of collected portfolios from students over all these years that fills boxes and boxes in my garage, and [pointing to a filing cabinet behind her] this filing cabinet is filled with portfolios from last year that I'll empty out and take home, too. And then you have portfolios—I mean, there are portfolios . . . *everywhere!*

It was a warm afternoon in early August 1998, when I went to Jennifer Johnson's portable classroom at Ruff, one of those temporary classrooms which symbolized overcrowding and were really permanent campus fixtures, for an interview with three original project participants. I had not been on the Ruff campus since the summer of 1996, when I left for a teaching position elsewhere. My aim for the interview was to find out what had become of the portfolio system since the project year. Although I was sure that I would hear about portfolios of some sort, chameleons that they are, I also fully expected to hear that the system as it had been practiced in the 1994–95 school year had fallen by the wayside like a piano left behind on a steep trail.

Given that Governor Wilson had successfully leveraged a legislative mandate for a statewide standardized, norm-referenced, multiple-choice test in October 1997 (DeFao, 1998); given that a professor from a California State University college of education with a voice listened to by policymakers had proclaimed that "Portfolios are dead" (Under-wood, 1997); and given that "whole language" and anything associated with it, like portfolios, had been thoroughly discredited in the eyes of the public by politicians and journalists "hooked on phonics" (Woo & Colvin, 1998), I expected at best to hear that remnants of project-year portfolio practices existed here and there, and at worst to hear about distortions or caricatures of the original system. California may have traveled "beyond the bubble" as the decade of the 1990s began (California Education Summit, 1989a, 1989b), but no one could mistake the trip "back to the bubble" that had occurred as the decade ended.

In June 1998, for example, the Department of Education had issued a draft version of a new framework (Simmons & Kameenui, 1998) to guide instruction in a new direction in the public schools. This new framework was decidedly different from the document prepared under Superintendent Honig ten years earlier—so different, in fact, that the title itself had been changed from "English/Language Arts" in 1987 to "Reading/Language Arts" in 1998, a change which captured the profound philosophical shift that had taken place among policy-makers (see McCormick, 1994, for a discussion of the relationship between "reading" and "English").

No longer was there a call in the framework to develop students who would share "a common background of core works that speak to all of us in the American society" (Glass & Gottsman, 1987, p. 6). The 1980s emphasis on literature as a humanizing, socializing force had been replaced by a 1990s emphasis on literacy as a saleable commod-ity. The new framework called on the schools to create students capa-ble of functioning as "knowledge" workers in the twenty-first century to replace a disappearing blue-collar class:

> In 1993, Peter Drucker described the advent of the "knowledge" society, a society in which "knowledge" workers will replace blue-collar workers as the dominant class in the 21st century. According to Drucker, the skills society will require are more sophisticated, print-oriented skills than currently required of the American work force. America will be greatly challenged in general to develop competitive "knowledge" workers. Particularly challenged will be those students we refer to as vul-nerable learners, that is, those children who by virtue of their instructional, socioeconomic, experiential, physiological, and neurological characteristics bring different and often additional requirements to instruction and curriculum (Simmons & Kameenui, 1996). (Simmons & Kameenui, 1998, p. 3)

Honig's concern with "cultural literacy"—in the vein of T. S. Eliot and Matthew Arnold—was gone. In its place was a concern for "the need to develop competence in the English language arts to ensure they will be able to access [listen and read] information with ease, apply [speak and write] language skills at levels demanded by the 21st century, and appreciate the literature and liberty that fluency and flexibility with the English language beholds" (Simmons & Kameenui, 1998, p. 3).

Moreover, the CLAS test's emphasis on the assessment of "resistant" readers—critical readers who not only understood the content of texts, but challenged and probed—was gone. As we have seen, the new framework talked about creating "knowledge" workers in schools that could accommodate the physiological and neurological needs of all learners through the use of research-based, scientific, highly technical instructional scripts. To assess this new aim, the CLAS strategy would be completely inappropriate; the Governor's newly mandated off-the-shelf, multiple-choice model would fit the bill.

This philosophical shift at the state level had had its impact on the Ruff district and on Charles Ruff Middle School. Interview data suggest that the district's use of a common list of works of core literature in every school had been abandoned. Individual schools now were free to select core works for their individual sites—provided that selections could be shown to have the appropriate readability level using the Fry Readability Formula. The following excerpt, in which Jennifer described the nature of discussions about book adoptions, represents what had happened with respect to the district's policy for approval of literary works:

> *Jennifer:* The district was just *adamant* about Fry's Readability level. And . . . a book had to *fry* . . . at a certain grade level. It was just awful!!! Or it couldn't be that level. So we argued and argued and argued about *Giver* because *Giver* moved down to seventh grade because it fried at a seventh-grade level—actually, it fried at a sixth-grade level, readability-wise. But we argued and argued and argued about concept development and the appropriateness of this book for sixth graders. . . .

But as the excerpt presented above from my August 1998 interview with Jennifer Johnson and Maria Madsen and with Sylvia Sampson, a project-year examination teacher, suggests, the set of assessment agreements made by the Ruff English teachers in 1994, and made manifest by examined student portfolios, was not dead, despite its assumption that readability was as much a matter of reader interest, purpose, and persistence as it was a matter of textual linguistic difficulty. "I mean, there are portfolios . . . *everywhere!*" Jennifer said, and when I got the chance to look at some of them, as subsequent data will show, I could see clearly that they were real Ruff portfolios, not cosmetic imitations. Although the system was not what one might call the picture of health, it was nonetheless still alive in the thinking of some of the teachers, and more than a few classrooms of Ruff adolescents were still organized around its values and practices.

Jennifer and Maria, two portfolio teachers from the original project, remained at the site. Martha Goldsmith, the third portfolio teacher, left Ruff in 1996 to finish a master's program and was teaching at a middle school in a northern California town seventy-five miles away. Martha had tried to transplant the system among a resistant faculty—and, according to Maria, a resistant group of parents. Sylvia Sampson and two other original examination teachers still worked at Ruff—one as an English teacher, the second as a special reading teacher—and interview data suggest that the English teacher had been actively using original aspects of the system in some way in her practice each year since the project. Ralph, the fourth examination teacher, left Ruff the year after the project to work elsewhere, and no one knew what had happened to him. Several other English teachers, who had not formally participated in the project but had been working on staff in 1994, had also used aspects of the system in their teaching and had served as examination teachers for their colleagues. Two English teachers hired in 1996 had also decided to "play on our team," as Sylvia put it.

For the past three years, almost all Ruff English students had been "doing portfolios" each year in one fashion or another, though such "doing" was not always faithful to the original system of agreements, particularly not among some of those English teachers with the longest tenure in the department. According to Jennifer, however, only one English teacher refused to use anything that she would categorize as a portfolio practice. Even the newly hired teachers had been brought into the system as both portfolio and examination teachers. Although not all of the teachers who were using the system made the portfolio grade the sole determiner of the report-card grade, many had continued "swapping portfolios" at the end of each trimester to examine the student work of their colleagues, to write commentary, and to issue a portfolio grade using the rubric.

So there were several holdouts among the English faculty who resisted, as Sylvia said, "play[ing] on our team," but only one adamant refusal. Maria and Sylvia believed that part of the resistance could have been minimized if things had been done differently during the first year following the project. During that year, English Department policy had called for all teachers to use the system, but in a modified form, a plan which Sylvia described as flawed:

> *Sylvia:* To get them to do a portfolio, we said they could do one that represented the entire year, but no one took the time to develop a rubric that could be used for a yearlong portfolio, which would be very different from the rubric that is in place for the trimester portfolios. And that turned all those people off.

Whether the reason was this lack of fit between the trimester rubric and the end-of-year portfolio or something else, Maria and Sylvia agreed that neither those teachers who refused to join "the team"—nor their students—truly understood what the system was intended to do and therefore had little chance of ever accepting its assumptions:

> *Maria:* Those people didn't have the criteria in mind when they were asking kids to write entry slips and create entries, and so there were no goals, there were no challenging books, there were—you know, it was all very superficial, and the kids would get their portfolios back and get C's and D's, and then those teachers would think, well, this is bad, because my A students are getting D's.
>
> *Jennifer:* It [the system] doesn't work.
>
> *Maria:* Yeah.
>
> *Sylvia:* So when they [students] came to me from seventh grade and I had their portfolios, I had to explain to them, OK, now, did you set goals? And they'd say no, and so I'd say, so, automatically, *this* is all going to be low. Now, that's all going to go up immediately, because the first thing we do in here is set goals, and I'd have to explain to them how it didn't work when they put their yearlong portfolio together as a seventh grader—and *why* it didn't work—because they came in with that immediate negative, "I get an A in English and this is a D," you know.
>
> *Maria:* It's like the instrument was faulty rather than the music. Is that a good analogy?

Maria's analogy, together with Sylvia's comments, suggests that the instrument—the portfolio system—had been tuned and was ready for playing in concert; indeed, it could produce great music if it were properly played. But the music that came from it—the actual student work—was out of tune because the musicians—the teachers—didn't know how to play the instrument. For Sylvia, however, the instrument itself had not been properly prepared for the musicians. The department had given the teachers permission to play a different instrument altogether—a yearlong portfolio—and what was worse, the department had not specified a rubric for the alternate instrument's music. In the end, the mismatch led to the creation of music which sounded unsurprisingly little like what people expected to hear.

The evidence I am about to present will show quite clearly that the system as an instrument was, in fact, designed to create a particular kind of music, that is, the particular set of beliefs, values, habits, and competencies discussed in Chapter 7. It will also show that new Ruff teachers not involved in the system's original design and implementation learned to play the instrument quite well. This point is important because it suggests that local professional portfolio cultures can be entered successfully by newcomers, and that newcomers can become respected participants. The evidence—Maria might say the "music"—comes from what I consider a highly valid and reliable source: Actual student portfolios created by a student of a new teacher.

During the 1996–97 school year, the second year after the original project, Charles Ruff hired a new English teacher in her first year of practice, whom we will call Kathy Currie, to teach seventh-grade block classes. According to Maria, Kathy Currie did not understand how to use the portfolio system at first, but she learned by way of an apprenticeship. Most important, she learned by reading portfolios created by students of more experienced portfolio teachers who had internalized the system:

> *Maria:* So for staff development, I mean, for new teachers like
> [Kathy], who was curious and who wanted to do better but
> didn't quite understand how to make the portfolio work—
> she read people's portfolios and she said, "Oh! That's how
> you—That's how you—" and she just. . . . She was able to
> learn so much just by looking at other people and how
> other people approached the process.

To illustrate how Kathy Currie implemented the portfolio system in her seventh-grade classes, I will present data from the portfolios of one of her students, whom we will call Lori. As it happened, Lori went on to eighth grade and had Jennifer Johnson as a teacher. Because Lori was a student of the portfolio system in seventh grade and again in eighth grade, and because Jennifer Johnson kept Lori's portfolios in her filing cabinet (with the exception of the seventh-grade first-trimester portfolio, which is missing), I can present data with respect to Lori's growth over a two-year period. These data are related to her growth as a reader.

Lori's autobiography written for the winter 1997 portfolio scoring period contains clear evidence that Lori's teacher had devoted class time to goal-setting activities and that Lori responded. Lori wrote the following:

> Dear Evaluation Teacher,
>
> My reading goal for the second trimester is to explore mysteries and compare them with horror books to see the differences and similarities. I came to select this goal when I saw a mystery movie and I wanted to read the book.

As we have seen in the 1994–95 data, Ruff students were generally fascinated by horror, and Lori was no exception. We have also seen that Ruff students tended to begin their portfolio experiences either as non-readers or as leisure-escape readers. Lori read for leisure and escape.

Lori's goal statement represents a turning point for her as a reader and, as we will see, the beginning of a willingness to cross genre boundaries. She had experience with books by R. L. Stine and Christopher Pike, and she knew what to expect from them. Moreover, she knew how to apply her knowledge of horror to other books of the genre not written by Stine or Pike, as the following excerpt from a text-log entry dated October 15, 1996, illustrates (in this entry Lori was responding to a book titled *Sorority Sister* by Diane Hoh):

> This book is a Nightmare Hall book by Diane Hoh. This author seems familiar to me, but I never remember reading any books written by her, except this one. Nightmare Hall is like how R. L. Stine's books are. Like his are Fear Street and Diane Hoh's are Nightmare Hall. I can't really see why I shouldn't read this book because it seems like a good book and it is a thriller.

Although we can see in Lori's goal statement the beginning of a boundary crossing, this excerpt also shows that Lori resists the message from the portfolio culture that she change her habits and values as a reader: "I can't really see why I shouldn't read this book." Readers interested in generalizable points might note that this resistance was identified in the data during the original project (see "Between Two Worlds" in chapter 8); here it has been found again in the student of a new teacher.

Lori agreed to broaden her experiences with horror to include mystery, but she did not know what to expect from the new genre, nor did she know how to negotiate it. Ironically, though she enjoyed reading horror because it gave her "chills" (a word she used in a text-log entry), what really frightened her was trying something new. The following excerpt was taken from her second-trimester autobiography and appeared just after her goal statement:

> As I began to work to achieve my goal, I realized that I didn't know what kind of authors I should go for. I was scared if I tried a new author, I wouldn't enjoy it or it doesn't interest me. But I knew I had to try something new. So I started to explore new authors. . . . I learned that if I don't like the book, I can always abandon it and try something else.

It is hard to know from her portfolio what, precisely, Lori feared from discovering that a new author bored her. This excerpt may illustrate a common, if perhaps hidden, attitude about reading, that is, that it is somehow bad to begin a book and not finish it. Lori may have been afraid that she would be morally obligated to finish a book she didn't like, but she learned that such was not the case. This excerpt underlines the important role for ongoing assessment of a broad range of reading behaviors, especially among adolescents—in Lori's case, her assumption that once a reader selects a book, the reader must read it regardless of her interest in it.

To support the judgment of a high grade, the Ruff autobiography must go beyond merely making goal statements. Like students from the original portfolio-project year, Lori included language in her autobiography to help the examination teacher determine how well she had met her goals:

> My greatest accomplishment for this trimester was that I was able to explore different kinds of authors and genres. It is my greatest accomplishment because I finally got some nerves to try something different. . . .

Consider what might have happened to Lori's "nerve" had she not been in a classroom where abandonment was discussed and understood. If her personal reading habits had been separate from her reading instruction, as has often been the case in canon-driven or anthology-driven English instruction, she would likely have stayed close to books within the horror genre for quite some time.

Lori's "nerve" to try a new author and a new genre emerged in mid-seventh grade and was recognized and commented upon by her second-trimester examination teacher, a teacher who, like Lori's regular teacher, was fairly new to teaching. This examination teacher, who had been at Charles Ruff during the original project year as a long-term substitute and was later hired permanently, reinforced Kathy Currie's

work with Lori by urging Lori to go further with her reading, a reinforcement that sustained Lori through eighth grade. The following is
an excerpt from Lori's seventh-grade second-trimester commentary:

> In reading—what wonderful responses! You are giving evidence
> that you are reading, thinking and learning! I agree with [your
> teacher's] comments—you are definitely ready to move on to
> more challenging literature. This time you took quite a leap in
> your writing. Next trimester make a leap in your reading.

By the time that the spring 1997 portfolio scoring period had
arrived, Lori had taken another small step. In the previous portfolio,
she presented evidence of a struggle between familiar and unfamiliar
kinds of books, but she also had tried to broaden her interest in horror
ever so slightly by inching toward a sister genre, mystery. Third
trimester, Lori took an even bigger risk:

> Dear Evaluation teacher,
>
> For the third trimester, I set reading goals that were connected
> to my writing goals. This way it shows that I am going for com-
> plex goals. Also, my reading goal has two parts to it. My read-
> ing goal is to explore biographies of singers and other famous
> people, *and* compare the author's writing style. I came to select
> this goal when I wanted to explore books that weren't horror or
> mystery, so I went with biographies. . . . This stretched me as a
> reader because I am now completely hooked to another genre
> that I have never tried before. I took a shot at it, and it turned out
> that I am enjoying it.

Lori's willingness to risk during the second trimester paid big
dividends in the third trimester. One of the biographies that she
selected was a recommendation from her teacher, a book called *Hunger
of Memory: The Education of Richard Rodriguez.* The following excerpt
from her text logs was dated May 28, 1997. She had read for sixty-five
minutes that evening and had completed pages 63 to 94. Here is her
entry, a letter to Richard:

> Dear Richard,
>
> As I am reading your book, I was wondering how you could
> remember things from when you were in your childhood? I
> mean, it seems so long ago. You still remembered the time you
> were in first grade! I could barely remember what happened
> when I was in first grade. Things from so long ago, like how
> your grandmother's face looked on the day of her funeral, and
> the time you got on the bus with "ghetto black teens," you still
> remember. Is it because they had special meaning to you and

you kept it as a memory? If it is, you must have had a lot of memories kept inside your brain because this book has lots of things from your childhood. It's also good that you *could* remember your childhood so well, because you only get one childhood in a lifetime. You've kept yours really well and are sharing it with people.

Over the course of seventh grade, Lori broadened her reading horizons from a fascination with horror and "chills" to an appreciation of autobiography and "wonder."

Lori moved from Kathy Currie's seventh grade to Jennifer Johnson's eighth grade, but Lori did not leave behind what she had learned. The following excerpt was taken from her autobiography submitted with her first-trimester portfolio:

To start off with, I am an experienced person with portfolios. What I'm writing is an autobiography of myself as a reader and writer. In this letter, you will get to know me more in the areas of reading and writing. . . .

For reading, my goal is to explore Asian culture through reading short stories, novels, and folk tales, written by different Asian writers. I tried to set specific goals so that I know what I am heading toward. I see myself as a hard working reader, where I'm trying to read everyday for a longer period of time, pushing myself. At first I wanted to get away from the stage of reading R. L. Stine and Christopher Pike's horror/mystery books, where I was at the beginning of seventh grade. I do believe I got away from that genre by working hard. I tried to go out and discover new genres and thought about how I could challenge myself with them. . . .

The issue of abandonment, which had arisen in the middle of seventh grade when Lori was just beginning to move away from horror, came up again in her personal reading in this first-trimester eighth-grade portfolio. This time, however, Lori voiced no guilt about her decision to stop a book. On Jennifer's recommendation, Lori started to read *Fahrenheit 451* by Ray Bradbury. Consider the following excerpt from her text-log entry slip for this first eighth-grade portfolio:

Even though I have experimented with different books, I have abandoned two books. The first book was *Fahrenheit 451* by Ray Bradbury. I abandoned this book because I didn't really understand what it was talking about. It was rather complex. The second book was *Manzanar* by John Armor and Peter Wright. I abandoned the book because it didn't keep my interest. I tried really hard to focus on it but just couldn't. There were boring parts and when I was reading it, my mind was thinking "boring, boring." I knew I couldn't go on like that so I discontinued to read on.

Lori's text logs showed clearly that she had stopped reading these books, but she did not record her reasons in her text-log entries. Apparently, Lori added the above comments in her entry slip because Jennifer Johnson had written a comment in the margin of Lori's text logs: "Why did you stop reading?"

Lori's second-trimester goals involved reading memoirs by Annie Dillard, Maxine Hong Kingston, and Joan Didion. Lori wanted to write a memoir and believed that she would do a better job of it if she read works by these authors, who had been recommended to her by her examination teacher and by Jennifer Johnson. The following excerpt from second-trimester text logs illustrates how Lori began crossing boundaries beyond genre boundaries. This entry was written on December 30, 1997, in response to *China Men* by Maxine Hong Kingston:

> I think this part I just read is really interesting because it's about the laws, some of which is related to what I'm learning in history. There's a part about the Constitution and a little about the Fourteenth Amendment saying that it was adopted in 1868 saying naturalized Americans have the same rights as native-born Americans. It also talks about Supreme Court cases where someone was versing another, testing laws against or what the court ruled. . . . When I read about them in here, I think "Hey! What is this? I learned it in history." Wow! This book is not only related to reading, but to history too!!

By the third trimester of eighth grade, Lori appeared to have learned the ultimate lesson from her portfolios. Here is what she wrote in her autobiography:

> Through these two years of goal setting, I found that setting goals will help us accomplish what we set for ourselves and we will know what we're doing. It'll keep us organized in the present and in the future. And that's why I decided that I would continue to set goals in life and in school even though there's no teacher giving me a goals contract. I know that setting goals is a positive thing and there's no need for someone to tell me to do it, for I am doing this for myself.

In seventh grade, Lori learned that as a reader, she had a right to abandon a book if she decided she did not want to read it. In eighth grade, she learned that she also had the right to return to a book she had abandoned. The following excerpt from her third-trimester text logs illustrates this learning with respect to *Fahrenheit 451*:

> First off, to let you know, this is my second time picking this book up. In other words, at the beginning of the trimester, [Jennifer Johnson] recommended this book to me because I

thought about reading it for my reading goal. But I never did read past the first 5 pages because when I read it I couldn't understand it. Now reading it again for the second time I see a difference. I'm past the first few pages, and I am not having trouble in the area of understanding the book. In fact, I kind a like it because in a way it's similar to something I read in the past: *The Giver.* (They're both science fiction.) I think now I'm understanding the book better than the first time because by now I am a strong reader and learn many helpful reading strategies that I'm using to help me deepen my understanding. Right now when I read it, I read very slow to make sure I got everything, . . . I'm glad I got a second chance at the book because I realized that I improved as a reader. I kind of enjoy this book.

Lori started Bradbury's book on March 26, wrote a number of thoughtful text-log entries, and ended the book with a text-log entry on April 16 with the following:

> *Wow!!!* I can't believe I finally was able to finish this book. At first I thought I was never going to finish. . . . What [Bradbury] added to the end of the book, his "Afterward," really helped me catch and learn some things I didn't get while reading the story. For instance, like *owning* books wasn't the crime, it was *reading* them that got you into trouble. . . . If there wasn't [an Afterward] my thoughts and wonders would still be floating everywhere.

Lori's portfolios represent her experiences during the 1996–97 school year with a teacher new to Charles Ruff and during the 1997–98 school year with a portfolio teacher who participated in the original project. Data from her portfolios appear to support the conclusions that (1) the portfolio system had been maintained at Charles Ruff in at least some classrooms; (2) teachers new to the portfolio culture were able to enter it and use the system instructionally to accomplish the same pattern of results that was seen in the original project data; and (3) some sort of systematic, ongoing assessment strategy appears to be almost essential to instruction which aims not just to create competent literacy users, but to impact student engagement and identity as literacy users in schools.

Maria, Jennifer, and Sylvia agreed that the current school year (1998–99) would be the "true test" of the portfolio system. Maria had not been teaching English classes for the past two years but had been assigned to work in a "reading center" where she worked with the school's struggling readers. Sylvia was also assigned to the center for the 1998–99 school year, a move which would also take her out of the English classroom. Moreover, Jennifer would be teaching only two sections of eighth-grade English during the 1998–99 school year; she had been reassigned half-time as the school's reading specialist. This personnel arrangement meant that only one original project participant, an examination teacher, would be teaching English classes. If the system survives the 1998–99 school year, it will be because of the efforts of the original project participants beyond their assigned teaching duties and because of the efforts of the new teachers who have internalized the system.

Perhaps the best way to end this "epilogue" so that my readers aren't left with "thoughts and wonders still floating everywhere"—as Lori expressed her feelings when she finished *Fahrenheit 451*—is with a few words from Jennifer, Maria, and Sylvia. At the following point in the interview, I tried to summarize a few of the minor obstacles in the path of the portfolio system at Ruff for the teachers, in an attempt to find out what the system needed in order to last. Here is how the discussion went:

> *TU:* OK. So let's see here, you have experienced teachers who are not able to do portfolios because they are influenced by their [. . .]s, and then you have new teachers [who student-taught at Ruff] who go out and try to do portfolios at an alternate site and they have to have support groups. What do you need?
>
> *Jennifer* [long pause]: The system needs . . . Portfolios and teaching need time and support. And when we had the pilot year when we had 1274 money, we *had* that. We had each other. We had release time. We had time to score portfolios. It was a *pleasure!*
>
> *Maria:* —well—
>
> *Jennifer* [laughs]: —it *wasn't a pleasure?*
>
> *Maria* [smiles, kiddingly]: No! [short pause] Well, there were parts of it that I didn't like, but . . .
>
> *Jennifer:* But?
>
> *Maria* [speaking to me]: Anyway, it goes back to what you used to say about restructuring, that we need to restructure the whole way we use our time.
>
> *Jennifer:* Yep.
>
> *Maria:* Because what Sylvia and I are finding in the reading center after three weeks—actually after five weeks—not only do *teachers* need to find the support, but *kids* need that, too. They need to have quality time with their teachers to feel supported, and then it seems like with that as a foundation . . . kids who have spent good time with their teachers have gone on feeling a much greater degree of success,

assuming much more risk. They're the kind of kids who would fade into the background in your classroom, and they're doing OK. And it's because you went through it with them and helped them monitor it. And they know where to come when they need help. And . . . I just don't feel like we provide that for students at all. I mean, how can you when you have 150 kids? You can with some, but there's many more that will be lost.

Appendix

Method

Central and subsidiary questions investigated from the perspective of the ethnographer included the following: With reference to the students in the alternative classrooms, what changes in motivation could be observed over the course of the school year? What reasons did students give for exerting effort in their English class over the course of the year? How did students respond to their experiences in the portfolio classrooms? Again with reference to the students in the alternative classrooms, what evidence could be gathered to suggest that students did or did not come to behave in accordance with the role of readers and writers which the portfolio system constructed for them? With reference to the portfolio teachers, what impact would the portfolio-assessment system have on their curriculum and instruction?

The grounded-theory method of ethnographic research as discussed by Schatzman and Strauss (1973) was employed to answer the above questions. This method calls for careful development of a field record with observational, methodological, and theoretical notes which provide a detailed trail of findings linking together all of the elements of the explanatory theory that emerges during analysis with the empirical evidence that gave rise to them.

Gaining permission to enter and study the field occurred as follows: As a credentialed employee of the site who had been elected coordinator of the Performance Assessment Committee (by a vote of the other staff members on that committee, almost two years before the start of the portfolio experiment), I participated in discussions regarding site assessment practices and possible approaches to improving them long before anyone even imagined the experiment which ultimately took place. After almost eighteen months of vigorous debate about the appropriate role of learning outcomes within the school structure, the impact of the traditional grading system on teaching and learning, and other related matters, the assessment committee as a whole formulated a proposal for the portfolio experiment which went forward to the school leadership council for funding and approval.

Having shepherded the proposal through its conception to its final approval, I was named the coordinator of the experiment and was formally assigned by the site administrator to the duties of facilitating the scoring activities and overseeing the collection of data which would be reported to the school. Sometime after this formal assignment, I approached the site principal to secure permission to make use of the database, which I would generate as part of my job assignment, for a much more extensive and reflective purpose, i.e., my dissertation. This administrator was enthusiastically supportive of my request and stated that he believed that the experiment would produce a wealth of information with relevance well beyond the confines of Charles Ruff Middle School, though he agreed that the names of individuals as well as the name of the school and district should be changed in the final report. Subsequently, he assisted me in the process by providing supporting documentation that allowed me to meet the requirements of the Human Subjects Committee at a local university. I discussed the nature of my research with the three English teachers who had volunteered to teach in the portfolio classrooms and was granted virtually free access to their classrooms as well as almost unlimited opportunity to interview them.

In early July 1994, I started establishing a field record in accordance with the method articulated by Schatzman and Strauss (1973). By July 1995, this field record had grown to roughly 1,000 pages of expanded observational, methodological, and theoretical notes, with roughly 200 accompanying pages of analytic and reflective memos. Over the course of this year I observed in the portfolio classrooms for approximately seventy-five hours. During these observations I took raw notes on a portable computer and used a tape recorder to capture verbal data. After each observation, usually within one to two days following the event, I expanded these raw notes and included data recorded on tape. I also conducted and transcribed approximately 200 interviews (including what Schatzman and Strauss term "eavesdropping" and "situational conversation," as well as lengthier and more purposeful interviews) ranging from five minutes to three hours with the portfolio teachers, both separately and in a group, as well as with approximately forty different portfolio students, almost always in groups of three to five students.

During the actual scoring of the portfolios, I tape-recorded and transcribed the thinkalouds of each of the examination teachers in the process of assessing student portfolios, for a total of eight thinkaloud protocols. Data derived from documents included detailed looks at student portfolios in the process of construction as well as during and after assessment sessions; daily readings of the local newspaper for references to the school or to the district in which it sits or to state assessments; and daily readings of school as well as district communications, minutes from meetings, school bulletins, and other texts that appeared fortuitously (such as worksheets or other artifacts of lessons which I happened to find left behind near the site's photocopy machine).

Data analysis proceeded in accordance with the method explained by Schatzman and Strauss. During the development of the field record, I constructed extensive analytic memos that articulated connections among the data as they were being entered or expanded in the record. Each memo was given a title, and many of these titles later became categories in the more formal analysis of the data. Throughout the observational process, I was constantly alert to in vivo codes and kept detailed records of occurrences which I predicted might become categories in the formal analysis.

The formal analysis itself occurred in stages. First, I read through each page of the record, numbering and labeling each observational note; as I did this reading, I attempted to capture the gist of each observational note (or "unit of information" as Schatzman and Strauss termed them, p. 103) on a separate record, which later served as a sort of index to the record. Simultaneously, I entered the number of each observational note on other documents which held the names of codes as they had been spelled out on the analytic memos. Second, with the entire field record reduced to approximately thirty pages, including an index of sorts and a rough coding scheme cross-referenced to the record, I began to evaluate particular units of information to make judgments about which specific items ought to enter the composition. These judgments were made on the basis of several criteria, including the following in order of importance: representativeness (i.e., the degree to which the item accurately represented the category of items); completeness (i.e., the degree to which the item included specific and accurate information); and vividness (i.e., the degree to which the item could be expected to be memorable to the reader as the reader attempts to follow the train of thought).

Writing the report was done in stages. The discussion of portfolios in Chapter 3 was started long before the study actually began and continued to be revised until the final draft was completed. The sociocultural context portion was started during the middle of the 1994–95 school year. Early drafts of it were read by Ruff staff members who had little to do with the portfolio project (the technology coordinator, for example, who is mentioned in the section, read and responded to early versions). Later versions were read by the three portfolio-project teachers; questions regarding unknown or uncertain data were asked of teachers who had been on staff for many years. Each of the qualitative sections was read by the portfolio teachers; their insights and corrections were integrated in the final version. The Ruff principal read and responded to the entire draft in a semifinished form, and his comments were incorporated into the final report. Throughout the process, Sandra Murphy, Carl Spring, and P. David Pearson, members of my dissertation committee, read, reread, and critiqued all sections. This composition process was used to ensure that the empirical data were valid and reliable and that the logic was as sound as I could make it. All interpretations, inferences, and judgments are my responsibility and represent, as Guba and Lincoln (1989) described it, the output of one human instrument.

Grades: Reading	Consistency and Challenge	Control of Processes	Self-Assessment and Reflection	Knowledge and Work Products
A	—reading done habitually almost every day, often for long periods of an hour or so —readings not only entertain, but also challenge and stretch capabilities —reads widely; experiments with new authors and forms	—rereads and revises interpretations —supports views with references to the text —uses a variety of strategies and response types —shows persistence	—sets complex goals for reading and achieves them —applies personal/public criteria and supports judgments —analyzes own processes thoughtfully	—reads like a writer —creates organized, complete, and effective work products —learns new vocabulary regularly —pays attention to literary and stylistic features of texts —interprets shared readings personally and deeply
B	—reading done habitually almost every day, often for shorter periods of time —readings entertain, not so much challenge and stretch capabilities —less experimentation with new forms, though perhaps tries new authors	—tends to stick with one interpretation —supports views but may need to explain more thoroughly —uses less variety of strategies and response types —sometimes shows persistence; sometimes is satisfied when understanding could be improved	—sets complex goals for reading and works to achieve them —applies criteria to texts but with less clear support —analyzes own processes superficially	—creates organized and complete work products —shows some attention to learning new vocabulary —pays less attention to literary and stylistic features of texts —understands shared readings thoroughly

Table A. Reading Rubric

Table A. Reading Rubric (continued)

Grades: Reading	Consistency and Challenge	Control of Processes	Self-Assessment and Reflection	Knowledge and Work Products
C	—reading done at least once or twice a week, often for brief periods of ten to thirty minutes —readings mainly for entertainment —little evidence of concern for experimenting with new authors or forms	—interprets readings superficially —only occasional support for own views —relies on one or two strategies and response types —may give up easily or quickly when bored or challenged	—sets simple goals for reading and achieves them —applies criteria to texts mechanically —analyzes own processes with clichés; may use reflective-type terms with little understanding	—creates only superficially polished ones —occasionally shows interest in learning new vocabulary —rarely pays attention to style/literary features —understands shared readings superficially
D	—reading done quite sporadically —resists even readings that entertain —may not finish books	—sketchy interpretations —little if any support for views —relies on one strategy or response type	—sets simple goals and works to achieve them —seems uninterested in own learning and processes	—work products seem sloppy or "slapped together" —little interest in vocabulary development —evidence of exposure to shared readings
F	—little or no evidence of reading	—little evidence that the student interprets reading —little evidence of views	—may set up simple or no goals with little work —doesn't even go through the motions of voicing vague clichés	—few if any work products

Grades: Writing	Consistency and Challenge	Control of Processes	Self-Assessment and Reflection	Knowledge and Work Products
A	—writes fluently and elaborately for a variety of purposes, both formal and informal —selects personally interesting writing topics that stretch capabilities —experiments with drafts; tries out ideas to see how they look on the page; explains purposes and outcomes of experiments	—uses a variety of writing process tools and strategies —evidence of sophisticated and flexible planning of writing projects —draws on multiple sources to shape ideas —uses drafts to discover ideas, clarify language, and explore alternative possibilities —shows persistence	—sets complex goals for writing and achieves them —applies personal/public criteria to texts written by self and others during both process and product work —is alert to own thought processes during writing events and can recognize learnings	—writes like a reader —creates organized, complete, and effective work products in both content and form —evidence of habitual application of knowledge of conventions in final drafts —evidence of command of a variety of sentence structures; uses sentence structure to enhance the meaning
B	—writes less fluently or elaborately for formal and informal purposes —selects writing topics of personal interest; less concern with challenge —less evidence of experimenting with drafts or less explanation of purposes and outcomes	—uses some process tools and strategies —plans, but less sophistication and flexibility —may over-rely on one or more sources —less use of drafts for discovery and clarification —sometimes shows persistence when writing; sometimes is satisfied when piece could be improved	—sets complex goals for writing and works to achieve them —applies criteria to texts but less effectively —is sometimes alert to own thought processes during writing events but only occasionally recognizes new insights and learnings	—creates organized and complete work products in both content and form —shows attention to application of knowledge of conventions in final drafts, but less consistently —evidence of command of sentence structures but with less variety

Table B. Writing Rubric

Table B. Writing Rubric *(continued)*

Grades: Writing	Consistency and Challenge	Control of Processes	Self-Assessment and Reflection	Knowledge and Work Products
C	—writes to complete assignments —selects writing topics of personal interest, often concerned with ease —little evidence of purposeful experimentation	—mechanical use of process tools and strategies —plans are routinized and inflexible —usually relies on one source to shape ideas —usually sees drafts as products —usually is satisfied when piece could be improved	—sets simple goals for writing and achieves them —only vaguely applies criteria to texts —is rarely alert to own thought processes during writing and expresses clichés or vague learnings	—creates superficially polished work products —exhibits a basic knowledge of conventions in final drafts —sentence structure is serviceable but usually simple and/or repetitive —final drafts contain occasional surface errors
D	—evidence that writing is attempted —does not develop even topics that are personally interesting	—uses one or two process strategies —may have a vague plan —always sees drafts as products	—sets simple goals and works to achieve them —seems uninterested in own learning but voices vague clichés	—work products are slapped together —frequent, serious errors in conventions —final drafts look like rough drafts
F	—little evidence of writing —is satisfied with incomplete, unfinished, or no pieces of work	—little or no evidence of process strategies —drafts are not even seen as products	—may set simple or no goals with little work —doesn't even go through the motions of voicing vague clichés	—few if any work products

Works Cited

Allen, M. (1991). *Self-evaluation in writing placement.* Unpubl. manuscript. Maryville, MO: Northwest Missouri State University.

Alpert, B. (1991). Students' resistance in the classroom. *Anthropology & Education Quarterly, 22,* 350–365.

Ames, C. (1984). Achievement attributions and self-instructions under competitive and individualistic goal structures. *Journal of Educational Psychology, 76* (3), 478–487.

Anderman, E., & Maehr, M. (1994). Motivation and schooling in the middle grades. *Review of Educational Research, 64* (2), 287–309.

Anderson, P., & Rubano, G. (1991). *Enhancing aesthetic reading and response.* Urbana, IL: National Council of Teachers of English.

Apple, M. (1993). *Official knowledge: Democratic education in a conservative age.* London: Routledge.

Artley, A. S. (1975). Words, words, words. *Language Arts, 52,* 1067–1072.

Ash, R., Bruce, A., Brown, C., Cheong, J., Hanna, M. A., Kapinus, B., Kolanowski, K., Rivers, J., Roeber, E., & Selden, R. (1994). *Primary level assessment system/pilot: Pilot manual.* A collaborative project coordinated by the Council of Chief State School Officers, State Collaborative on Assessment and Student Standards. Pilot materials prepared by the Psychological Corporation.

Atwell, N. (1987). *In the middle: Writing, reading, and learning with adolescents.* Upper Montclair, NJ: Boynton/Cook.

Au, K. (1994). Portfolio assessment: Experiences at the Kamehameha elementary education program. In S. Valencia, E. Hiebert, & P. Afflerbach (Eds.), *Authentic reading assessment: Practices and possibilities* (pp. 103–126). Newark, DE: International Reading Association.

Au, K., Scheu, J., Kawakami, A., & Herman, P. (1990). Assessment and accountability in a whole literacy curriculum. *The Reading Teacher, 43* (8), 77–81.

Ballard, L. (1992). Portfolios and self-assessment. *English Journal, 81* (2), 46–48.

Barr, M., Ellis, S., Hester, H., & Thomas, A. (1990). *Patterns of learning: The primary language record and the national curriculum.* London: Centre for Language in Primary Education.

Barr, M., & Hallam, P. (1996). Teacher parity in assessment with the California learning record. In R. Calfee & P. Perfumo (Eds.), *Writing portfolios in the classroom: Policy and practice, promise and peril* (pp. 285–302). Mahwah, NJ: Erlbaum.

Bartine, D. (1989). Writer's meaning or reader's meaning. In D. Bartine, *Early English reading theory: Origins of current debates* (pp. 77–88). Columbia: University of South Carolina Press.

Belanoff, P. (1994). Portfolios and literacy: Why? In L. Black, D. Daiker, J. Sommers, & G. Stygall (Eds.), *New directions in portfolio assessment: Reflective practice, critical theory, and large-scale scoring* (pp. 13–25). Portsmouth, NH: Boynton/Cook.

Belanoff, P., & Elbow, P. (1986). Using portfolios to increase collaboration and community in a writing program. In P. Connolly & T. Vilardi (Eds.), *New methods in college writing programs: Theories in practice* (pp. 28–39). New York: Modern Language Association of America.

Bennett, R. (1993). On the meanings of constructed response. In R. Bennett & W. Ward (Eds.), *Construction versus choice in cognitive measurement: Issues in constructed response, performance testing, and portfolio assessment.* Hillsdale, NJ: Erlbaum.

Bereiter, C., & Scardamalia, M. (1987). An attainable version of high literacy: Approaches to teaching higher-order skills in reading and writing. *Curriculum Inquiry, 17* (1), 9–29.

Berlin, J. (1994). The subversions of the portfolio. In L. Black, D. Daiker, J. Sommers, & G. Stygall (Eds.), *New directions in portfolio assessment: Reflective practice, critical theory, and large-scale scoring* (pp. 56–68). Portsmouth, NH: Boynton/Cook.

Black, L., Daiker, D., Sommers, J., & Stygall, G. (Eds.), (1994). *New directions in portfolio assessment: Reflective practice, critical theory, and large-scale scoring.* Portsmouth, NH: Boynton/Cook.

Blau, S. (1993). *Building bridges between literary theory and the teaching of literature.* Rep. Ser. 5.6. Albany: Center for the Learning and Teaching of Literature, State University of New York.

Blau, S. (1994). *The California Learning Assessment System Language Arts Test: A guide for the perplexed.* Doc. prepared for the CLAS Language Arts Development Team. Sacramento: California State Department of Education.

Brandt, R. (1989). On curriculum in California: A conversation with Bill Honig. *Educational Leadership,47* (3), 10–13.

Breneman, B. (1998). Email communication.

Butler, R., & Nisan, M. (1986). Effects of no feedback, task-related comments, and grades on intrinsic motivation and performance. *Journal of Educational Psychology, 78* (30), 210–216.

Calfee, R., & Perfumo, P. (Eds.), (1996). *Writing portfolios in the classroom: Policy and practice, promise and peril.* Mahwah, NJ: Erlbaum.

California Assessment Policy Committee. (1991). *A new student assessment system for California schools. Executive summary report of the California Assessment Policy Committee.* Sacramento: California State Department of Education.

California Assessment Program's English–Language Arts Development Team [CAP]. (1992). *A sampler of English–language arts assessment: Elementary.* Sacramento: California State Department of Education.

California Educational Summit. (1989a, December). *Educational accountability: A driving force for school reform.* Discussion paper. Los Angeles: California Educational Summit.

California Educational Summit (1989b, December). *Educational assessment: Harnessing the power of information to improve student performance.* Discussion paper. Los Angeles: California Educational Summit.

California State Department of Education. (1986). *Writing assessment handbook: Grade 8.* Sacramento: California State Department of Education.

California State Department of Education. (1987). *California state framework for English–language arts.* Sacramento: California State Department of Education.

California State Department of Education. (1989). *Writing achievement of California eighth graders: Year two (1987–1988 annual report).* Sacramento: California State Department of Education.

California State Department of Education. (1992). *A rationale for the CLAS Language Arts exam.* Draft document. Sacramento: California State Department of Education.

California State Department of Education. (1994a, August 3). News release: CLAS statistical report released. Sacramento: California State Department of Education.

California State Department of Education. (1994b). *Scoring guide for the California Reading Assessment.* Sacramento: California State Department of Education.

Camp, R. (1992). Portfolio reflections in middle and secondary school classrooms. In K. Yancey (Ed.), *Portfolios in the writing classroom: An introduction* (pp. 61–79). Urbana, IL: National Council of Teachers of English.

Carini, P. (1994). Standards, judgment, and writing. *Assessing Writing, 1* (1), 29–65.

Cather, W. (1949/1988). *On writing: Critical studies on writing as an art.* Lincoln: University of Nebraska Press.

Cherry, R., & Meyer, P. (1993). Reliability issues in holistic assessment. In M. Williamson & B. Huot (Eds.), *Validating holistic scoring for writing assessment* (pp. 79–108). Cresskill, NJ: Hampton.

Chrispeels, J. H. (1997). Educational policy implementation in a shifting political climate: The California experience. *American Educational Research Journal, 34* (3), 453–481.

Claggett, M. F. (1994/1996). Reshaping the culture of testing: California's integrated reading and writing assessment. In *A measure of success: From assignment to assessment in English language arts* (pp. 1–13). Portsmouth, NH : Boynton/Cook.

Clay, M. M. (1979). *The early detection of reading difficulties.* (3rd ed.). Auckland, New Zealand: Heinemann.

Collins, R. (1979). *The credential society: An historical sociology of education and stratification.* New York: Academic Press.

Cooper, C., & Breneman, B. (1989). California's new writing assessment. *The Quarterly, 9,* 9–14, 22.

Cooper, W., & Brown, B. J. (1992). Using portfolios to empower student writers. *English Journal, 81* (2), 40–45.

Corsaro, W. A. (1985). *Friendship and peer culture in the early years.* Norwood, NJ: Ablex.

Covington, M. (1992). *Making the grade: A self-worth perspective on motivation and school reform.* New York: Cambridge University Press.

Crooks, T. (1988). The impact of classroom evaluation practices on students. *Review of Educational Research, 58* (4), 438–481.

Crowley, S. (1989). *A teacher's introduction to deconstruction.* Urbana, IL: National Council of Teachers of English.

Cunningham, P. (1989). Will this experiment work? *The California Reader, 23* (1), 3–7.

Daggett, W. (1993). The skills students need for success in the workplace. *Palmetto Administrator* (Winter), 3–24.

Daggett, W. (1994) Today's students, yesterday's schooling. *The Executive Educator, 16* (6), 18–21.

Deci, E. L. (1975). *Intrinsic motivation.* New York: Plenum.

DeFao, J. (1998, June 30). Some school test data due today. *Sacramento Bee,* Section B, p. 1.

Delandshere, G., & Petrosky, A. (1994). Capturing teachers' knowledge: Performance assessment (a) and post-structuralist epistemology, (b) from post-structuralist perspective, (c) and post-structuralism, (d) none of the above. *Educational Researcher, 23* (5), 11–18.

Deyhle, D. (1987). Learning failure: Tests as gatekeepers and the culturally different child. In H. Trueba (Ed.), *Success or failure? Learning and the language minority student* (pp. 85–108). Cambridge, MA: Newberry House.

Dias, P. (1989). A test-driven literary response curriculum. In J. Milner & L. Milner (Eds.), *Passages to literature: Essays on teaching in Australia, Canada, England, the United States, and Wales* (pp. 39–52). Urbana, IL: National Council of Teachers of English.

Dias, P., & Hayhoe, M. (1988). *Developing response to poetry.* Philadelphia: Open University Press.

Diener, C., & Dweck, C. (1978). An analysis of learned helplessness: Continuous changes in performance, strategy, and achievement cognitions following failure. *Journal of Personality and Social Psychology, 36* (5), 451–462.

Dweck, C., & Leggett, E. (1988). A social-cognitive approach to motivation and personality. *Psychological Review, 95* (2), 256–273.

Elbow, P. (1994). Will the virtues of portfolios blind us to their potential dangers? In L. Black, D. Daiker, J. Sommers, & G. Stygall (Eds.), *New directions in portfolio assessment: Reflective practice, critical theory, and large-scale scoring* (pp. 40–56). Portsmouth, NH: Boynton/Cook.

Emig, J. (1971). *The composing processes of twelfth graders.* Urbana, IL: National Council of Teachers of English.

Everhart, R. (1983). *Reading, writing, resistance.* Norwood, NJ: Ablex.

Faigley, L. (1989). Judging writing, judging selves. *College Composition and Communication, 40* (4), 395–413.

Faigley, L. (1992). *Fragments of rationality: Postmodernity and the subject of composition.* Pittsburgh: University of Pittsburgh Press.

Flood, J., & Lapp, D. (1989). Reporting reading progress: A comparison portfolio for parents. *The Reading Teacher, 42* (7), 508–514.

Frederickson, J., & Collins, A. (1989). A systems approach to educational testing. *Educational Researcher, 18* (9), 27–32.

Freedman, S. (1993). Linking large-scale testing and classroom portfolio assessments of student writing. *Educational Assessment, 1* (1), 27–52.

Fullan, M. (1991). The student. In *The new meaning of educational change* (pp. 170–190). New York: Teachers College Press.

Gearhart, M., Herman, J., Baker, E., & Whittaker, A. (1993). *Whose work is it? A question for the validity of large-scale portfolio assessment.* CSE Tech. Rep. 363. Los Angeles: CRESST Institute on Education and Training, University of California.

Geertz, C. (1995). *After the fact: Two countries, four decades, one anthropologist.* Cambridge, MA: Harvard University Press.

Glass, M. L., & Gottsman, J. (1987). *English-language arts framework for California public schools kindergarten through grade twelve.* Sacramento: California State Department of Education.

Gomez, M., Graue, M., & Bloch, M. (1991). Reassessing portfolio assessment: Rhetoric and reality. *Language Arts, 68* (8), 620–628.

Goodlad, J. (1984). *A place called school.* New York: McGraw-Hill.

Graves, D. (1992). Portfolios: keep a good idea growing. In D. Graves & B. Sunstein (Eds.), *Portfolio portraits* (pp. 1–12). Portsmouth, NH: Heinemann.

Greenberg, K. (1992). Validity and reliability issues in the direct assessment of writing. *WPA: Writing Program Administration, 16* (1/2), 7–22.

Guba, E. & Lincoln, Y. (1989). *Fourth generation evaluation.* Newberry Park, CA: Sage.

Herman, J., Gearhart, M., & Aschbacher, P. (1996). Portfolios for classroom assessment: Design and implementation issues. In R. Calfee & P. Perfumo (Eds.), *Writing portfolios in the classroom: Policy and practice, promise and peril* (pp. 285–302). Mahwah, NJ: Erlbaum.

Hayamizu, T., & Weiner, B. (1991). A test of Dweck's model of achievement goals as related to perceptions of ability. *Journal of Experimental Education, 59* (3), 226–234.

Hillocks, G., Jr. (1987). Synthesis of research on teaching writing. *Educational Leadership, 44* (8), 71–82.

Hirsch, E. D., Jr. (1967). *Validity in interpretation.* Chicago: University of Chicago Press.

Hirsch, E. D., Jr. (1988). *Cultural literacy: What every American needs to know.* Boston: Houghton Mifflin.

Honig, B. (1986). *Recommended readings in literature kindergarten through grade eight.* Sacramento: California State Department of Education.

Honig, B. (1987). How assessment can best serve teaching and learning. In *Assessment in the service of learning: Proceedings of the 1987 ETS Invitational Conference* (pp. 1–9). Princeton, NJ: Educational Testing Service.

Jamentz, C. (Dir.). (1993). *Charting the course toward instructionally sound assessment: A report of the alternative assessment pilot project.* San Francisco: California Assessment Collaborative.

Johnston, P. (1989). Constructive evaluation and the improvement of teaching and learning. *Teachers College Record, 90* (4), 509–528.

Johnston, P., Afflerbach, P., & Weiss, P. (1993). Teachers' assessment of the teaching and learning of literacy. *Educational Assessment, 1* (2), 91–117.

Jordan, S., & Purves, A. (1996). The metaphor of the portfolio and the metaphors in portfolios: The relation of classroom-based to large-scale assessment. In R. Calfee & P. Perfumo (Eds.), *Writing portfolios in the classroom: Policy and practice, promise and peril* (pp. 179–202). Mahwah, NJ: Erlbaum.

Kennedy, C. (1985). *Evolution of the California assessment program: 1958–1985.* [Provided to the researcher by the author, who is a consultant for the California State Department of Education.]

Koretz, D., Klein, S., McCaffrey, D., & Stecher, B. (1993). *Interim report: The reliability of Vermont portfolio scores in the 1992–93 school year.* CSE Tech. Rep. 370. Los Angeles: CRESST/RAND Institute on Education and Training, University of California.

Koretz, D., Stecher, B., Klein, S., McCaffrey, D., & Deibert, E. (1993). *Can portfolios assess student performance and influence instruction? The 1991–92 Vermont experience.* CSE Tech. Rep. 371. Los Angeles: CRESST/RAND Institute on Education and Training, University of California.

Langer, J. (1985). Levels of questioning: An alternative view. *Reading Research Quarterly, 20* (5), 586–602.

Langer, J. (1987). Envisionment: A reader-based view of comprehension. *The California Reader, 20* (3), 4–6.

Langer, J. (1989). *The process of understanding literature.* Rep. Ser. 2.1. Albany: Center for the Learning and Teaching of Literature, State University of New York.

LeMahieu, P., Eresh, J., & Wallace, R. (1992). Using student portfolios for a public accounting. *The School Administrator, 49* (11), 8–15.

Loban, W. (1987). Literature and the basic skills. *The California Reader, 20* (3), 15–17.

Loofbourrow, P. (1994). Composition in the context of the CAP: A case study of the interplay between composition assessment and classrooms. *Educational Assessment, 2* (1), 7–49.

Lucas, C. (1988a). Toward ecological evaluation: Part one. *The Quarterly of the National Writing Project and the Center for the Study of Writing, 10* (1), 1–3, 12–16.

Lucas, C. (1988b). Toward ecological evaluation: Part two. *The Quarterly of the National Writing Project and the Center for the Study of Writing, 10* (2), 4–10.

Lucas, C. (1992). Introduction: Writing portfolios—changes and challenges. In K. Yancey (Ed.), *Portfolios in the writing classroom: An introduction* (pp. 1–12). Urbana, IL: National Council of Teachers of English.

MacLeod, J. (1987). *Ain't no makin' it: Leveled aspirations in a low-income neighborhood.* Boulder, CO: Westview.

Marzano, R. J. (1992). *Assault on the freedom to teach and learn.* [Draft of a paper circulated in California prior to the passage of legislation revoking California's performance-based assessment system.]

Mayher, J., & Boomer, G. (1990). *Uncommon sense: Theoretical practice in language education.* Portsmouth, NH: Boynton/Cook.

McCormick, K. (1994). *The culture of reading and the teaching of English.* Urbana, IL: National Council of Teachers of English.

McDonnell, L. M. (1994). Assessment policy as persuasion and regulation. *American Journal of Education, 102* (4), 394–420.

McKenna, M., & Kear, D. (1990). Measuring attitude toward reading: A new tool for teachers. *The Reading Teacher, 43* (9), 626–639.

Mehan, H. (1979). The structure of classroom events and their consequences for student performance. In *Learning lessons: Social organization in the classroom* (pp. 59–87). Cambridge, MA: Harvard University Press.

Miall, D., & Kuiken, D. (1995). Aspects of literary response: A new questionnaire. *Research in the Teaching of English, 29* (1), 37–58.

Midgley, C. (1993). Motivation and middle level schools. In M. Maehr & P. Pintrich (Eds.), *Advances in motivation and achievement: Motivation and adolescent development* (pp. 217–275). Greenwich, CT: JAI Press.

Miholic, V. (1994). An inventory to pique students' metacognitive awareness of reading strategies. *Journal of Reading, 38* (2), 84–86.

Mitchell, R. (1992a). Assessing writing in California, Arizona, and Maryland. In *Testing for learning: How new approaches to evaluation can improve American schools* (pp. 27–49). New York: Free Press.

Mitchell, R. (1992b). Moderation: How other countries support teachers' judgments. In *Testing for learning: How new approaches to evaluation can improve American schools* (pp. 161–164). New York: Free Press.

Morrow, L., & Weinstein, C. (1986). Encouraging voluntary reading: The impact of a literature program on children's use of library centers. *Reading Research Quarterly, 21* (3), 330–346.

Moss, P. (1994a). Validity in high stakes writing assessment: Problems and possibilities. *Assessing Writing, 1* (1), 109–128.

Moss, P. (1994b). Can there be validity without reliability? *Educational Research, 23* (2), 5–12.

Murphy, S. (1994, August 1). *Portfolios and curriculum reform: Patterns in practice.* [Draft of an unpublished manuscript.]

Murphy, S., & Ruth, L. (1993). The field testing of writing prompts reconsidered. In M. Williamson & B. Huot (Eds.), *Validating holistic scoring for writing assessment.* (pp. 237–265). Cresskill, NJ: Hampton.

Murphy, S., & Smith, M. A. (1992). Looking into portfolios. In K. Yancey (Ed.), *Portfolios in the writing classroom: An introduction* (pp. 49–60). Urbana, IL: National Council of Teachers of English.

Myers, J. (1992). The social contexts of school and personal literacy. *Reading Research Quarterly, 27* (4), 297–333.

Myers, M. (1980). *A procedure for writing assessment and holistic scoring.* Urbana, IL: National Council of Teachers of English.

Myers, M. (1996). Sailing ships: A framework for portfolios in formative and summative systems. In R. Calfee & P. Perfumo (Eds.), *Writing portfolios in the classroom: Policy and practice, promise and peril* (pp. 149–178). Mahwah, NJ: Erlbaum.

National Assessment of Educational Progress [NAEP]. (1990). *Guidelines for selecting passages for the 1992 NAEP assessment of reading* [Document circulated by Educational Testing Service (ETS) to passage contributors during spring 1990.]

Nell, V. (1988). The psychology of reading for pleasure: Needs and gratifications. *Reading Research Quarterly, 23* (1), 6–50.

New Standards Project [NSP]. (1993a). *Man and his message.* [A reading/writing task; for information contact the National Center for Education and the Economy, New York, NY.]

New Standards Project [NSP]. (1993b). *Scoring guide for reading.* [For information contact the National Center for Education and the Economy, New York, NY.]

New Standards Project [NSP]. (1994). *Student portfolio handbook: Field trial version.* [For information contact the National Center for Education and the Economy, New York, NY.]

Nicholls, J., Cobb, P., Wood, T., Yackel, E., & Patashnick, M. (1990). Assessing students' theories of success in mathematics: Individual and classroom differences. *Journal for Research in Mathematics Education, 21* (2), 109–122.

Nicholls, J., Patashnick, M., Cheung, P. C., Thorkildsen, T., & Lauer, J. (1989). Can achievement motivation succeed with only one conception of success? In F. Halisch & J.H.L. van der Berken (Eds.), *International perspectives on achievement and task motivation* (pp. 189–201). Amsterdam: Swets & Zeitlinger.

Ogbu, J. (1992). Understanding cultural diversity and learning. *Educational Researcher, 21* (8), 5–14.

O'Masta, G., & Wolf, J. (1991). Encouraging independent reading through the reading millionaires project. *The Reading Teacher, 44* (9), 656–662.

Pearson, P. D. (1994). Commentary on California's new English–language arts assessment. In S. Valencia, E. Hiebert, & P. Afflerbach (Eds.), *Authentic reading assessment: Practices and possibilities* (pp. 218–227). Newark, DE: International Reading Association.

Peters, C. (1975). A comparative analysis of reading in four content areas. In G. H. McNinch & W. D. Miller (Eds.), *Reading: Convention and inquiry.* Clemson, SC: National Reading Conference.

Purves, A. (1989). *The reconstruction of education and examinations.* [Notes drafted by Alan Purves on May 24, 1989, and circulated to the members of the CAP Development Team later that year.]

Resnick, L., & Resnick, D. (1992). Assessing the thinking curriculum. In B. Gifford & M. O'Connor (Eds.), *Changing assessments: Alternative views of aptitude, achievement, and instruction* (pp. 37–75). Boston: Kluwer.

Rief, L. (1990). Finding the value in evaluation: Self-assessment in a middle school classroom. *Educational Leadership, 47* (6), 24–29.

Rosenblatt, L. (1938/1983). *Literature as exploration* (4th ed.). New York: The Modern Language Association of America.

Rosenblatt, L. (1978). *The reader, the text, the poem: The transactional theory of the literary work.* Carbondale: Southern Illinois University Press.

Rosenblatt, L. (1983). The literary transaction: Evocation and response. *Theory into Practice, 21* (4), 268–277.

Rosenblatt, L. (1991). Literature—S.O.S.! *Language Arts, 68* (6), 444–448.

Round Table. (1989). Involving students in evaluation. *English Journal, 78* (7), 75–77.

Schatzman, L., & Strauss, A. (1973). *Field research: Strategies for a natural sociology.* Englewood Cliffs, NJ: Prentice-Hall.

Schwartz, J. (1991). Let them assess their own learning. *English Journal, 80* (2), 67–73.

Shannon, P. (1990). Introduction. In *The struggle to continue: Progressive reading instruction in the United States* (pp. 1–19). Portsmouth, NH: Heinemann.

Simmons, D., & Kameenui, E. (1998). *Draft reading—Language arts framework for California.* Sacramento: California State Department of Education.

Simmons, J. (1992). Portfolios for large-scale assessment. In D. Graves & B. Sunstein (Eds.), *Portfolio portraits* (pp. 96–113). Portsmouth, NH: Heinemann.

Sizer, T. (1984). *Horace's compromise: The dilemma of the American high school.* Boston: Houghton Mifflin.

Spiegel, D. L. (1981). *Reading for pleasure: Guidelines.* Newark, DE: International Reading Association.

Spivey, N. (1989). *Construing constructivism: Reading research in the United States.* Occ. Paper No. 12. Berkeley and Pittsburgh: Center for the Study of Writing, University of California, and Carnegie Mellon University.

Sutherland, M. (1993). Sweden. In J. Nisbet (Ed.), *Curriculum reform: Assessment in question* (pp. 91–103). Paris: Centre for Educational Research and Innovation, Organization for Economic Co-operation and Development (OECD).

Thelin, W. (1994). The connection between response styles and portfolio assessment: Three case studies of student revision. In L. Black, D. Daiker, J. Sommers, & G. Stygall (Eds.), *New directions in portfolio assessment: Reflective practice, critical theory, and large-scale scoring* (pp. 113–125). Portsmouth, NH: Boynton/Cook.

Underwood, T. (1995). *The impact of a portfolio assessment system on the achievement, instruction, and motivation of seventh and eighth grade English-Language Arts students in a northern California middle school.* Unpubl. diss. Davis, CA: University of California–Davis.

Underwood, T. (1997). Portfolios on the precipice. *Assessing Writing, 4* (2), 225–234.

Valencia, S., Au, K., Scheu, J., & Kawamaki, A. (1990). Assessment of students' ownership of literacy. *The Reading Teacher, 44* (2), 154–156.

Valencia, S., McGinley, W., & Pearson, P. D. (1989/1990). Assessing literacy in the middle schools. In G. Duffy (Ed.), *Reading in the middle school* (2nd ed., pp. 63–104). Newark, DE: International Reading Association. [Read in prepublication draft form.]

Vavrus, L. (1990). Put portfolios to the test. *Instructor, 100* (1), 48–53.

Vygotsky, L. (1934/1986). *Thought and language.* Ed. Alex Kozulin. Cambridge, MA: Massachusetts Institute of Technology Press.

Watson-Gegeo, K. (1988). Ethnography in ESL: Defining the essentials. *TESOL Quarterly, 22* (4), 576–590.

Weiss, B. (1994). California's new English–language arts assessment. In S. Valencia, E. Hiebert, & P. Afflerbach (Eds.), *Authentic reading assessment: Practices and possibilities* (pp. 197–217). Newark, DE: International Reading Association.

Wiggins, G. (1994). The constant danger of sacrificing validity to reliability: Making writing assessment serve writers. *Assessing Writing, 1* (1), 129–139.

Wilgoren, J. (1994, May 6). Newport-Mesa schools may boycott CLAS test. *Los Angeles Times* [Orange County edition], 1.

Witte, S. with Vander Ark, C. (1992). *WSAS communications/language arts performance assessment: The Wausau workshop (August 10–14, 1992).* Madison: Wisconsin Student Assessment System, Wisconsin State Department of Public Instruction.

Wolf, D. (1987/88). Opening up assessment. *Educational Leadership, 45* (4), 24–29.

Wolf, D. (1989). Portfolio assessment: Sampling student work. *Educational Leadership, 46* (7), 35–39.

Woo, E., & Colvin, R. L. (1998, May 17). Lower standards, money, and changing student body are the challenges. *Los Angeles Times* [Orange County edition], Section 5, p. 1.

Zessoules, R., & Gardner, H. (1991). Authentic assessment: Beyond the buzz-word and into the classroom. In V. Perrone (Ed.), *Expanding student assessment* (pp. 47–72). Alexandria, VA: Association for Supervision and Curriculum Development.

Index

Author

Terry Underwood taught in both elementary and secondary classrooms in California for ten years before becoming a teacher of language and literacy at California State University, Sacramento. He has been a consultant for the California Writing Project since 1987 and was a member of the development team that created California's CLAS reading examination. He worked on the development of the New Standards Project's portfolio assessment system between 1991 and 1996 during the time that NCTE was affiliated with the NSP, and he has published several articles and chapters on literacy assessment and instruction. Underwood was recognized with a Promising Researcher award from NCTE in 1996 for a paper based on his dissertation, which he completed at the University of California at Davis in 1995. He, his wife, Joanne, and their daughter, Karen, live in Roseville, California.

This book was typeset in Palatino and Optima by
Precision Graphics of Champaign, Illinois.
The typeface used on the cover and spine was Adobe Garamond.
The book was printed on 60-lb. Lakewood by Bookcrafters/Sheridan Books.